INSPIRE / PLAN / DISCOVER / EXPERIENCE

LONDON

DK EYEWITNESS

LONDON

CONTENTS

DISCOVER 6

Welcome to London 8
Reasons to Love London 10
Explore London 14
Getting to Know London 16

London Itineraries 26
London Your Way 32
A Year in London 58
A Brief History 60

EXPERIENCE 66

Whitehall and Westminster 68

Mayfair and St James's 86

Soho and Trafalgar Square 102

Covent Garden
and the Strand 118

Holborn and the
Inns of Court 132

Bloomsbury and Fitzrovia 146

King's Cross, Camden
and Islington 160

The City 170

Shoreditch and Spitalfields 192

Southwark and Bankside 202

South Bank 216

Chelsea and Battersea 230

South Kensington
and Knightsbridge 240

Kensington, Holland Park
and Notting Hill 260

Regent's Park
and Marylebone 274

Hampstead and Highgate 286

Greenwich and
Canary Wharf 298

Beyond the Centre 310

NEED TO KNOW 332

Before You Go 334
Getting Around 336
Practical Information 340

Index 342
Acknowledgments 350

Left: The skyscraping Shard in Southwark
Previous: The bustling streets of Piccadilly Circus
Front cover: Sunset at the London Eye on the South Bank

DISCOVER

An aerial view of London

Welcome to London..8

Reasons to Love London.........................10

Explore London...14

Getting to Know London..........................16

London Itineraries..26

London Your Way..32

A Year in London..58

A Brief History..60

WELCOME TO
LONDON

Built on pomp and ceremony, London has become a cosmopolitan capital. This diverse city has it all: amazing art and ground-breaking music, royal palaces and historic pubs, futuristic skyscrapers and picturesque parks. Whatever your dream trip to London includes, this DK Eyewitness Travel Guide is the perfect companion.

1 Enjoying the view on Hampstead Heath.

2 A typical London pub.

3 Admiring art at the National Gallery.

4 Royal Festival Hall on the South Bank.

Steeped in history, from the imposing fortress of the Tower of London to graceful Buckingham Palace, it's easy to tread in the footsteps of kings and queens in London. The city is a cultural colossus, brimming with free museums and art galleries, from the National Gallery, with its Renaissance masterpieces, to the Tate Modern's cutting-edge performance works. London also boasts a vibrant music scene and the world's busiest theatre district, the West End. It's a paradise for foodies, where you can sample street food from around the world, as well as dine in an enticing array of Michelin-starred restaurants. Countless wonderful green spaces punctuate the city's heart, including eight royal parks, and swathes of bucolic bliss such as Hampstead Heath are never too far away.

The city's charms extend beyond its centre. Head to places such as Brixton or Richmond to experience the diverse personalities of London's urban villages. Alternatively, escape the crowds at Kew Gardens or the Queen Elizabeth Olympic Park, ambling along the winding trails and landscaped flowerbeds.

With so many different things to discover and experience, London can seem overwhelming. We've broken the city down into easily navigable chapters, with detailed itineraries, expert local knowledge and colourful, comprehensive maps to help you plan the perfect visit. Whether you're staying for a weekend, a week or longer, this Eyewitness guide will ensure that you see the very best London has to offer. Enjoy the book, and enjoy London.

REASONS TO LOVE
LONDON

It's a world in a city. It's a buzzing metropolis. It has a story to tell on every corner. Ask any Londoner and you'll hear a different reason why they love their city. Here, we pick some of our favourites.

1 PRICELESS MUSEUMS AND GALLERIES

Take a turn through Ancient Egypt or meet a roaring dinosaur at one of London's unbeatable museums – and all without spending a penny.

WALKING THE THAMES PATH 2

With 45 km (28 miles) of riverside walkways between Richmond in the west and the Thames Barrier in the east, there is no better way to see the sights.

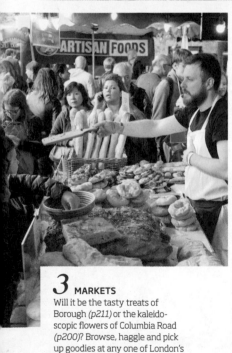

3 MARKETS

Will it be the tasty treats of Borough *(p211)* or the kaleidoscopic flowers of Columbia Road *(p200)*? Browse, haggle and pick up goodies at any one of London's many markets.

POMP AND CEREMONY *4*
Time your trip with the Opening of Parliament, the Lord Mayor's Show or the extravagant Trooping the Colour to see London's traditions at their finest.

INCREDIBLE ARCHITECTURE *5*
There are architectural treats all over the city. Discover staggering skyscrapers, Brutalist art centres and even a majestic Hindu temple.

NOTTING HILL CARNIVAL *6*
Europe's largest street festival is an exuberant celebration of Afro-Caribbean culture that turns Notting Hill into one enormous party *(p270)*.

THE SOUTH BANK 7

Hugging a curve of the River Thames, the South Bank is filled with accessible-to-all institutions of theatre, film, art and music, and buzzing bars perfect for a sundowner.

PARKS AND GARDENS 8

In a city that hums with traffic and noise, it may be a surprise to find green spaces at every turn - so many in fact that London is petitioning for National Park City status.

9 THEATRELAND

From Shakespeare to Pinter, London has always enjoyed a wonderful theatrical tradition, no more so than in the heart of the West End. Book a show for a first-class evening out (p129).

10 GLOBAL RESTAURANT SCENE

Thanks to its multicultural population, London has an enviable array of culinary experiences to tantalize the tastebuds of any foodie.

HOUSES OF PARLIAMENT 11

The Mother of Parliaments, housed in the Gothic Palace of Westminster, is a city icon *(p76)*. Explore the moody interior and discover centuries of turbulent and fascinating history.

A CITY OF PUBS 12

One of Britain's enduring institutions, the pub is ubiquitous on London's streets. And the choice is staggering – from traditional affairs to innovative craft-beer breweries.

EXPLORE
LONDON

This guide divides London into 17 colour-coded sightseeing areas, as shown on the map below. Find out more about each area on the following pages. For areas beyond the main city centre see p310.

CAMDEN

London Zoo

Regent's Park

REGENT'S PARK AND MARYLEBONE
p274

MARYLEBONE

PADDINGTON

KENSINGTON, HOLLAND PARK AND NOTTING HILL
p260

NOTTING HILL

MAYFAIR

MAYFAIR AND ST JAMES'S
p86

HOLLAND PARK

Kensington Gardens

Hyde Park

Green Park

Kensington Palace

SOUTH KENSINGTON AND KNIGHTSBRIDGE
p240

Buckingham Palace

Holland Park

KNIGHTSBRIDGE

KENSINGTON

Science Museum

Natural History Museum

Victoria and Albert Museum

CHELSEA AND BATTERSEA
p230

SOUTH KENSINGTON

Ranelagh Gardens

CHELSEA

River Thames

Battersea Park

BATTERSEA

UNITED KINGDOM

Edinburgh

North Sea

Belfast

GREAT BRITAIN

IRELAND

NETHER-LANDS

Birmingham

Cardiff

LONDON

BELGIUM

Atlantic Ocean

FRANCE

KING'S CROSS, CAMDEN AND ISLINGTON
p160

ISLINGTON

KING'S CROSS

British Library

FINSBURY

BLOOMSBURY AND FITZROVIA
p146

SHOREDITCH

BLOOMSBURY

CLERKENWELL

SHOREDITCH AND SPITALFIELDS
p192

British Museum

Museum of London

HOLBORN AND THE INNS OF COURT
p132

St Paul's Cathedral

CITY

SOHO AND TRAFALGAR SQUARE
p102

COVENT GARDEN AND THE STRAND
p118

TEMPLE

THE CITY
p170

Tower of London

National Gallery

Tate Modern

River *Thames*

WAPPING

St James's Park

SOUTH BANK
p216

London Eye

SOUTHWARK AND BANKSIDE
p202

City Hall

Westminster Abbey

Houses of Parliament

SOUTHWARK

WHITEHALL AND WESTMINSTER
p68

WESTMINSTER

LAMBETH

Imperial War Museum

Tate Britain

FURTHER AFIELD

HAMPSTEAD AND HIGHGATE
p286

GREENWICH AND CANARY WHARF
p298

0 kilometres 1
0 miles 1

N

GETTING TO KNOW
LONDON

The UK's bustling capital is best known for its iconic sights, regal architecture and cool, urban streets and neighbourhoods. Unsurprisingly, many of London's highlights are in its centre but, more unusually, there are visitor-friendly enclaves to discover all over the city.

PAGE 68

WHITEHALL AND WESTMINSTER

The seat of government for a millennium, Westminster is synonymous with two of the most stunning buildings in London: the Houses of Parliament and Westminster Abbey. The area is packed with a curious mixture of civil servants and sightseers, many of them making their way up and down Whitehall, the grand street linking Parliament Square and Trafalgar Square. You'll find few locals here, with its traditional pubs mostly the haunts of government workers.

Best for
Sightseeing and iconic London landmarks

Home to
Westminster Abbey, Houses of Parliament, Tate Britain

Experience
A tour of the tombs of royalty at Westminster Abbey

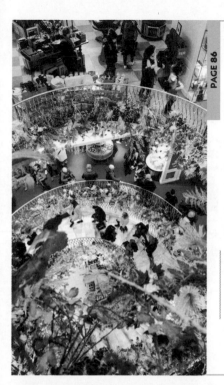

PAGE 86

MAYFAIR AND ST JAMES'S

Home to some of London's wealthiest individuals (the word Mayfair screams "money"), neither of these elite areas are exclusively for the rich, with some good, affordable restaurants, cosy and welcoming pubs, and delightful gardens dotted around. South of ritzy, if traffic-clogged, Piccadilly, the streets of St James's are often surprisingly quiet, given this is the heart of London. There are historical buildings aplenty but, really, this is the place to shop for designer fashion and mingle with the moneyed.

Best for
Designer fashion and high-end men's tailoring

Home to
Buckingham Palace, Royal Academy of Arts

Experience
A shopping spree on Mayfair's Bond Street

PAGE 102

SOHO AND TRAFALGAR SQUARE

Trafalgar Square can lay strong claim to being the epicentre of touristic London, a well-placed launching pad for much of what the city has to offer. Nearby is the liveliest part of the West End, with clumsily commercialized Leicester Square, lantern-strewn Chinatown and cool, unconventional Soho, the main LGBT+ district of London. Many of Soho's streets are replete with excellent independent restaurants, bars and theatres, making it the perfect spot for an evening out.

Best for
Eating out and a buzzing, lively atmosphere

Home to
National Gallery, National Portrait Gallery, Chinatown

Experience
A night of theatre in the West End

→

PAGE 118

COVENT GARDEN AND THE STRAND

The distinctive Covent Garden is always crowded, attracting visitors and locals in equally large numbers. A dense mix of markets, independent shops and restaurants side by side with fashion chain stores and street performers looking for applause, there's usually a spirited family-friendly atmosphere. Running along its southern border is the Strand, a busy road mostly worth visiting for grand Somerset House, with its large and elegant courtyard – often used for special events – cafés, restaurant and riverside views.

Best for
The buzz on Covent Garden Piazza

Home to
Covent Garden Piazza and Central Market, Somerset House

Experience
The brightly painted warehouses of Neal's Yard

PAGE 132

HOLBORN AND THE INNS OF COURT

This is one of the calmest areas of central London. The traditional home of the legal profession, the relative absence of shops and restaurants means there are almost as many lawyers as visitors. The Inns of Court themselves are subdued havens of tranquillity, a maze of alleyways and gardens overlooked by city residents. Add to this the excellent small museums and the lovely Lincoln's Inn Fields, and you have a great place to escape the chaos and crowds.

Best for
Hidden and quiet corners in the heart of London

Home to
Inns of Court, Sir John Soane's Museum

Experience
A picnic in the green squares of the Inns of Court

BLOOMSBURY AND FITZROVIA

Though not exactly avant-garde, these relatively genteel districts have a pleasingly bohemian, laid-back air. Parts of Fitzrovia are densely packed with an enjoyable mix of restaurants, akin to Soho but turned down a few notches. Bloomsbury is the student quarter, home to several university institutions, a variety of independent bookshops and large garden squares. Its most famous location by far is the British Museum, but elsewhere Bloomsbury is characterized by a pleasing sense of studious calm.

Best for
A laid-back, cultured atmosphere and a strong literary heritage

Home to
British Museum

Experience
Some of the world's greatest treasures at the British Museum

KING'S CROSS, CAMDEN AND ISLINGTON

Imaginatively converted from a downbeat industrial landscape into a collection of culinary, commercial and artsy hotspots, King's Cross has undergone staggering transformation in recent years. Not entirely finished, it's still gaining reputation – the same of which cannot be said of neighbouring Camden, where the alternative market and raucous venues keep the place thriving day and night. Adding yet more to the mix is well-heeled Islington, a more bourgeois district full of gastropubs.

Best for
Canal walks and a wide range of shopping and dining options

Home to
Camden Market, St Pancras Station, British Library

Experience
Off-beat fashion and food at Camden Market

$\rightarrow$

PAGE 170

THE CITY

The towering skyscrapers of the City make up London's traditional financial district, where corporates in suits scurry around during the week, making it a bustling place at lunchtimes but an eerily deserted one during the weekend. Also the historical heart of the city, with traces of the Roman occupation in places, the sights are dispersed over a relatively wide area, but there are plenty of them, including London's highest concentration of medieval and early modern churches, crowned by the most famous church of all, St Paul's Cathedral.

Best for
Getting up close to London's staggering history

Home to
St Paul's Cathedral, Tower of London, Barbican Centre

Experience
The gore and glory of the centuries-old Tower of London

PAGE 192

SHOREDITCH AND SPITALFIELDS

These districts have attracted and spawned a once cutting-edge, much caricatured and now simply trendy local population. Though gentrification has firmly set in there is still an alluring energy here, particularly in lively Shoreditch. It's not entirely hipster-centric though, with Brick Lane home to a large Bangladeshi community, and markets like Old Spitalfields and Columbia Road continuing traditions that stretch way back beyond the latest incarnation of the neighbourhood.

Best for
Feasting on street food and people-watching

Home to
Columbia Road Flower Market, Brick Lane

Experience
The hustle and bustle of some of London's top markets

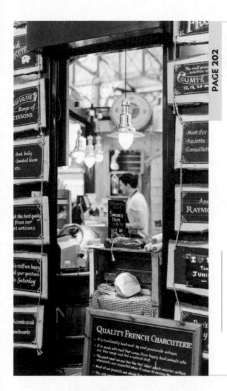

PAGE 202

SOUTHWARK AND BANKSIDE

Over the river from the City, Bankside, in the borough of Southwark, contains some of the most popular tourist attractions on the Thames. Tate Modern and Shakespeare's Globe along with waterside restaurants, pubs and Borough Market keep this stretch of the Thames Path happily congested most days. The recently developed area emanating out from London Bridge station has plenty of new places to eat, a few of them in Western Europe's tallest building, the Shard.

Best for
Urban river walks and riverside sightseeing

Home to
Tate Modern, Shakespeare's Globe

Experience
Striking and strange modern art at the Tate Modern

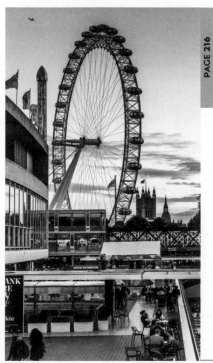

PAGE 216

SOUTH BANK

At night this is the liveliest part of the river, but it is cultural institutions rather than nightclubs that draw in the after-dark crowds. The Southbank Centre's concert halls and gallery alongside the National Theatre and British Film Institute form a striking line-up of architecture along the river. Any gaps are filled mostly with mediocre chain restaurants, though bookstalls, a skate park and a food market provide a more homespun angle. Always busy in the daytime too, the views from the South Bank promenade – and from atop the London Eye – have cemented it as one of London's must-visit areas.

Best for
A sundowner and an evening's entertainment

Home to
Southbank Centre, Imperial War Museum, London Eye

Experience
A stroll along the Thames Path

→

PAGE 230

CHELSEA AND BATTERSEA

Sitting on opposite sides of the Thames are wealthy Chelsea and energetic Battersea. Flashy sedans and 4WD vehicles, known locally as Chelsea tractors, ply Chelsea's main shopping street, King's Road, where upmarket fashion boutiques sit next door to more humdrum high-street stores. Away from King's Road the area is largely residential, though there are some decent pubs, worthwhile museums and gardens. The glorious park, trendy shops and varied restaurants of Battersea are a welcome retreat from the touristy sights of central London.

Best for
Upmarket shopping and riverside parks and gardens

Home to
Saatchi Gallery, Battersea Park

Experience
A spot of shopping along the King's Road

PAGE 240

SOUTH KENSINGTON AND KNIGHTSBRIDGE

London's museum quarter, South Kensington is home to three of the largest and best museums in the city, exhibiting stunning natural history, science and decorative arts collections. In keeping with the spirit of learning that pervades here, the wide streets house several important royal colleges and societies. In contrast, Knightsbridge, just up the road, oozes ostentatious wealth and is the location of one of the city's most iconic department stores, Harrods.

Best for
World-class free museums

Home to
Victoria and Albert Museum, Natural History Museum, Science Museum

Experience
The weird and wonderful skeletons and species inside the Natural History Museum

PAGE 260

KENSINGTON, HOLLAND PARK AND NOTTING HILL

From well-to-do High Street Kensington, the neighbourhoods to the north drift uphill through expensive townhouses, some original little museums and Holland Park. Partially wooded and beautifully landscaped, the park reflects its upmarket location with its pricey restaurant, and outdoor operas. To its north is Notting Hill, more touristy than High Street Kensington, in part because of the eponymous film, but also because of its market on Portobello Road.

Best for
Markets, parks and beautiful neighbourhoods

Home to
Design Museum

Experience
Browsing for bargains on Portobello Road

PAGE 274

REGENT'S PARK AND MARYLEBONE

The residents of Marylebone are generally less aristocratic than their Mayfair counterparts, but this is still a genteel area with one of London's more high-brow high streets. There is a distinct change in tone on the main road between here and Regent's Park to the north, where the massive queues for Madame Tussauds are accompanied by non-stop traffic. This all melts pleasantly away in the attractive park itself, with its canalside location providing universal appeal.

Best for
Georgian architecture, open-air theatre

Home to
London Zoo

Experience
The splendid shelves of the marvellous Daunt Books

$\rightarrow$

PAGE 286

HAMPSTEAD AND HIGHGATE

Separated by the rolling fields and woodlands of Hampstead Heath and the atmospheric Highgate Cemetery, two of the biggest draws for visitors, the "villages" of Hampstead and Highgate have maintained much of their quaintness and independence, despite London's rapid urban expansion. The jumbled streets graced with boutique shops and upscale restaurants that make up the old villages are great for a stroll in a part of the city where the pace is noticeably slower.

Best for
London villages and vast swathes of heathland

Home to
Hampstead Heath, Highgate Cemetery

Experience
A dip in the chilly Hampstead bathing ponds

PAGE 298

GREENWICH AND CANARY WHARF

Separated by the river, but joined by a foot tunnel underneath it, Greenwich and Canary Wharf are as different from one another as it gets. Built around the old docks in the 1980s, the business district of Canary Wharf lacks soul but is full of hidden history and dockside walking routes, the sum of which makes it unlike anywhere else in the city. In contrast, Greenwich has history seeping from its pores, populated as it is by a swathe of prominent royal and historical buildings and museums, an ancient park and a handsome town centre.

Best for
Maritime London

Home to
National Maritime Museum, Cutty Sark, Greenwich Park, Royal Observatory

Experience
The home of Greenwich Mean Time atop Greenwich Park

BEYOND THE CENTRE

Though it has a distinct city centre, London's sprawling capital reaches far beyond the banks of the Thames. Make the effort to venture out to the suburbs and you'll find the locals: urban families and young professionals, multinational and multicultural, all fiercely protective of their backyard, and with good reason. There are some big-name attractions out here – royal palaces, stately homes and lush gardens to name a few – but a trip beyond the centre is really a thrilling opportunity to get to know the locals behind this multifaceted city.

Best for
Local life and getting off the beaten path

Home to
Hampton Court, Kew Gardens, Warner Bros. Studio Tour: The Making of Harry Potter

Experience
The sights, sounds and smells of energetic Brixton

←

1 Looking towards iconic Tower Bridge.

2 Tate Modern, housed in a former power station.

3 St Paul's Cathedral.

4 The London Eye.

With so much to see and do in London it can be difficult knowing where to start. Here we suggest a few itineraries to help you get the most out of your visit.

24 HOURS

Morning

By following the river you can fit an awful lot into one day without having to travel too far or rely on public transport. Begin at Butler's Wharf; located close to Tower Bridge (p186) and lined with decent river-facing restaurants, it's a great spot for breakfast. From there, walk across the world-famous bridge to the Tower of London (p178) and immerse yourself for a few hours in a thousand years of royal history and scandal. Ready for lunch? Follow the river to London Bridge and cross back over to the south side where you can pick up tasty street food or a gourmet picnic from Borough Market (p211).

Afternoon

Wander through the streets of Southwark past the Golden Hinde and through Clink Street. Soon you'll reach Shakespeare's Globe (p208) and the Tate Modern (p206). Stop at the Millennium Bridge to enjoy a picture-perfect view of St Paul's Cathedral (p174) before heading into the gigantic old power station to admire – or puzzle over – modern art. Check out the views from the top floor of the Blavatnik Building before having a coffee in the gallery's cafe (the view from here isn't bad either). Revitalized, continue along the Thames Path, around a bend in the river, to the South Bank (p216). Pause to watch skateboarders and browse the popular second-hand book stall under Waterloo Bridge before joining the queues for the London Eye (p226), which is open until at least 6pm on most days of the year.

Evening

It's a half-hour walk back along the river to Southwark (p202). Have a spot of dinner at one of the many restaurants in the area – Roast, within Borough Market, is a good choice (p212) – before ending the day with a pint at London's last galleried pub, the 17th-century George Inn (p211).

←

1 Canalboats meandering along Regent's Canal

2 The Cenotaph

3 Renting bikes in Hyde Park

4 A street performer in Covent Garden

2 DAYS

Day 1

Morning Have a full English breakfast in Art Deco style at the St Pancras Brasserie, right inside St Pancras station. It's a short stroll to the innovatively resurrected King's Cross quarter (p165), where you can wander the city's newest independent hub, grab a coffee from one of the cafés in Granary Square and relax in Camley Street Natural Park. From here, follow the winding Regent's Canal path to infamous Camden Market (p168) for quirky, offbeat shopping and a casual lunch.

Afternoon From Camden Town Tube station take the Northern Line down to Embankment – from there it's just a 600-m (2,000-ft) walk along the north bank of the river to the Houses of Parliament (p76), one of the great wonders of London, and only another 300-m (1,000-ft) to the architecturally and historically awe-inspiring Westminster Abbey (p72).

Evening Make your way up Whitehall, past 10 Downing Street (p81) and the Cenotaph (p81), towards Trafalgar Square (p114). Once at the square stroll up through always-bustling Chinatown (p112) to the edge of Soho, the West End's most vibrant and eclectic restaurant district. Get a taste of one of London's current culinary crazes by dining on the delectable Peruvian tapas at Casita Andina (p115). It's just a few hundred metres from here to Ronnie Scott's, the city's most famous archetypal jazz club, as well as some of London's best bars.

Day 2

Morning Have a traditional English breakfast at the atmospheric Café in the Crypt (p115), below St Martin-in-the-Fields church just off Trafalgar Square. Afterwards, cross the road to the National Gallery (p106) and explore one of the world's greatest art collections. Pick up something delicious for lunch from one of the many cafés in nearby Soho.

Afternoon From here, head back south to cross lively Piccadilly Circus and thread through the regal streets of St James's to the beautifully landscaped St James's Park. Wander past the pelicans on the lake and over the blue bridge, a great spot for photos of Buckingham Palace (p90). If they're open, visit the grandiose State Rooms in the palace itself; otherwise admire the precious art collection at the Queen's Gallery or the ornate carriages at the Royal Mews. From the palace, at the other end of Constitution Hill, pick up bikes (p339) and see out the daylight hours cycling around the expansive Hyde Park (p257).

Evening Park the bikes at the docking station in Knightsbridge and hop on the Piccadilly Line to the always bustling Covent Garden (p122). Enjoy the street performers in the atmospheric piazza and then settle into dinner accompanied by opera singers at Sarastro on Drury Lane, in the heart of Theatreland. See out the evening with a drink – and great views – on the riverside terrace of Somerset House (p124).

7 DAYS

Day 1

Morning Start at the Shard – there's no better vantage point from which to survey the city (p212). Down at street level, stroll along the cobbled alleys of Southwark and pick up lunch at Borough Market (p211).

Afternoon Head west along the Thames Path, popping into the cavernous Tate Modern (p206) to see what's new in the world of modern art.

Evening Finish up at the Southbank Centre (p220) for a spin on the London Eye and, afterwards, dinner and drinks.

Day 2

Morning Choose from three of the city's top museums: the Natural History Museum (p248), the Science Museum (p250) or the Victoria and Albert (p244). Any one could occupy you for a day, but as they're free split your time across two or perhaps all three.

Afternoon Have a picnic in nearby Hyde Park (p257) before returning to another of the museums for the afternoon.

Evening If you've pre-booked tickets, enjoy a performance at the refined Royal Albert Hall (p252).

Day 3

Morning Head east to the City and explore the history of the capital at the Museum of London (p183).

Afternoon Have lunch at the historic Leadenhall Market (p188). Afterwards, take the Docklands Light Railway to Greenwich (p298) to discover centuries of maritime history.

Evening Walk to the top of Greenwich Park to enjoy the sunset.

Day 4

Morning Take the Tube north to enjoy the alternative vibe at Camden Market (p168). Browse the stalls until lunchtime – there's plenty here to feast on.

Afternoon Head to the characterful villages of Highgate and Hampstead. Walk between the two via the heath (p290) and Highgate Cemetery (p292).

① Leadenhall Market.
② The Southbank Centre in the sunshine.
③ Camden Market and its food stalls.
④ Deer graze at lush Richmond Park.
⑤ Columbia Road Flower Market.

Evening Have a relaxed dinner at one of Hampstead's excellent pubs, such as the Holly Bush (p295).

Day 5

Morning Travel south to Dulwich Picture Gallery (p325) in upper-crust Dulwich Village, taking in the gorgeous park (p325) over the road.

Afternoon Catch a train at West Dulwich station for livelier Brixton. Do the full circuit of the Brixton Village and Market Row arcades (p328), a foodie's haven, before settling down for a late lunch.

Evening Stick about in Brixton for a spot of live music at one of its venues, catch a film at the Ritzy cinema or simply chill out in Pop Brixton, a complex of shipping containers packed with street food start-ups and bars.

Day 6

Morning Catch the train from London Waterloo to Kew Bridge; from here it's a short walk to the gardens of Kew (p318).

Afternoon Follow the river path at a relaxed pace to the attractive riverside town of Richmond (p329). Have lunch on the go or, better yet, take a picnic to the expansive Richmond Park.

Evening Keep close to the Thames and enjoy a riverside dinner as the evening draws in.

Day 7

Morning Sunday morning is the only time Columbia Road Market (p200) operates and it's well worth a visit, whether or not you want to buy flowers. Here you'll catch sight of the sellers or "barrow boys" flaunting their impressive displays of flowers and foliage.

Afternoon Check out what's on at the Barbican (p182) or Rich Mix (p200), both of which have an ever-changing roster of film screenings, exhibitions and talks.

Evening Spend the evening in super-cool Shoreditch. There are plenty of trendy places to eat, drink and relax in, not least on Brick Lane (p197), the curry capital of Europe.

TOP
DISCOVER London Your Way

DIVERSE DISTRICTS

Brick Lane
AKA the "curry capital of Europe" and home to a large Bangladeshi community.

Ealing
The unofficial Polish capital of Britain – over 6 percent of people here speak Polish.

Stockwell
Nicknamed "Little Portugal", there are over 27,000 Portuguese in the local area.

Stamford Hill
London's largest community of ultra-Orthodox Jews live here.

Southall
Home to the biggest Punjabi population outside of India.

Did You Know?

One in three people who live in London were born in another part of the world.

LONDON IS
A WORLD CITY

Sit on the Tube and listen. You'll hear conversations in Polish, Chinese, Yoruba and 300 other languages besides. These are the voices of London, one of the most wonderfully multicultural cities in the world. Wherever you go, you'll find slices of life from every continent begging to be explored.

Places of Worship

Lighting up neighbourhoods from east to west are spectacular places of worship, many of them open to the public and each one a crash-course in understanding the cultural traditions they serve. From the largest Hindu temple in Europe *(p322)* to the towering mosque in Regent's Park *(p282)*, these architectural anomalies spice up the urban landscape wherever they stand.

→

BAPS Shri Swaminarayan Mandir, an incredible Hindu temple in Neasden

Festivals

Aside from the popular Chinese New Year and Notting Hill Carnival, there are plenty of festivals that showcase London's locals. St Patrick's Day in March is widely celebrated with all-out revelry, as is Australia Day in January, less raucous in numbers only. Plaza Latina in August unites the Latin American communities for parades and merriment, and the fireworks of Diwali in the autumn sparkle over the city's skies. Whenever you visit, there's sure to be something to celebrate.

←

Entertainers contribute to the party atmosphere at the Notting Hill Carnival

↑ Vibrant Chinatown, the original home of London's Chinese population

Welcome to the Neighbourhood

West Indian barbershops to the south, Turkish grocers to the north, London's diversity is palpable whichever way you turn. Head to the East End to find the traditional heart of immigrant London, where so many have settled and dispersed into the cultural soup that is London.

A snapshot of ↑ modern London in Brixton Market

Ceremonies and Traditions

A number of centuries-old royal ceremonies and traditions continue today, despite the sometimes baffling outfits and proceedings. Most famous is the Changing the Guard, which takes place daily at Buckingham Palace and Horse Guards Parade on Whitehall. Once a year, in June, the far more elaborate military parade Trooping the Colour is staged to celebrate the Queen's birthday. Tickets must be booked online (www.household division.org.uk).

→ Queen Elizabeth II waving to the crowd during the military parade Trooping the Colour

LONDON FOR
ROYALTY

London has been the royal capital of the UK for almost a thousand years and most of the royal family, including the Queen, live in the city. Over the centuries, successive monarchs have done much to shape the character of the city, from the landscaping of royal parks to the landmarks they left behind.

The Legacy of Victoria and Albert

We have much to thank Queen Victoria and her husband Prince Albert for. The Christmas tree, housing projects for the poor and the superb museums in South Kensington are just some of the things accredited to the forward-thinking pair. Give them a nod at the Queen Victoria Memorial outside Buckingham Palace and the Albert Memorial in Hyde Park.

← The stunning Natural History Museum, a legacy of Prince Albert

Tower of London

At times a royal palace, at others a prison and place of execution for fallen monarchs or rejected courtiers, the story of the Tower of London (p178) is to some extent the story of the English monarchy itself. Built by William the Conqueror in the late 11th century, this was where Anne Boleyn awaited her fate after falling out of Henry VIII's favour and was later beheaded. Curiously, for 600 years it was also home to the royal menagerie, a collection of exotic wild animals, including lions and an elephant, gifted to the monarchy. It is now one of London's most popular attractions.

↑ Trooping the Colour, a parade to celebrate the Queen's birthday

💬 INSIDER TIP
Sneak Preview

You can catch members of the Household Cavalry leaving the barracks on the south side of Hyde Park at 10:28am on weekdays and 9:28am on Sundays on their way to the Changing the Guard at Horse Guards Parade.

↑ The stark image of the Tower of London

Royal Palaces

Go behind the scenes of royal households to discover how the upper echelons of power have lived over the centuries. Hampton Court (p314) is arguably the most impressive with its long and rich history, while Kew Palace (p318), surrounded by its beautiful gardens, is relatively modest by royal standards. Pop by the famous Buckingham Palace (p90), the official London residence of the monarch since 1837, to say hello to the Queen – if the Royal Standard flag is flying, she's at home.

← Visitors exploring the interior of Hampton Court Palace

Royal Parks

During a day of sightseeing take a detour to the former stomping grounds of kings and queens. Boat on the lake in the expansive Hyde Park *(p257)*, wander landscaped gardens at Kensington *(p256)* or take in the view of famed Buckingham Palace from St James's Park *(p95)*. Venture a little further out and spend the day exploring the rural landscapes of Richmond Park *(p328)*. A hike up the hill in Greenwick Park *(p303)* provides sweeping views over the city of London, the perfect end to any day.

Relaxing by the lakeside in the vast Hyde Park

LONDON FOR
GREEN SPACES

With its eight million trees and 3,000 parks, London is one of the greenest capitals in Europe. There's even a campaign to grant it National Park City status. Take a break from the city hubbub and venture to any one of these green spaces.

An English City Garden

The English have long had an unabashed love affair with their gardens. The green-fingered should make their way to the gorgeous scenic gardens that surround manor houses like Chiswick House *(p331)* and Syon House *(p329)*. If it's respite you're after, any of the public garden squares throughout the city will do, particularly those in Bloomsbury *(p154)*. The breathtaking Kew Gardens *(p318)* crowns them all and is a must for any budding gardener.

The exquisite Kew Gardens, a veritable haven for the green-fingered

47
—
Percentage of green space in Greater London, most of which is open to the public.

Back to Nature

There are more than 40 nature reserves and pockets of woodland across London, some of them not so far away from the centre. Go bird-watching at Walthamstow Wetlands, hunt for creepy-crawlies at Camley Street Natural Park *(p165)* or walk through woodland at the ancient Highgate Wood.

→

Sifting for creepy-crawlies at the Camley Street Natural Park

A Walk on the Wild Side

Linking a lot of the city's green spaces together, along rivers, canals, old train tracks and park paths, is the Capital Ring, a painstakingly plotted 126-km (78-mile) circular walking route. Signposted throughout the route, it's worth downloading a map for one of the 15 sections from the TfL website *(tfl.gov.uk)*.

→

A couple of couples on the Capital Ring trail

Football in London

The capital city of the country that invented the game has more professional football clubs and large football stadiums than any other on the planet. Premier League games are usually booked up well in advance, mostly with corporate guests and season ticket holders. Your best hope of watching some action is to try to book in a cup match, particularly a League Cup game, when tickets are not only more widely available but a bit cheaper too.

Ecstatic Arsenal players and fans celebrating a goal

LONDON FOR
SPORTS FANS

Britain is a nation of sports fans and its capital is no exception. London, the only city to have hosted the Olympic Games three times, puts on a dazzling range of sporting events and tournaments, from football to boxing and everything in-between.

An Olympic Legacy

Head to the Queen Elizabeth Olympic Park *(p312)* and relive the magic of the 2012 London Olympics. There are frequent events here ranging from international track cycling competitions to all-star basketball championships, plus a range of first-class facilities, fit for any budding Olympian.

→

The Queen Elizabeth Olympic Park, with the ArcelorMittal Orbit

Sports Museums and Stadium Tours

London's sporting heritage is unparalleled, with legendary areas dotted all over. Given their long histories they all have stories to tell, and a tour is the best way to hear them. Walk through the player's tunnel at Wembley, go behind the scenes at the home of rugby in Twickenham or explore the grass courts of Wimbledon. The oldest sporting museum in the world, the MCC Museum at Lord's cricket ground, is a must-visit for fans.

←

England's national stadium, Wembley

The Sporting Calendar

The Six Nations Rugby tournament kickstarts the year, with some games held at Twickenham. The hotly contested Boat Race brings in spring, followed swiftly by the London Marathon and people's favourite the FA Cup Final. Expect strawberries and sunburn in summer, as crowds watch Wimbledon and cricket internationals. After the frenzy of the transfer window, the Premier League kicks off in mid-August. Rugby Union Internationals and the ATP World Tour Finals round off the year.

→

Pounding the pavements for the London Marathon *(above)* and enjoying a game of tennis at Wimbledon *(inset)*

The gorgeous ↑
Albert Bridge,
illuminated at night

LONDON
ON THE RIVER

Like many cities, London grew up around its river. The Romans used it as a line of defence, the Victorians established it as the world's largest port and the city today claims it as a cultural hotspot. Take to the water to see London landmarks from a different angle.

Follow the Thames Path

Twisting and turning along the river through London and out into the countryside is the Thames Path. Starting far to the west of the city in the Cotswold Hills, this National Trail's London section stretches from the flood-plains of Richmond *(p329)* to the Thames Barrier *(p327)*, hardly ever losing sight of the river. The best stretch for sightseeing is between Tower Bridge and Westminster Bridge, but there are some pretty sections, dotted with pubs and full of greenery, between Hammersmith Bridge and Kew Bridge in the west.

→
A section of
the Thames Path,
running past City Hall

Spanning the River

For centuries, right up until 1750, London Bridge was the only bridge across the Thames in London. Now there are more than 30 – and tunnels too. Instantly recognizable is Tower Bridge *(p186)*, with its twin towers and famous drawbridge. A favourite for many Londoners is the attractive 19th-century Albert Bridge, near Battersea Park *(p238)*, spectacular at night when it is illuminated by thousands of lights. The somewhat eerie Greenwich Foot Tunnel *(p305)* links the Isle of Dogs, the home of Canary Wharf, and Greenwich – it's an unusual way to get from one bank to the other. Snap great shots or take in the view of the riverscape from the Golden Jubilee Bridges, each flanking graceful Hungerford Bridge *(p222)*.

← A legend of London, the turreted Tower Bridge

EAT

Dine at one of these top riverside locations.

Skylon

Cool, refined restaurant on the first floor of the Royal Festival Hall.

🏠 Southbank Centre
ⓦ skylon-restaurant.co.uk

£££

Sea Containers

Tuck into a bottomless breakfast or Sunday roast on the marvellous riverside terrace.

🏠 20 Upper Ground SE1
ⓦ seacontainers restaurant.com

£££

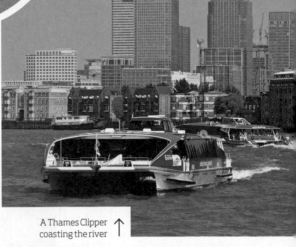

A Thames Clipper coasting the river ↑

From the Water

Board a Thames Clipper rather than a sightseeing boat to cruise the river and see the sights for a fraction of the price. There are four main routes, all of them covering the busiest section of the river between the London Eye and London Bridge. There are boats roughly every 15 minutes at peak times.

LONDON
ON TAP

Londoners, like most Brits, come together in pubs. They eat and drink in them, they chat and dance in them, and they watch comedy and sport in them. And whether you're on the river, in a park or on a busy street, no matter the neighbourhood, there will be a pub just round the corner.

Brewing a Beer

While London's craft brewers come up with ever more inventive beer styles, be sure to try traditional draught "real" ale, hand-pumped from casks and served at cellar temperature. Still, London's taste for hoppy IPAs shows no sign of dissipating, and there are more than a hundred microbreweries and brewpubs across the city. Tackle the Bermondsey Beer Mile on a Saturday to try some of the best.

→

Some of the London-brewed ales on offer at a local pub

A Traditional Public House

The title of "oldest pub in London" is claimed by quite a number of pubs. Though very few pub interiors are more than 200 years old, there have been pubs and inns in the city for over a millennium and there are certainly a select few establishments whose current building dates to the 16th century. Look out for timber-framed interiors and compartments separated by frosted glass screens - the classic tells of a Victorian-era pub.

← The Victorian Market Porter pub, found in Southwark

DRINK

Hoop and Grapes
This 17th-century pub is one of the oldest still standing in London.

🏠 47 Aldgate High Street 🚇 Aldgate East 🌐 nicholsonspubs.co.uk

Ye Olde Mitre
Elizabeth I danced around the cherry tree still standing at this 16th-century pub.

🏠 Ely Place 🚇 Farrington 🌐 yeolde mitreholborn.co.uk

↑ A pint of London Pride, one of the most popular brews in the United Kingdom

Pub Lunch

Since the 1990s, there has been a gastropub explosion in London. Though many pubs have stuck to traditional pub grub, some can compete with top restaurants for quality. Among those most renowned for their food are the Anchor & Hope in Waterloo, the Harwood Arms in Fulham and the Marksman in Hackney.

↑ Serving up an impressive Sunday roast dinner at a London gastropub

Independent Cinemas

Intimate arthouse venues, Golden Age auditoriums, brick-lined railway arch establishments and trendy industrial-style spaces are just some of the places you can watch big screen films around the city. The historic Regent Street Cinema, the Electric Cinema on Portobello Road, with its diner and leather armchairs, and the Art Deco Phoenix in East Finchley, which opened in 1912, are among the most memorable. Look out, too, for a branch of the excellent cinema chains Picturehouse, Curzon and Everyman.

INSIDER TIP
Summer Cinema Tickets

Tickets for summer screenings go on sale months in advance and often sell out. The best site to check for multiple venues is thelunacinema.com. Screenings are rarely cancelled so don't expect refunds if it rains, and bring an umbrella.

The plush setting of the Electric Cinema on Portobello Road ↑

LONDON FOR
FILM BUFFS

From the grimy, sinister streets of Victorian London to the romantic home of middle-class bumblers and eccentrics, the capital has been the backdrop to countless movies over the decades. Here, we round up the best of London's film scene.

Big Screen Scenes

Finding the streets of London familiar? It's no surprise, given the city's role in film. Hugh Grant wooed Julia Roberts in *Notting Hill* and Cillian Murphy faced a post-apocalyptic Westminster in *28 Days Later*. James Bond fans will recognize landmarks at every turn, particularly after Bond's high-speed chase down the Thames. And let's not forget a certain boy wizard, who boarded the train to Hogwarts at King's Cross Station (look out for the staged Platform 9¾, see p165).

←

Film fans on their way to Hogwarts at Platform 9¾

British Film Institute

The British Film Institute (BFI) aims to promote and preserve film-making in the UK. Its head-quarters at the BFI Southbank building *(p223)* are equipped with a four-screen cinema, a film shop and a publicly accessible film archive. The BFI organizes the London Film Festival, which runs for 12 days every October at cinemas around the city.

←

The shop at the
British Film Institute

Summer Cinema

Every summer, dates are set for outdoor cinema seasons. Among the big names is the central courtyard at Somerset House. Rooftops are a favourite, with screenings at the Bussey Building in Peckham and the Queen of Hoxton pub in Shoreditch, among others. Look out for the Luna Cinema, which has a jampacked summer schedule at over a dozen parks and gardens as well as royal palaces.

→

Settling down to watch an
open-air film screening at
Somerset House

Classical, Opera and Ballet

The classical music calendar in London is dominated every year by the Proms, eight weeks of summer concerts climaxing at the Royal Albert Hall (p252). There is plenty going on for the rest of the year – check out programmes at the Royal Festival Hall (p223), the Barbican (p182) and Wigmore Hall (p283). For opera and ballet, head to the sumptuous London Coliseum (p129) and the Royal Opera House (p125).

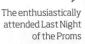

→

The enthusiastically attended Last Night of the Proms

 INSIDER TIP
Getting Tickets

Head to the TKTS booth on Leicester Square for on-the-day last-minute and discounted tickets for some first-rate West End productions.

LONDON FOR
LIVE SHOWS

"When a man is tired of London, he is tired of life," Samuel Johnson famously declared and that is as true in the 21st century as it was in the late 1700s. With an overwhelming choice of live entertainment, from a thriving comedy circuit to world-class theatre, visitors to London really are spoilt for choice.

Take Me to Church

There is much more to church music than stuffy choirs and organ recitals. Free lunchtime concerts are common and St Martin-in-the-Fields (p114) has weekday concerts. It also stages regular jazz concerts at its Café in the Crypt. St John's on Smith Square (p83) in Westminster has ticketed concerts almost every afternoon or evening. Frequently named the city's best live music venue, the Union Chapel in Islington is a special place to hear world and contemporary music.

→

A performance at the atmospheric Union Chapel

Did You Know?

Licensed Tube station buskers must pass auditions judged by music industry professionals.

Pub Performances

Some of the future greats of British music started their careers gigging on the London pub circuit, and legendary venues like the Windmill in Brixton and the Dublin Castle in Camden still host regular live performances. London's pubs also play a major role on the comedy circuit, at pubs like the Bedford in Balham and the Camden Head.

← A band playing at the Dublin Castle in Camden

A City of Theatre

The West End is the city's answer to Broadway, and commercial theatre, much of it of a very high standard, is in rude health. Independent theatre is thriving too. The National Theatre (p227) and the Barbican (p182) provide audience-pulling platforms for first-time directors and experimental productions, injecting an extra dose of creativity into London's theatre scene.

→ The long-running Les Misérables in the West End

A Fashion Mecca

When it comes to style, London is a city where just about anything goes. Iconic designers to look out for include Vivienne Westwood and the late couturier Alexander McQueen, a graduate of Central Saint Martins, the London art and design school renowned for churning out superstar designers. Check out the experimental and the edgy at London Fashion Week, which takes place in February and September.

←

A Vivienne Westwood show presenting her unique collection

LONDON IN
FASHION

London is Europe's undisputed heavyweight champion of shopping. Perhaps best known for its luxurious department stores, the city's thriving markets also provide much to delight in. In these festivals of independent retail, the walk through is at least as much fun as the eventual purchase.

Hit the High Street

Oxford Street is a bustling 2 km- (1 mile-) long parade of over 300 shops and stores. Find here the staples of the British wardrobe, with flagship stores for perennial favourites John Lewis, Marks & Spencer and Topshop. On adjoining Regent Street are famous national and international names, such as Hackett, Barbour and Ted Baker.

→

The ever-popular Oxford Street

Embrace Your Independents

On every corner there are chances to find something unique, whether high-end goods or vintage bargains. For the best suits in the city, head for the unbeatable tradition of Savile Row and Jermyn Street. Independent boutiques abound in Notting Hill and Hampstead, while for vintage and alternative fashion you can't do much better than Brick Lane and Camden.

←

Browsing the wares at a vintage shop in trendy Notting Hill

↑ Cutting-edge tailoring at a London boutique

TOP 5 LONDON MARKETS

Camden Lock Market
A canalside market, best for alternative fashion.

Portobello Road
A long road lined with antiques-loaded stalls.

Old Spitalfields Market
A covered market with themed days, like vinyl.

Columbia Road Market
Cut flowers, plants and seedlings at great prices on Sunday mornings.

Petticoat Lane Market
Historic street market, with great leather goods.

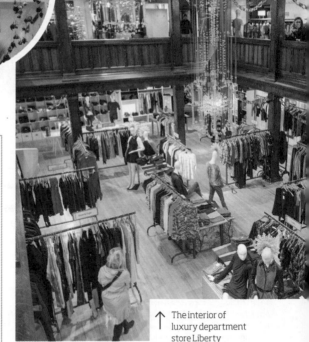

↑ The interior of luxury department store Liberty

World-Class Department Stores

You can shop till you drop in London's top department stores – and certainly your jaw will drop when you see some of the prices. The sheer extravagance of Harrods is absolutely worth braving the crowds for, as is the historic Liberty, housed in a Tudor revival building. Selfridges, second only to Harrods in size, has built a reputation not just for the staggering breadth and quality of its stock, but for its artistic and innovative window displays.

LONDON
ON THE ROOF

London is in the midst of a tall building boom, and as fast as the towers shoot up, so the trend for socializing up high thrives. Popping up on London's rooftops are open-air cinemas, adventure playgrounds for adults and buzzing bars – and all with superlative views of the cityscape.

Sky-High Jinks

Take to the rooftops for an evening of summer entertainment. Roof East in Stratford is a riotous activity playground with mini-golf, batting cages and lawn bowls surrounded by the obligatory street food pop-ups. Rooftop Film Club shows classic movies from a height, supplying their audience with wireless headphones and rows of deckchairs to settle back in. Choose from one of three venues and book your ticket in advance.

$\rightarrow$

A screening of *Saturday Night Fever* at Peckham's Rooftop Film Club

Rooftop Gardens

Some of the most delightful rooftops are those with gardens, a number of which are open to the public. Book (free of charge) to see the terraced palms and ferns of the Sky Garden *(p187)*, or walk through the landscaped flowerbed of the Crossrail Place Roof Garden in Canary Wharf. The greenery of the Queen Elizabeth Hall Roof Garden may be modest, but its riverside location in one of London's most dynamic cultural districts more than makes up for it.

←

The Sky Garden's panoramic views and the Crossrail Place Roof Garden *(inset)*

EAT

SUSHISAMBA London
An inventive menu, served 38 floors up.

⌂ 110 Bishopsgate, EC2
Ⓦ sushisamba.com

£ £ £

Oxo Tower Restaurant
Thameside location and a modern British menu.

⌂ Barge House St, SE1
Ⓦ harveynichols.com

£ £ £

Madison
In-your-face views of St Paul's from the terrace.

⌂ One New Change, EC4
Ⓦ madisonlondon.net

£ £ £

Take in the View

The Shard *(p212)*, western Europe's tallest building, provides miles of eye-busting views from its 72nd-floor viewing platform. The price of a ticket is high too, but you can opt for one of the bars on a slightly lower floor, where the view is the cost of a cocktail. Even closer to earth are some of the city's more long-lived buildings; the viewing galleries of St Paul's and Westminster cathedrals present captivating vistas along with a satisfying sense of history.

↑ The lights and landmarks of London, as seen from the Shard

EAT

Rainforest Café
Its jungle decorations
will delight little ones.

⌂ 20 Shaftesbury Ave
🖥 therainforest
cafe.co.uk

£££

Giraffe World Kitchen
Lively, with a menu to
satisfy all tastes.

⌂ Southbank Centre
🖥 giraffe.net

£££

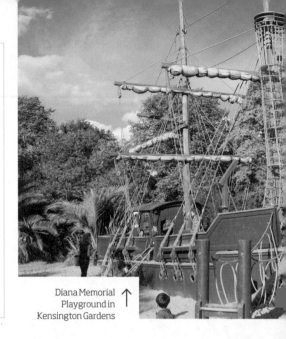

Diana Memorial ↑
Playground in
Kensington Gardens

LONDON FOR
FAMILIES

You won't struggle to find places geared up for kids in this city, with its
innovative museums, abundance of expansive parks and family-friendly
restaurants. Although some attractions are a little pricey, there's a huge
range of free and low-cost activities to be found.

Rainy-Day Activities

Given the unpredictable
British climate, it's lucky that
some of the most entertaining experiences for kids are
indoors. The standout is
the Science Museum *(p250)*,
a veritable world of wonder
that pairs well with a trip to
the Natural History Museum
(p248). A far less wholesome
experience is to be had at
the London Dungeon *(p228)*,
where gory moments in the
city's history are brought to
life. The similarly macabre
Clink Prison Museum *(p212)*
will delight fiendish teenagers.

←

Coming face-to-face with
the specimens at the Natural
History Museum

Let Off Steam

The hundreds of parks in London – both large and small – provide, at the very least, a space for kids to run around. Take your pick of St James's Park *(p95)*, Holland Park *(p266)*, Regent's Park *(p279)* and Kensington Gardens *(p256)*, all of which have playgrounds. As well as climbing frames, swing sets and slides, Hyde Park also has a lido and a boating lake *(p257)*. Don't miss Coram's Fields *(p157)* in Bloomsbury, a park designed solely for children and young people, with adventure play areas, a city farm and a paddling pool.

 INSIDER TIP
Kids Go Free

Under-11s can travel for free on public transport when they're accompanied by an adult and can gain admission to most attractions for a reduced price. At many sights, entry is free for under-5s.

Urban Safari

Inexpensive or free, London's city farms are great places for families on a budget. One of the biggest is Mudchute Park and Farm, near Canary Wharf (www.mudchute.org), home to over 100 animals. For more exotic creatures, head to the children's zoo at Battersea Park *(p238)*, which counts monkeys, snakes and emus among its residents, while for the biggest beasts make a beeline for London Zoo *(p278)*.

$\rightarrow$

Feeding the donkeys at Mudchute Park and Farm

Acting Up

From traditional puppet shows to cutting-edge plays, there are plenty of theatres for children. The marionette shows at the Puppet Theatre Barge in Little Venice *(p270)* and Richmond offer a unique, floating setting, while the Unicorn Theatre in London Bridge puts on around 20 kids' shows a year *(www.unicorntheatre.com)*.

 $\leftarrow$

A performance at the Puppet Theatre Barge

Dickensian London

Inspired by the city and its people, Charles Dickens is inextricably linked to London. Read *The Pickwick Papers* and *Oliver Twist* to get you in the mood, then tour the streets he made famous with Charles Dickens Walks and Tours (*dickenslondontours. co.uk*). To get to know the man himself, visit his Bloomsbury house, now the Charles Dickens Museum (*p155*).

Victorian interior of the Charles Dickens Museum

LONDON FOR
BOOKWORMS

If you're a lover of books you'll be a lover of London. Writers and readers alike have much to celebrate in the city, with the world's largest library and Europe's largest bookshop, a thriving independent bookshop scene and a literary heritage stretching back centuries.

Recommended Reads

Dickens classics aside, there are plenty of London-set novels to devour. George Orwell's *Keep the Aspidistra Flying* is a portrayal of city poverty. There's a strong sense of place in Zadie Smith's *White Teeth* and Sam Selvon's *The Lonely Londoners*, both examinations of the immigrant experience. John Lanchester's *Capital* explores the dynamics on a London street around the 2008 financial crisis.

→

Browsing at the Foyles store, Charing Cross Road

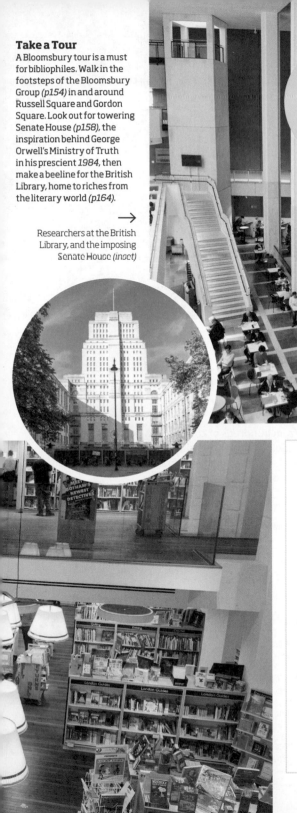

Take a Tour

A Bloomsbury tour is a must for bibliophiles. Walk in the footsteps of the Bloomsbury Group *(p154)* in and around Russell Square and Gordon Square. Look out for towering Senate House *(p158)*, the inspiration behind George Orwell's Ministry of Truth in his prescient *1984*, then make a beeline for the British Library, home to riches from the literary world *(p164)*.

→

Researchers at the British Library, and the imposing Senate House *(inset)*

Did You Know?
___

If you read five books a day, it would take 80,000 years to work your way through the British Library.

SHOP

Foyles

This renowned store, one of London's biggest, is a haven for booklovers with a history dating back to 1903, when brothers William and Gilbert began the venture by selling the textbooks they didn't need. The five-story flagship store on Charing Cross Road includes a jazz music concession, an excellent foreign language books section and over 6 km (4 miles) of shelving.

⌂ 107 Charing Cross Rd
ⓦ foyles.co.uk

LONDON FOR
FOODIES

You can sample food from hundreds of countries in every imaginable setting and on any budget in London. Shining with Michelin-starred restaurants, the city is also in the midst of a sparks-flying street food explosion. Here, we explore some of its must-eats.

Festival Seasoning

For more food stalls than you can wave a bread stick at, time your visit to coincide with one of the city's summer food festivals. In May, Feria de Londres at the Southbank Centre celebrates Spanish cuisine and culture. In June, bag a ticket for Taste of London, a fine-dining jamboree in Regent's Park (london.taste festivals.com). Looser and livelier are the StrEATlife festivals held between May and August at Alexandra Palace (p322). The vibe is more like a music festival here, with DJs and bands providing the soundtrack for grazing while gazing out over London.

$\rightarrow$

Trying out nibbles at the Taste of London festival

Eat the Street

There are plenty of restaurants jumping on the street food bandwagon, but genuine on-the-hoof eats - sold from market stalls, shipping containers, trucks and more - are popping up wherever there are crowds of people. The best-known option - although on the pricey side - is Borough Market *(p211)*. The Southbank Centre Food Market *(p222)* is also slap-bang in the middle of the tourist circuit and sells breads and cheeses, as well as a mix of British and international dishes. For a more authentic street experience, head to Leather Lane Market *(p143)*, Berwick Street Market *(p116)*, Camden Market *(p168)* or Maltby Street Market *(www.maltby.st)*.

Street stall at Borough Market selling freshly baked breads

TOP 5 LONDON FOOD HUBS

Brixton Village and Market Row
Old market arcades now heaving with cafés and restaurants *(p328)*.

Flat Iron Square
Food counters in a set of railways arches *(p212)*.

The Prince
A polished street food hub with alfresco dining *(theprincelondon.com)*.

Feast Bar & Kitchen
Street food in the old BBC TV Centre *(feastbar andkitchen.com)*.

Bang Bang Oriental
A specialist Asian cuisine food hall *(bang bangoriental.com)*.

↑ Le Gavroche, and a dish from the Connaught Restaurant *(inset)*

Fine Dining

With over 70 Michelin-starred restaurants, the fine dining scene is booming. Most of the extravagant eateries are found in the West End, the City, Kensington and Knightsbridge. They tend to be formal affairs, but there are hipper exceptions, such as industrial chic tapas joint Barrafina *(p115)* and Cantonese favourite Hakkasan *(hakkasan.com)*. Most of these places build their reputation on their chefs, like Michel Roux of Le Gavroche *(le-gavroche.co.uk)* and Gordon Ramsay, whose eponymous restaurant is one of only three in the city with three Michelin stars *(gordonramsayrestaurants.com)*.

A YEAR IN
LONDON

JANUARY

London Art Fair (*mid-Jan*). Top-notch modern and contemporary art show.

△ **Chinese New Year** (*late Jan*). Chinatown celebrates the new year with a parade, performances and plenty of food.

FEBRUARY

△ **Six Nations** (*early Feb to mid-Mar*). This Rugby Union tournament takes place in Ireland, France, Scotland, Wales, Italy and England's Twickenham, near London.

MAY

FA Cup Final (*mid-May*). The annual conclusion of the oldest cup tournament in world football is held at Wembley Stadium.

△ **Chelsea Flower Show** (*late May*). A five-day horticultural show at the Royal Hospital Chelsea.

International Cricket (*late May*). The cricket season kicks off; catch it at Lord's or the Oval.

JUNE

△ **Trooping the Colour** (*mid-Jun*). A show of extravagant military pageantry for the Queen's Birthday Parade.

Open Garden Squares Weekend (*mid-Jun*). More than 200 private gardens open up to the public for one weekend only.

Royal Academy of Arts Summer Exhibition (*Jun–Aug*). Hundreds of works are exhibited in one of the most popular art events of the year.

SEPTEMBER

Totally Thames (*all month*). A month-long festival featuring events along and on the river.

△ **Open House Weekend** (*mid- or late Sep*). Citywide iconic and little-known buildings open their doors to the public free of charge for one weekend only.

OCTOBER

△ **London Film Festival** (*mid- to late Oct*). Some 300 British and international films are screened at cinemas large and small around the city.

MARCH

△ **The Boat Race** (late Mar or early Apr). The Oxford and Cambridge University rowing crews take to the river in this annual race that runs from Putney Bridge to Chiswick Bridge.

APRIL

△ **London Marathon** (mid Apr). Thousands pound the city's streets, from Blackheath to the Mall, as they tackle the gruelling 42.2-km (26.2-mile) course.

Queen's Birthday gun salute (21 Apr). A 41-gun salute at Hyde Park and 62-gun salute at the Tower of London herald the Queen's birthday.

JULY

Wimbledon Lawn Tennis Championships (early to mid-Jul). The only Grand Slam tournament played on grass.

△ **Pride in London** (early Jul). The culmination of London's Pride Festival, thousands parade through the streets of London to celebrate the LGBT+ community.

The Proms (mid-Jul to mid-Sep). An eight-week festival of classical and orchestral music, concluding with the over-the-top, uproarious Last Night of the Proms.

Buckingham Palace State Rooms open to the public (mid-Jul to late Sep).

AUGUST

Film4 Summer Screen at Somerset House (2 wks in Aug). Open-air cinema screenings in Somerset House's Fountain Court.

△ **Notting Hill Carnival** (last weekend of Aug). Europe's largest street festival is a riotous celebration of Afro-Caribbean music and culture.

NOVEMBER

Lord Mayor's Show (2nd Sat). A procession of bands, floats and military detachments accompany the Lord Mayor in his gold state coach as it makes its way through the City.

Remembrance Sunday (2nd Sun). A ceremony giving thanks to those who died fighting in any conflict from World War I onwards. The Cenotaph is the focus of London's main ceremony.

△ **London Jazz Festival** (mid-Nov). Big names, local acts and the broadest possible definition of jazz characterize this eclectic festival.

DECEMBER

Hyde Park Winter Wonderland (late Nov to early Jan). Festive markets, fairground rides and a huge outdoor ice rink attract crowds to London's largest inner-city park.

△ **New Year's Eve Fireworks** (31 Dec). A spectacular display of fireworks lighting up the Houses of Parliament, the London Eye and the South Bank.

A BRIEF
HISTORY

Founded by the Romans, London changed hands many times in its first thousand years. Devastated by fire, plague and war during the subsequent millennium, the city rebuilt itself every time to become a centre of world trade and the largest metropolis on the planet.

Roman London

The first permanent settlement on land within what is now London was established after the first Roman invasion of Britain in 55 BC, though it was not cemented until almost a century later, following another, greater invasion in AD 43. The Romans bridged the river and built their administrative headquarters, Londinium, on the north bank, the present site of the City of London. The Roman occupation lasted some 350 years, but following its withdrawal in the early 5th century during the decline of the Roman Empire, the city lay more or less abandoned.

1 A map of London from 1570. ↑

2 Work begins on Westminster Abbey.

3 The Battle of 1066.

4 Thousands were killed by the Black Death of 1348.

Timeline of events

55 BC
Julius Caesar invades Britain

AD 43
Londinium founded

AD 61
Londinium is sacked by the Iceni, British Celts led by their queen Boudicca

200
Romans build a wall around the city

410
Romans withdraw from Britain

Saxons and Vikings

Saxon and Viking invaders fought over the city over the following centuries, during which time its importance fell below that of others like Winchester and Canterbury. It wasn't until 1016 that it recovered its status as the capital under King Canute. Edward the Confessor, one of the last Anglo-Saxon kings of England, moved the base for royal government to the City of Westminster, a distinction that remains to this day. Edward also founded Westminster Abbey where, following the subsequent Norman invasion, William the Conqueror was crowned in 1066.

Norman and Medieval London

William allowed the City of London a degree of independence, reliant as he and his successors were on the City's backing, with all its wealth, for the maintenance of power. City tradesmen set up their own institutions and guilds and the first City of London mayor was appointed in 1189. By the early 14th century London enjoyed a period of relative prosperity, though much of the population, thought to be around 80,000 by this time, lived in poverty. This number was cut in half by the arrival of the bubonic plague, known as the Black Death, in 1348.

WHERE TO SEE MEDIEVAL LONDON

The Tower of London's White Tower is likely the most complete 11th-century palace in Europe, while the Museum of London (p183) contains medieval artifacts. Manuscripts, including the Domesday Book, are found at the British Library (p164). A 14th-century rose window is all that remains of Winchester Palace near the Clink (p212).

872

The Danes occupy London

1066

Edward the Confessor buried, and William the Conqueror crowned on Christmas Day

1209

Old London Bridge completed

1348

The Black Death kills half of the London population

1381

Peasants' Revolt

Tudor London

The Tudors' reign began in 1485 with Henry VII. They established peace throughout England, allowing art and commerce to flourish. Under Elizabeth I, explorers opened up the New World, installing London as the world's foremost trade market. It was also during Elizabeth's reign that the foundations of England's great theatrical and literary traditions were firmly laid. The Globe Theatre was erected in 1576 and premiered many of Shakespeare's plays.

Religious Strife and Civil War

Just two years after Elizabeth I's death Catholic conspirators, led by Guy Fawkes, attempted to assassinate King James I by blowing him up in the Houses of Parliament. An anti-Catholic backlash followed and religious conflict, married to a power struggle between Parliament and the monarch, led to Civil War in 1642. London, a Parliamentarian stronghold, became a key battleground. Parliamentarian victory in 1649 established an English Commonwealth dominated by Puritans under Oliver Cromwell. Their rule was, however, short lived and the monarchy was restored under Charles II in 1660.

↑ Charles I beheaded by the Parliamentarians, led by Oliver Cromwell

Timeline of events

1585
Shakespeare arrives in London

1642
Civil War begins and Charles I decamps from London

1649
Charles I beheaded at Whitehall, Commonwealth established

1660
Monarchy restored under Charles II

1665
The Great Plague kills 100,000

3

Devastation and Reconstruction

On 2 September 1666 a fire broke out at a bakery in Pudding Lane, near London Bridge. It raged for five days, destroying much of the City of London. The post-fire reconstruction formed the basis of the modern-day City of London. As settlements spread beyond the original walled city, the City of London was soon stretching as far as the previously separate City of Westminster.

Expansion

The foundation of the Bank of England in 1694 spurred growth and transformed London into a global financial powerhouse. By the middle of the 18th century London was the largest city in Europe and within a hundred years had become the most populous and wealthiest in the world. The prospect of jobs and money lured millions of the dispossessed from the countryside and from abroad. They crowded into insanitary dwellings, many just east of the City, where docks provided employment. From the 1820s the fields and villages that ringed the city, places like Brompton, Islington and Battersea, filled rapidly with terraced housing for the growing numbers of people.

1 Queen Elizabeth I, who oversaw great change in the city. ↑

2 Guy Fawkes, plotting King James I's downfall.

3 The Great Fire of London, 1666.

Did You Know?
———
After the Great Fire, Sir Christopher Wren designed 51 new churches for the city, plus St Paul's Cathedral.

1710
Christopher Wren's St Paul's cathedral is completed

1826
London University established

1666
The Great Fire of London devastates the City

1801
The first census records a London population of over one million

1802
West India Dock is built, the beginning of a major expansion of London docklands

Victorian London

Much of London today is Victorian. In this golden age of British engineering, many of the city's iconic buildings and structures – the modern Houses of Parliament, Tower Bridge, St Pancras station, the Royal Albert Hall and the London Underground – were built. In 1855 the Metropolitan Board of Works was created, the beginnings of a form of local government. Its chief engineer, Joseph Bazalgette, designed a ground-breaking underground sewer system which did much to alleviate the filth and stink in the streets and the river, reducing the outbreaks of cholera that had accompanied urban expansion. By the end of the 19th century, 4.5 million people lived in inner London and another 4 million in its immediate vicinity.

World Wars and Postwar Reconstruction

During World War I, Zeppelin airships bombed the city, but the damage and number of casualties was nothing as compared to the devastation wreaked during World War II. Much of London, particularly central areas, was flattened, first by the bombing during the Blitz of 1940–41 and then towards the end of the war by V-1 and V-2 rockets, early forms of cruise missiles. The

↑ Winston Churchill, prime minister during World War II

Timeline of events

1836
First London rail terminus opens at London Bridge

1837
Queen Victoria makes Buckingham Palace her London residence

1858
Smelliness of the Thames forces parliament into recess

1851
The Great Exhibition is held in Hyde Park

1863
World's first underground railway opens between Paddington and Farringdon

substantial rebuilding that followed the war coincided with the decline of the docks and other Victorian industries. Enormous housing estates sprung up around the city, some of which remain today. Still around too is the Royal Festival Hall, built on the banks of the Thames for the 1951 Festival of Britain, a celebration of British technology and culture. The hall is now part of the Southbank Centre, along with a few striking Brutalist buildings. Mass immigration from the former colonies of Britain's rapidly disappearing empire, and from the Indian subcontinent and the West Indies, contributed to the city's ever diverse population.

London Today

The city saw in the new millennium with a swathe of grand building projects – the London Eye, Tate Modern and the ill-fated Millennium Dome – and cranes continue to dominate the skyline in a city that never seems finished. Indeed, regeneration reverberates around the city as it grapples to combat a housing crisis and toxic pollution levels. Despite a number of terror attacks and this cosmopolitan city's disquiet over Britain's decision to leave the European Union, the enduring spirit of the city's inhabitants and sense of community prevails.

1 The Great Exhibition of 1851.

2 Sleeping in a Tube station during World War II.

3 The Festival of Britain.

4 Opening ceremony, 2012 Olympics.

Did You Know?

The Millennium Dome cost over £700 million to construct.

1908
London hosts the Olympic Games

2000
Ken Livingstone becomes London's first directly elected mayor

2005
Major terrorist attack takes place on London's transport system

1951
Festival of Britain held on the South Bank

2012
London hosts the Olympic Games for the third time

EXPERIENCE

Looking towards St Paul's Cathedral

Whitehall and Westminster 68

Mayfair and St James's 86

Soho and Trafalgar Square 102

Covent Garden and the Strand 118

Holborn and the Inns of Court 132

Bloomsbury and Fitzrovia 146

King's Cross,
Camden and Islington 160

The City 170

Shoreditch and Spitalfields 192

Southwark and Bankside 202

South Bank 216

Chelsea and Battersea 230

South Kensington
and Knightsbridge 240

Kensington, Holland Park
and Notting Hill 260

Regent's Park and Marylebone 274

Hampstead and Highgate 286

Greenwich and Canary Wharf 298

Beyond the Centre 310

WHITEHALL AND WESTMINSTER

Whitehall and Westminster have been at the centre of political and religious power in England for a thousand years. King Canute, who ruled at the beginning of the 11th century, was the first monarch to have a palace on what was then an island in the swampy meeting point of the Thames and its vanished tributary, the Tyburn. Canute built his palace beside the church that, some 50 years later, Edward the Confessor would enlarge into England's greatest abbey, giving the area its name (a minster is an abbey church). Over the following centuries the offices of state were set up in the vicinity, many of them in Whitehall. This grand street took its name from the Palace of Whitehall that once stood there, established by Henry VIII in the early 16th century as a residence of the royal court. The palace burnt down in 1698 but Whitehall remained at the heart of government, its buildings now occupied by the Ministry of Defence, the Foreign Office, Cabinet Office and several other prestigious government departments.

WHITEHALL AND WESTMINSTER

Must Sees
1. Westminster Abbey
2. Houses of Parliament
3. Tate Britain

Experience More
4. Big Ben
5. Jewel Tower
6. St Margaret's Church
7. Parliament Square
8. Downing Street
9. Churchill War Rooms
10. Banqueting House
11. Horse Guards Parade
12. Household Cavalry Museum
13. Guards Museum
14. Westminster Cathedral
15. St John's Smith Square

Stay
1. Artist Residence

WHITEHALL AND WESTMINSTER

0 metres   300
0 yards   300
N

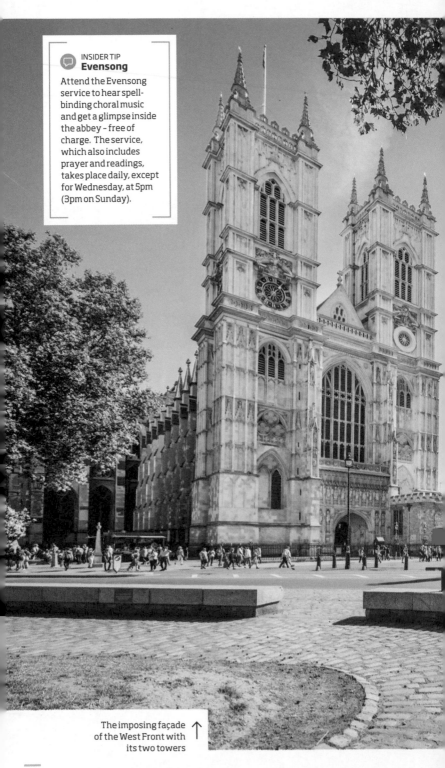

💬 INSIDER TIP
Evensong

Attend the Evensong service to hear spellbinding choral music and get a glimpse inside the abbey – free of charge. The service, which also includes prayer and readings, takes place daily, except for Wednesday, at 5pm (3pm on Sunday).

The imposing façade ↑
of the West Front with
its two towers

❶

WESTMINSTER ABBEY

📍 I7 🏠 Broad Sanctuary SW1 🚇 St James's Park, Westminster 🚆 Victoria, Waterloo 🕐 Check website for specific parts of the church 🌐 westminster-abbey.org

The final resting place of 17 of Britain's monarchs and numerous political and cultural icons, the glorious Gothic Westminster Abbey is the stunning setting for coronations, royal marriages and Christian worship.

Within the abbey walls are some of the best examples of medieval architecture in London and one of the most impressive collections of tombs and monuments in the world. Half national church, half national museum, the abbey is part of British national consciousness. Many of the leading lights from British history are buried or memorialized here, including poets and politicians, writers and scientists.

History of the Abbey

The first abbey church was established as early as the 10th century, by St Dunstan and a group of Benedictine monks. The present structure dates largely from the 13th century; the new French-influenced design was begun in 1245 at the behest of Henry III. It survived Henry VIII's 16th century onslaught on Britain's monastic buildings due to its unique role as the royal coronation church.

←

Statue of Richard I, known as Richard the Lionheart, facing the rear of Westminster Abbey

CORONATION

The abbey has been the fittingly sumptuous setting for all royal coronations since 1066. The last occupant of the Coronation Chair was the present monarch, Elizabeth II. She was crowned in 1953 and many watched the event on TV: this was the first televised coronation.

Inside the Abbey

The abbey's interior presents an exceptionally diverse array of architectural and sculptural styles, from the austere French Gothic of the nave, through the stunning complexity of Henry VII's Tudor chapel, to the riotous invention of the later 18th-century monuments. The latest addition is the 2018 Weston Tower, which provides access to the triforium and its Queen's Diamond Jubilee Galleries, packed with historical treasures.

The West Front towers were designed by Nicholas Hawksmoor.

① Monument to William Shakespeare in Poets' Corner.

② Executed by Elizabeth I in 1587, Mary Queen of Scots was reburied in Henry VII's Lady Chapel by her son James I (James VI of Scotland) in 1612.

③ The Westminster Abbey choir sing from their stalls in the quire every day. The original quire stalls were medieval, but the ones you see now date from 1848.

Timeline

1050
△ New Benedictine abbey church begun by Edward the Confessor

1245
New church begun to the designs of Henry of Reyns

1269
△ Body of Edward the Confessor is moved to a new shrine in the abbey

1540
△ Monastery dissolved on the orders of King Henry VIII

The stonework here is Victorian.

The north transept's three chapels contain some of the abbey's finest monuments.

St Edward's chapel houses the shrine of Edward the Confessor.

The Queen's Diamond Jubilee Galleries are 16 m (52 ft) above the abbey floor.

The Lady Chapel, with a superb vaulted ceiling.

The octagonal Chapter House contains 13th-century tiles.

The south transept contains Poets' Corner, where famous literary figures are commemorated.

The cloisters were built mainly in the 13th and 14th centuries.

↑ Cross-section of Westminster Abbey, revealing the interior

Massive flying buttresses help spread the weight of the nave.

The nave – 31 m (102 ft) tall – is the highest in England.

1745
▲ West towers completed

1838
▲ Queen Victoria's coronation

1953
Elizabeth II's coronation is beamed to televisions across the nation

2011
▲ Prince William and Catherine Middleton marry in the abbey

② 🏛 🎨 🖥 🛍

HOUSES OF PARLIAMENT

📍 I7 🏠 London SW1 🚇 Westminster 🚆 Victoria ⛴ Westminster Pier
🕐 For details on visiting and to buy tickets, check website 🔒 Recesses: mid-Feb, Easter, Whitsun, summer (late Jul–early Sep), conference (mid-Sep–mid-Oct), mid-Nov, Christmas 🌐 parliament.uk/visit

At the heart of political power in England is the Palace of Westminster. Built in Neo-Gothic style it lies beside the Thames near Westminster Bridge and makes an impressive sight, especially with the distinctive Elizabeth Tower.

For over 500 years the Palace of Westminster has been the seat of the two Houses of Parliament, called the Lords and the Commons. The Commons is made up of elected Members of Parliament (MPs) of different political parties; the party – or coalition of parties – with the most MPs forms the Government, and its leader becomes prime minister. MPs from other parties make up the Opposition. Commons debates are impartially chaired by an MP designated as Speaker. The Government formulates legislation which must be agreed to in both Houses before it becomes law.

↑ The Houses of Parliament, designed by Sir Charles Barry

→ The Gothic Revival masterpiece of the Palace of Westminster

Government and Opposition parties face each other across the Commons Chamber.

The vast bell named Big Ben was hung in 1858 and chimes on the hour.

Entrance to Westminster Hall

1605
▽ Guy Fawkes and others try to blow up the king and Houses of Parliament

1941
▽ Chamber of House of Commons destroyed by World War II bomb

Timeline

1042
△ Work starts on first palace for Edward the Confessor

1834
△ Palace destroyed by fire; only Westminster Hall and the Jewel Tower survive

People who come to meet their MP wait under a ceiling of rich mosaics in the Central Lobby.

The Lords Chamber is upholstered in red.

Sovereign's entrance

Westminster Hall is one of the surviving parts of the original Palace of Westminster, dating from 1097.

↑ The green leather benches of the Commons Chamber, where the government sits

TATE BRITAIN
THE NATIONAL
COLLECTION OF
BRITISH ART

The stately façade ↑
of Tate Britain, home
of British art

③ 🚴 🍴 🖥 🏛

TATE BRITAIN

📍I9 🏠 Millbank SW1 🚇 Pimlico 🚆 Victoria, Vauxhall ⛴ Millbank Pier
🕐 10am–6pm daily (till 10pm last Fri, every month except Dec)
📅 24–26 Dec 🌐 tate.org.uk

The nation's largest collection of British art, spanning the 16th to the 21st centuries, is held in a fabulous Neo-Classical building facing the river. The works include sculpture and modern installation pieces, plus a separate wing given over to the moody paintings of British artist J M W Turner.

The gallery exhibits a broad range of British art, from Tudor portraits and 18th-century landscapes to a large sculpture collection and modern art. Displays change frequently and the gallery's broad definition of British art stretches to work by non-British artists who spent time in the country, such as Canaletto and James Whistler. The gallery opened in 1897, founded on the private collection of the sugar merchant Henry Tate and works from the older National Gallery. The Tate includes seven rooms added to display the paintings of J M W Turner, one of Britain's most revered artists. The Turner Bequest, as it is known, was left to the nation by Turner on his death in 1851. It is displayed in its own wing, called the Clore Gallery, and consists of some 300 oil paintings, 300 sketchbooks and about 20,000 watercolours and drawings. Major temporary exhibitions here always draw huge crowds.

↑ Turner's *Peace – Burial at Sea* (1842), a tribute to his friend and rival David Wilkie

↑ Inside the gallery, where art graces every corner

TURNER PRIZE

Every other year, Tate Britain exhibits the shortlisted works for the prestigious and often controversial Turner Prize, which was established in 1984. Representing all visual arts, four contemporary artists are shortlisted annually on the basis of their work during the preceding year, before a panel of judges picks the winner. Among the most sensational of the boundary-testing winners have been Damien Hirst's *Mother and Child, Divided* (1995) and the ceramics of Grayson Perry *(right)* in 2003.

EXPERIENCE MORE

④

Big Ben

 I7 🏛 Bridge St
SW1 🚇 Westminster
🌐 parliament.uk/bigben

Big Ben is not the name of
the world-famous four-faced
clock in the 96-m (315-ft)
tower that rises above the
Houses of Parliament, but of
the resonant 13.7-tonne bell
inside the tower on which the
hour is struck. It is thought to
be named after the First
Commissioner of Works Sir
Benjamin Hall. Cast at
Whitechapel Bell Foundry in
1858, it was the second giant
bell made for the clock, the
first having become cracked
during a test ringing. The
clock is the largest in Britain,
its four dials 7 m (23 ft) in
diameter and the minute
hand 4.2 m (14 ft) long, made
in hollow copper for lightness.
The tower itself was renamed
the Elizabeth Tower in 2012 in
honour of Queen Elizabeth II
in her Diamond Jubilee year.

A symbol the world over,
Big Ben has kept exact time
for the nation more or less
continuously since it was first
set in motion in May 1859.

Now, however, it stands silent,
closed for essential building
works until 2021 – tours are
suspended for the duration.

---

⑤

Jewel Tower

 I7 🏛 Abingdon St SW1
🚇 Westminster ⏰ Apr-
Sep: 10am-6pm daily; Oct:
10am-5pm daily; Nov-
Mar: 10am-4pm Sat & Sun
🌐 english-heritage.org.uk

This 14th-century building
and Westminster Hall (p77) are
the only remaining vestiges of
the old Palace of Westminster,
having survived a fire in 1834.
The tower was built in 1365 as
a stronghold for Edward III's
treasure and today houses a
fascinating exhibition called
"Parliament Past and Present",
which relates the history of
Parliament. The display on the
upper floor is devoted to the
history of the tower itself.

The tower served as the
Weights and Measures office
from 1869 until 1938 and
another small display relates
to that era. Alongside are the
remains of the moat and a
medieval quay.

⑥

St Margaret's Church

📍 I7 🏛 Broad Sanctuary SW1
🚇 Westminster ⏰ 9:30am-
3:30pm Mon-Fri, 9:30am-
1:30pm Sat, 2:30-4:30pm
Sun 🌐 westminster-abbey.
org/st-margarets-church

This late-15th-century church
has long been a favoured
venue for political and society
weddings, such as Winston
and Clementine Churchill's.
Although much restored, the
church retains some Tudor

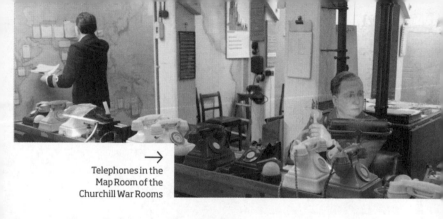

→ Telephones in the Map Room of the Churchill War Rooms

features, notably a stained-glass window commemorating the marriage of King Henry VIII and his first wife, Catherine of Aragon.

7

Parliament Square

📍 I7 🏠 SW1 🚇 Westminster

Laid out in 1868 to provide a more open aspect for the new Houses of Parliament, the square today is hemmed in by heavy traffic. Statues of statesmen are dominated by Winston Churchill, glowering at the House of Commons. On the north side, Abraham Lincoln stands in front of the mock-Gothic Middlesex Guildhall. Millicent Fawcett – a campaigner for women's suffrage – is the only female represented in the square.

8

Downing Street

📍 I6 🏠 SW1 🚇 Westminster 🚫 To the public

Sir George Downing (1623–84) spent part of his youth in the American colonies. He was the second person to graduate from the nascent Harvard College, before returning to

← The Elizabeth Tower, seen from Albert Embankment

fight for the Parliamentarians in the English Civil War. In 1680, he bought land near Whitehall Palace and built a street of houses. Four of these survive, though they are much altered. King George II gave No 10 to Sir Robert Walpole in 1732. Since then it has been the official residence of the British prime minister.

9

Churchill War Rooms

📍 I7 🏠 Clive Steps, King Charles St SW1 🚇 Westminster, St James's Park ⏰ 9:30am–6pm daily (last adm: 5pm) 🚫 24–26 Dec, 1 Jan 🌐 iwm.org.uk

This intriguing slice of 20th-century history is a warren of rooms below the Treasury building, where the War Cabinet met during World War II, when German bombs were falling on London. The War Rooms include living quarters for key ministers and military leaders and the Cabinet Room, where strategic decisions were taken. They are laid out as they were when the war ended, with Churchill's desk, communications equipment and maps for plotting military strategy. The Churchill Museum is a multimedia exhibit recording Churchill's life and career, and the display "Undercover: Life in Churchill's Bunker" features personal stories, objects and interviews with those who worked in the War Rooms. Booking ahead is recommended to avoid long queues.

THE CENOTAPH

On Remembrance Sunday every year – the Sunday nearest 11 November – ceremonies held around the UK honour those who have lost their lives serving in conflicts since World War I. The Cenotaph, a monument on Whitehall completed in 1920 by Sir Edwin Lutyens, is the focal point of London's remembrance service, when members of the royal family and other dignitaries place wreaths of red poppies at its base.

Henry VIII's jousting ↑
grounds, now Horse
Guards Parade

Banqueting House

I6 ⬛ Whitehall SW1
⬛ Embankment, Charing
Cross, Westminster
🕙 10am–5pm daily (last
adm: 4:15pm) 🚫 24–26 Dec
& 1 Jan ⬛ hrp.org.uk

This delightful building is of
great architectural importance.
It was the first built in central
London to embody the
Classical Palladian style that
designer Inigo Jones brought
back from his travels in Italy.
Completed in 1622, its
disciplined stone façade
marked a startling change
from the Elizabethans' fussy
turrets and unrestrained
external decoration.

Rubens's ceiling paintings,
a complex allegory on the
exaltation of James I, were
commissioned by his son,
Charles I, in 1630. This blatant
glorification of royalty was
despised by Oliver Cromwell
and the Parliamentarians,
who executed King Charles I
on a scaffold just outside
Banqueting House in 1649.
Eleven years later, the English
monarchy was restored with
the coronation of Charles II.

The building is used today
for official functions, and may
close early when these are
scheduled: check the website
for details.

Horse Guards Parade

⬛ I6 ⬛ Whitehall SW1
⬛ Westminster, Charing
Cross, Embankment

This is where the Trooping the
Colour ceremony (p58) takes
place each year, but you can
see royal pageantry in action
daily: Changing the Life Guard
takes place at 11am (10am
on Sunday), and there's a
guard inspection at 4pm.

This was Henry VIII's tiltyard
(tournament ground); nearby
is a trace of the "real tennis"
court where the king is said to
have played the precursor of
modern lawn tennis. The
elegant buildings, completed
in 1755, were designed by
William Kent. On the opposite
side, the ivy-covered Citadel is
a bomb-proof structure built in
1940 beside the Admiralty.
During World War II, it was
used as a communications
headquarters by the Navy.

> ### QUEEN ANNE'S GATE
>
> Not far from St James's Park Tube station is Queen Anne's
> Gate, a well-preserved street lined with spacious
> terraced houses, many of which are Grade I listed. Most
> date from 1704 and are notable for the ornate canopies
> over each front door. At the east end of the street are
> houses built some 70 years later, some sporting blue
> plaques that record former residents, such as Lord
> Palmerston, a prime minister during the Victorian era.
> It is rumoured that the British Secret Service, MI5, was
> formerly based in this unlikely spot.

working stables, and kids (big and small) can try on uniforms.

13

Guards Museum

📍H7 🏠Birdcage Walk SW1 🚇St James's Park 🕐10am-4pm daily (last adm: 3:30pm) 🚫Mid-Dec-end Jan & for ceremonies 🌐theguardsmuseum.com

Entered from Birdcage Walk, this museum is under the parade ground of Wellington Barracks, headquarters of the five Foot Guards regiments. A must for military buffs, the museum illustrates battles in which the Guards have taken part, from the English Civil War (1642–8) to the present. Weapons and colourful uniforms are on display, as are some fascinating models.

14

Westminster Cathedral

📍H8 🏠Victoria Street SW1 🚇Victoria 🕐7am-7pm Mon-Fri, 8am-7pm Sat & Sun; check website for service times 🌐westminster cathedral.org.uk

One of London's rare Byzantine buildings, this cathedral was designed by John Francis Bentley for the Catholic

12

Household Cavalry Museum

📍I6 🏠Horse Guards, Whitehall SW1 🚇Charing Cross, Westminster, Embankment 🕐Apr-Oct: 10am-6pm daily; Nov-Mar: 10am-5pm daily 🚫Good Fri, 20 Jul, 24-26 Dec; occasionally for ceremonies 🌐household cavalrymuseum.co.uk

A collection of artifacts and interactive displays cover the history of the senior regiments based at Horse Guards, from their role in the 1815 Battle of Waterloo to their service in Afghanistan in the early 21st century. Visitors can see the

diocese and completed in 1903. Its 87-m- (285-ft-) high red-brick bell tower, with horizontal stripes of white stone, has a superb viewing gallery at the top (there is a charge to take the lift). The rich interior decoration, with marble of varying colours and intricate mosaics, makes the domes above the nave seem incongruous. They were left bare because the project ran out of money. Eric Gill's dramatic reliefs of the 14 Stations of the Cross, created during World War I, adorn the piers of the nave. The organ is superb; there are often free recitals on Sundays at 4:45pm.

15

St John's Smith Square

📍I8 🏠Smith Sq SW1 🚇Westminster 🕐For concerts only 🌐sjss.org.uk

A masterpiece of English Baroque architecture, Thomas Archer's plump church looks as if it is trying to burst from the confines of the square. Today principally a concert hall, it has an accident-prone history: completed in 1728, it was burned down in 1742, struck by lightning in 1773 and destroyed by a World War II bomb in 1941. There is a basement restaurant, open on weekdays for lunch and on concert evenings.

The Life Guards, part of the royal Household Cavalry →

A SHORT WALK
WHITEHALL AND WESTMINSTER

Distance 2 km (1.25 miles) **Nearest Tube**
St James's Park **Time** 30 minutes

London has comparatively little monumental
architecture, but a stroll through the historic
seat of both the government and the established
church uncovers broad, stately avenues designed
to overawe with pomp. On weekdays the streets
are crowded with members of the civil service,
while at weekends they teem mainly with tourists,
visiting some of London's most famous sights.

The meticulously
preserved War
Rooms were
Winston Churchill's
World War II
headquarters (p81).

The Treasury is
where the nation's
finances are
administered.

Statues of famous
statesmen, such as
Benjamin Disraeli,
stand in Parliament
Square (p81).

Central Hall is a florid example of
the Beaux Arts style, built in 1911 as
a Methodist meeting hall. In 1946
the first General Assembly of the
United Nations was held here.

Westminster Abbey
is London's most
important church (p72).

Society weddings
often take place in St
Margaret's Church (p80).

Westminster School
was founded in
Dean's Yard in 1540.

Richard I's statue, by Carlo
Marochetti (1860), depicts
the 12th-century Coeur de
Lion (Lionheart).

Kings once stored their
most valuable possessions in
the Jewel Tower (p80).

The Burghers of Calais
is a cast of Auguste Rodin's
original in Calais.

KING CHARLES

STOREY'S GATE

GREAT GEORGE STREET

BROAD SANCTUARY

ST MARGARET STREET

GREAT COLLEGE ST

ABINGDON ST

British prime ministers have lived on Downing Street since 1732 (p81).

FINISH

A mounted guard is ceremonially changed at Horse Guards Parade every day (p82).

Dover House, a stately mansion dating from 1787, now houses the Scotland Office.

Inigo Jones designed the elegant Banqueting House, which has a Rubens ceiling, in 1622 (p82).

Earl Haig, the British World War I chief, was sculpted by Alfred Hardiman in 1936.

Edwin Lutyens's Cenotaph dates from 1920 (p81).

DOWNING ST

WHITEHALL

RICHMOND TERRACE

PARLIAMENT STREET

Richmond House is William Whitfield's prize-winning 1980s building for the Department of Health.

VICTORIA EMBANKMENT

Westminster Pier is a starting point for riverboat excursions.

Portcullis House provides offices for Members of Parliament.

BRIDGE STREET

START

Boudicca, the British queen who resisted the Romans, was portrayed by Thomas Thornycroft in the 1850s.

Westminster station

The Houses of Parliament and Big Ben were designed by Charles Barry in 1834, when the Palace of Westminster burned down (p76).

WHITEHALL AND WESTMINSTER

Locator Map
For more detail see p70

→ The Burghers of Calais statue, by the Houses of Parliament

| 0 metres | 100 |
| 0 yards | 100 |

N

MAYFAIR AND ST JAMES'S

The exclusivity of these most gentrified of London districts, with their royal connections, stretches back centuries. St James's Palace was the first royal residence to be constructed on this patch of land, built in the 1530s by Henry VIII, who also laid out the hunting grounds that would become St James's Park. During the 17th century several large mansions were added as aristocrats sought proximity to the royal court. Mayfair did not emerge as a tangible district until the late 17th century when the annual May Fair, held around present-day Shepherd Market, was moved here. The fair was abolished in 1764, having earned a reputation for debauchery and rowdiness that did not sit well with the wealthy residents moving to the area as the city expanded westwards. Three great squares were built and Mayfair became the property of a small number of landed estates, the most significant of which, the Grosvenor Estate, remains in the hands of the Grosvenor family to this day.

MAYFAIR AND ST JAMES'S

Must Sees
1. Buckingham Palace
2. Royal Academy of Arts

Experience More
3. Pall Mall
4. St James's Palace
5. Spencer House
6. St James's Square
7. St James's Park
8. St James's Church
9. The Mall
10. Institute of Contemporary Arts
11. Marlborough House
12. Green Park
13. Queen's Chapel
14. Wellington Arch
15. Apsley House
16. Handel & Hendrix in London
17. Grosvenor Square
18. Faraday Museum

Eat
①. The Ritz

Stay
②. Claridge's

Shop
③. Fortnum & Mason

Wallace Collection

Wigmore Hall

REGENT'S PARK AND MARYLEBONE
p274

John Lewis

Selfridges

Bond Street

OXFORD STREET

Marble Arch

OXFORD STREET

BAYSWATER ROAD

Marble Arch

Speaker's Corner

16 Handel & Hendrix in London

2 BROOK'S MEWS

17 Grosvenor Square

SOUTH KENSINGTON AND KNIGHTSBRIDGE
p240

BROOK GATE

CULROSS ST

GROSVENOR GATE

MAYFAIR

BERKELEY SQUARE

St George's Gardens

Hyde Park

PARK LANE

PICCADILLY

SHEPHERD MARKET

Apsley House

15 HYDE PARK CORNER

Hyde Park Corner

14 Wellington Arch

CONSTITUTION

DUKE OF WELLINGTON PLACE

Buckingham Palace Gardens

GROSVENOR PLACE

CHELSEA AND BATTERSEA
p230

BELGRAVE SQUARE

BELGRAVIA

State guests are presented and royal christenings take place in the Music Room.

The Victorian Ballroom, used for state banquets and ceremonies.

② (160 m) ①

→

Buckingham Palace, official home of the British monarch

❶ 🖫

BUCKINGHAM PALACE

📍G7 ⌂SW1 🚇St James's Park, Victoria 🚂Victoria 🕐State Rooms and Garden: mid-Jul-Sep 9:30am-7pm (till 6pm in Sep); selected dates Dec-May, check website 🌐rct.uk

The Queen's official London residence is one of the capital's best recognized landmarks. Visit its opulent state rooms for a glimpse at how the royals live.

Both administrative office and family home, Buckingham Palace is the official London residence of the British monarchy. The palace is used for ceremonial occasions for visiting heads of state as well as the weekly meeting between the Queen and Prime Minister. John Nash converted the original Buckingham House into a palace for George IV (reigned 1820–30). Both he and his brother, William IV (reigned 1830–37), died before work was completed, and Queen Victoria was the first monarch to live at the palace. She added a fourth wing to incorporate more bedrooms and guest rooms.

↑ Exhibits in the Queen's Gallery, including fine porcelain and Old Masters

The Throne Room holds thrones used by Queen Elizabeth II and the Duke of Edinburgh during her coronation.

Traditionally, the royal family waves to the crowds from the palace balcony during public ceremonies.

← Soldiers taking part in the Trooping the Colour ceremony

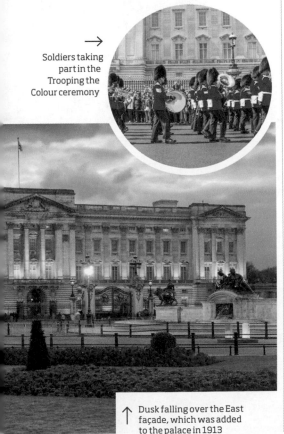

↑ Dusk falling over the East façade, which was added to the palace in 1913

①

The Queen's Gallery

G7 **St James's Park, Victoria** **10am-5:30pm daily (mid-Jul-Sep: 9:30am-5:30pm; last adm: 4:15pm)** **Between exhibitions, check website**

The royal family possesses one of the finest and most valuable art collections in the world, including works by Johannes Vermeer and Leonardo da Vinci. The Queen's Gallery hosts a rolling programme of the Royal Collection's most impressive masterpieces, with temporary exhibitions featuring fine art, porcelain, jewels, furniture and manuscripts.

②

Royal Mews

G7 **St James's Park, Victoria** **Apr-Oct: 10am-5pm daily; Nov, Feb-Mar: 10am-4pm Mon-Sat** **Subject to closure at short notice, check website; Dec-Jan**

Head to the Royal Mews to discover plenty of royal pomp. Stables and coach houses, designed by Nash in 1825, accommodate the horses and coaches used by the royal family on state occasions. The Mews' extensive collection of coaches, motorcars and carriages include the Irish state coach, bought by Queen Victoria for the State Opening of Parliament; the open-topped 1902 royal landau, used to give the crowds the best view of newlywed royal couples; and the glass coach, also used for royal weddings. The newest coach is the Diamond Jubilee State Coach, built in 2012. The star exhibit is the Gold State Coach: built for George III in 1761, with panels by Giovanni Cipriani, it has been used at every coronation since 1821.

2 🍴 🖥 🛍

ROYAL ACADEMY OF ARTS

📍H6 🏛Burlington House, Piccadilly W1 ⊜Piccadilly Circus, Green Park
🕐10am-6pm daily (till 10pm Fri) 🔒24-26 Dec 🌐royalacademy.org.uk

Though it holds one of the nation's great art collections, the Royal Academy of Arts is most renowned for its blockbuster temporary exhibitions, as well as its popular annual Summer Exhibition.

A storied art institution that holds one of the country's most prestigious collections of British art, the Royal Academy of Arts (RA) celebrated its 250th anniversary in 2018. It has always been led by its elected and appointed Royal Academicians, artists themselves, whose works make up the bulk of the permanent collection and who help to deliver the Royal Academy Schools' programme. The collection is displayed across two Italianate buildings, palatial Burlington House and Burlington Gardens. The two are linked by a bridge, built to mark the anniversary. Several new galleries including the Vaults and the Collection Gallery were opened for the occasion too.

↑ The exterior of the Royal Academy of Arts

→ Considering works on display during the annual Summer Exhibition

1. Sir Joshua Reynolds attempted to rival Dutch master Rembrandt with this self-portrait painted in c 1780.

2. The only marble sculpture by Michelangelo in Britain is his *Taddei Tondo*; carved in 1504–5, it depicts the Virgin and Child with the Infant St John.

3. The Collection Gallery features Giampetrino's 16th-century copy of Leonardo da Vinci's *The Last Supper*.

THE SUMMER EXHIBITION

The highlight of the RA calendar and among the most talked-about events in British art is the Summer Exhibition, held annually since 1769. Anyone can submit their work, for a fee, to be considered for the show, making it a potentially career-changing event for unknown artists, though established artists exhibit too. Over a thousand entries are selected, ranging from painting, printmaking and sculpture to photography, film and architecture, and displayed to the public, for an admission charge, between June and August in the main galleries of Burlington House. Most of the works displayed are for sale.

Did You Know?

As well as a gallery, the RA is an independent fine art school - it was Britain's first, founded in 1769.

EXPERIENCE MORE

3 Pall Mall

 H6 SW1 🚇 Charing Cross, Piccadilly Circus, Green Park

This dignified street is named for the game of pall-mall – a cross between croquet and golf – which was played here in the 17th century. For close to 200 years, Pall Mall has been at the heart of London's clubland. Exclusive gentlemen's clubs were formed here for members of the elite.

The clubhouses now amount to a textbook of the most fashionable architects of their era. At the east end, on the left is the colonnaded entrance to No 116, Nash's United Services Club (1827). This was the favourite club of the Duke of Wellington and now houses the Institute of Directors. Facing it, on the other side of Waterloo Place, is the Athenaeum (No 107), designed three years later by Decimus Burton, and long the powerhouse of the British establishment. Next door are two clubs by Sir Charles Barry, mastermind of the Houses of Parliament (p76): the Travellers' at No 106 and the Reform at No 104. The clubs' stately interiors are well-preserved but only members and their guests are admitted.

4 St James's Palace

H6 Pall Mall SW1 🚇 Green Park 🚫 To the public 🌐 royal.uk

Built by Henry VIII in the late 1530s on the site of a former leper hospital, this palace was a primary royal residence only briefly, mainly during the reign of Elizabeth I and in the late 17th and early 18th centuries. In 1952, Queen Elizabeth II made her first speech as monarch here, and foreign ambassadors are still officially accredited to the Court of St James's. Its northern gatehouse, seen from St James's Street, is one of London's great Tudor landmarks. The palace remains a royal residence for, among others, the Princess Royal and Princess Alexandra, and its State Apartments are used during official state visits.

5

Spencer House

H6 27 St James's Pl SW1 🚇 Green Park 🕐 Sep-Jul: 10am-5:30pm Sun (last adm: 4:30pm) 🌐 spencerhouse.co.uk

This Palladian palace, built in 1766 for the first Earl Spencer,

an ancestor of the late Diana, Princess of Wales, has been completely restored to its 18th-century splendour (thanks to an £18 million renovation project). It contains some wonderful paintings and contemporary furniture. The house is open to the public on Sundays, for guided tours only.

6 St James's Square

H6 SW1 🚇 Green Park, Piccadilly Circus

London's squares, quadrangles of elegant homes surrounding gated gardens, are among the city's most attractive features. St James's, one of London's earliest, was laid out in the 1670s and lined by exclusive houses for those whose business made it vital for them to live near St James's Palace. Many buildings date from the 18th and 19th centuries and have had many illustrious residents. During World War II, generals Eisenhower and de Gaulle both had headquarters here.

Today, No 10 on the north side, Chatham House (1736), is home to the Royal Institute for International Affairs. In the northwest corner, at No 14, is

←

The elegant Spencer House, on the edge of Green Park

→ The royal St James's Park, famed for its floral displays

the **London Library** (1896), a private lending library founded in 1841 by historian Thomas Carlyle *(p235)* and others. It offers guided tours at 6pm on some weekdays. The gardens in the middle contain an equestrian statue of William III, here since 1808.

London Library

🕐 For public tours; check website 🔵 londonlibrary. co.uk

---

7 🖵

St James's Park

📍 H6 🏠 SW1 🚇 St James's Park 🕐 5am–midnight daily 🔵 royalparks.org.uk

In summer, office workers sunbathe in between the flowerbeds of the capital's most ornamental park. In winter, the sunbathers are replaced with overcoated civil servants discussing affairs of state as they stroll by the lake, eyed by its resident ducks, geese and pelicans (which are fed at 2:30pm daily).

Originally a marsh, the park was drained by Henry VIII and incorporated into his hunting grounds. On his return from exile in France, Charles II had it remodelled in the more continental style as pedestrian pleasure gardens, with an aviary along its southern edge (hence Birdcage Walk, the name of the street that runs alongside the park where the aviary once was).

It is a hugely popular place to escape the city's hustle and bustle, with an appealing view of Whitehall rooftops and Buckingham Palace, a restaurant open daily and an attractive lake.

---

8 🖵

St James's Church

📍 H6 🏠 197 Piccadilly W1 🚇 Piccadilly Circus 🕐 8am–7pm daily 🔵 sjp.org.uk

Among the many churches Christopher Wren designed, this is said to be one of his favourites. It has been altered

↑ Stained glass at the Wren-designed St James's Church

over the years and was half-wrecked by a bomb in 1940, but it maintains its essential features from 1684 – the tall, arched windows and a thin spire (a 1966 replica of the original). The ornate screen behind the altar is one of the finest works of the 17th-century master carver Grinling Gibbons. The artist and poet William Blake and Georgian prime minister Pitt the Elder were both baptized here.

The church hosts concerts, talks and events, and houses a popular café. The outer courtyard hosts a food market on Monday and Tuesday, an antiques market on Tuesday and a crafts market from Wednesday to Saturday.

Tourists thronging the Mall en route to Buckingham Palace ↑

 9

The Mall

📍H6 🏠SW1 🚇Charing Cross, Piccadilly Circus, Green Park

This broad triumphal approach to Buckingham Palace was created by Aston Webb when he redesigned the front of the palace and the Victoria Memorial in 1911. It follows the course of the old path at the edge of St James's Park, laid out in the reign of Charles II, when it became London's most fashionable promenade. Down both sides of the Mall the national flags of foreign heads of state fly during their official visits. The annual London Marathon (p59) finishes on the Mall, amid a mass of crowds who cheer as enthusiastically for the weary stragglers at the end as they do for the elated runners at the front.

 10

Institute of Contemporary Arts

📍I6 🏠The Mall SW1 🚇Charing Cross, Piccadilly Circus 🕐Noon–11pm Thu & Sun; Fri & Sat noon–midnight; exhibition space: noon–9pm Tue–Sun 🚫Public hols 🌐ica.art

The Institute of Contemporary Arts (ICA) was established in 1947 to offer British artists some of the facilities available to artists at the Museum of Modern Art in New York. Originally on Dover Street, it has been situated in John Nash's Neo-Classical Carlton House Terrace (1833) since 1968. With its entrance on the Mall, this extensive warren contains exhibition spaces, a cinema, auditorium, bookshop, art gallery, bar and restaurant. It also hosts concerts, theatre and dance performances, and lectures. A modest fee applies to non-members, providing all-day access to most exhibitions and events.

11 Ⓜ

Marlborough House

📍H6 🏠Pall Mall SW1 🚇St James's Park, Green Park 🕐Only for prebooked group tours 🌐thecommonwealth.org/marlborough-house

Marlborough House was designed by Christopher Wren for the Duchess of Marlborough and completed

---

EAT

Afternoon Tea at the Ritz

The poshest afternoon tea in town is accompanied by a pianist and harpist. Expect sandwiches, scones, cakes and tea. No trainers or jeans.

📍G6 🏠150 Piccadilly W1 🌐theritz london.com

££££

---

in 1711. It was substantially enlarged in the 19th century and used by members of the royal family. From 1863 until he became Edward VII in 1901, it was the home of the Prince and Princess of Wales and the social centre of London. The building now houses the Commonwealth Secretariat.

 12

Green Park

🔲 G6 🏠 SW1 🚇 Green Park, Hyde Park Corner 🌐 royal parks.org.uk

Once part of Henry VIII's hunting grounds, this was, like St James's Park, adapted for public use by Charles II in the 1660s and is a natural, undulating landscape of grass and trees (with a fine spring show of daffodils). It was a favourite site for duels during the 18th century: in 1771 the poet Alfieri was wounded here by his mistress's husband, Viscount Ligonier, but then rushed back to the Haymarket Theatre in time to catch the last act of a play. Today the park is a popular place to take a breather from the city.

 13

Queen's Chapel

🔲 H6 🏠 Marlborough Rd SW1 🚇 Green Park 🌐 royal.gov.uk

This chapel by architect Inigo Jones was built for Charles I's French wife, Henrietta Maria, in 1627. Originally intended to be part of St James's Palace, it was the first Classical church to be built in England. George III married Charlotte of Mecklenburg-Strelitz here in 1761. Grinling Gibbons and Wren contributed to the interior. The chapel is only open for Sunday services from Easter to the end of July, at 8:30am and 11:15am.

SHOPPING ARCADES

On and around Piccadilly are four arch-fronted shopping arcades built in the 19th and early 20th centuries. These elegant covered walkways were the luxury shopping malls of their day, and are still home to the same kinds of top-drawer retailers. The first one to open, in 1819, was the Burlington Arcade, setting the template for the other three: the Royal, Princes and Piccadilly Arcades.

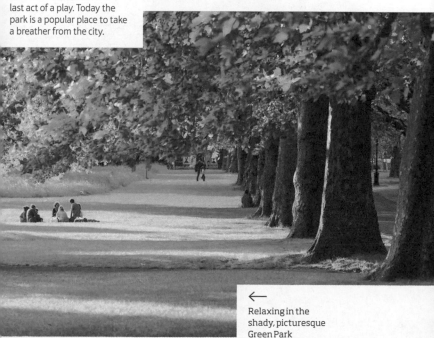

← Relaxing in the shady, picturesque Green Park

14

Wellington Arch

F7 Hyde Park Corner
SW1 Hyde Park Corner
Apr–Sep: 10am–6pm
daily; Oct: 10am–5pm daily;
Nov–Mar: 10am–4pm daily
1 Jan, Good Fri, 24–26 & 31
Dec english-heritage.
org.uk

After nearly a century of debate about what to do with the patch of land in front of Apsley House, Wellington Arch, designed by Decimus Burton, was erected in 1828 (it was moved to its current position in the 1880s). The sculpture by Adrian Jones of Nike, winged goddess of Victory, was added in 1912. Before it was installed Jones seated three people for dinner in the body of one of the horses.

Exhibitions are held in the inner rooms of the arch. A viewing platform beneath the sculpture has great views over the royal parks and the gardens of Buckingham Palace.

AUCTION HOUSES

Venerable Sotheby's, Bonhams and Christie's head the list of auction houses dotted around Mayfair and St James's. All three were founded in the 18th century and have overseen the sale of many of the most treasured and expensive antiques and works of art on the planet. In 1836 Bonhams sold a collection of furniture from Buckingham Palace; Van Gogh's *Sunflowers* sold at Christie's in 1987 for £24.75 million; and in 2016 Sotheby's New Bond Street auction rooms sold David Bowie's art collection for almost £33 million.

15

Apsley House

F7 Hyde Park Corner W1
Hyde Park Corner Apr–
Oct: 11am–5pm Wed–Sun;
Nov–Mar: 10am–4pm Sat &
Sun 1 Jan, 24–26 & 31 Dec
english-heritage.org.uk

Apsley House, or Number One London, as it is also known, at the southeast corner of Hyde Park, was completed by Robert Adam for Baron Apsley in 1778. Fifty years later it was enlarged and altered by the architect Benjamin Dean Wyatt to provide a grand home for the Duke of Wellington. His dual career as both soldier and politician brought him victory against his archenemy Napoleon at Waterloo (1815) and two terms as prime minister (1828–30 and 1834). Against sumptuous silk hangings and gilt decoration is the duke's art collection: works by Goya, Velázquez, Titian and Rubens hang alongside displays of porcelain, silver and furniture. Ironically, the duke's memorabilia is dominated by Canova's colossal statue of Napoleon.

Handel & Hendrix in London

📍 G5 🏠 25 Brook St W1 🚇 Bond Street 🕐 11am–6pm Mon–Sat 🌐 handelhendrix.org

A pair of Georgian houses on Brook Street have a couple of notable, very different, musical connections. The composer George Frideric Handel lived at No 25 from 1723 until his death in 1759, and his rooms have been restored to the early Georgian appearance they would have had during the composer's time, with portraits and musical instruments on display. The museum hosts changing exhibitions and regular recitals in an intimate performance space. In 1968, Jimi Hendrix moved into the

↑ A bust of Handel at the Handel & Hendrix in London museum

attic apartment next door. These rooms were used for a time as offices by the museum, but have now also been lovingly restored to resemble Hendrix's former apartment, complete with 1960s decor.

17 Grosvenor Square

📍 F5 🏠 W1 🚇 Bond Street

Mayfair has long been home to some of the grandest addresses in all of London, most notably in a series of prestigious squares, originally laid out in the early 18th century and still retaining many Georgian buildings. Grosvenor Square is the

largest, and has had ongoing political connections with the USA since John Adams – the second US president – lived at No 9 between 1785 and 1789. The west side is dominated by the former US Embassy. Having closed in 2017, the Eero Saarinen-designed Brutalist building is being redeveloped as a luxury 137-room hotel by lauded David Chipperfield Associates, slated to open in 2023. A statue of Franklin D Roosevelt – the 32nd US president – stands at the centre of the square.

18 Faraday Museum

📍 G5 🏠 The Royal Institution, 21 Albemarle St W1 🚇 Green Park 🕐 9am–5pm Mon–Fri 🔒 24 Dec–3 Jan 🌐 rigb.org

Michael Faraday was one of the 19th-century pioneers of the uses of electricity. Part of the Royal Institution, a body dedicated to scientific study, the museum includes a recreation of Faraday's laboratory and some of his scientific apparatus, as well as exhibits on the work of other great scientists.

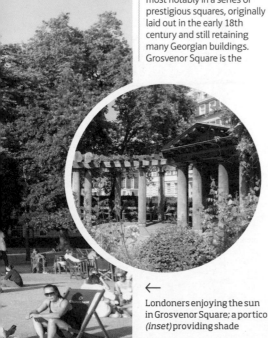

← Londoners enjoying the sun in Grosvenor Square; a portico *(inset)* providing shade

A SHORT WALK
ST JAMES'S

Distance 2.5 km (1.5 miles) **Nearest Tube**
Green Park **Time** 25 minutes

After Henry VIII built St James's Palace in the 1530s,
the area around it became the centre of fashionable
London, and it has remained so ever since. Its historic
streets, squares and arcades attract a thoroughly
international – and extremely wealthy – set.
A walk through the district will take you past the
flagship stores of exclusive global brands and
classic British names that have served royalty
and aristocracy for centuries, as well as the Royal
Academy and many independent art galleries.

The Albany mansion has been one of London's smartest addresses since it opened in 1803.

Sir Joshua Reynolds founded the Royal Academy of Arts in 1768. Now it mounts large popular exhibitions (p92).

Uniformed beadles discourage unruly behaviour in the Burlington Arcade, a 19th-century mall (p97).

Fortnum & Mason was founded in 1707 by one of Queen Anne's footmen (p95).

Named after César Ritz, and opened in 1906, the Ritz Hotel still lives up to his name.

An ancestor of Princess Diana built Spencer House in 1766 (p94).

Did You Know?

Hatchards on Piccadilly is London's oldest bookshop, opened in 1797.

Clarence House was designed by John Nash for William IV, and is now Prince Charles's London home.

0 metres 100
0 yards 100
N ↑
START

Piccadilly derives its name from the ruffs, or "pickadills", worn by 17th-century dandies.

Piccadilly Circus station

Jermyn Street is one of London's most elegant streets, lined with shops for style-conscious men.

Locator Map
For more detail see p88

MAYFAIR AND
ST JAMES'S

The crowds and dazzling neon lights make Piccadilly Circus the West End's focal point

FINISH

The organ in Christopher Wren's favourite church, St James's, was brought here from Whitehall Palace in 1691 (p95).

Pall Mall's famous clubs provide a haven for businessmen (and a few women) (p94).

William III's statue dominates St James's Square (p94).

King Street is lined with art galleries.

The Tudor St James's Palace is still the Royal Court's official headquarters (p94).

St James's Square, with the statue of William III at its centre

SOHO AND TRAFALGAR SQUARE

Formerly used as royal hunting grounds, Soho was first developed in the late 17th century by wealthy landowners. Its aristocratic residents, in contrast to those in neighbouring Mayfair, soon moved on and their influence on the character of the area went with them. Instead, the district became synonymous with bohemians and immigrants. French Huguenots, Jews, Greeks, Italians, Maltese, Chinese and others all came to Soho in significant numbers between the end of the 17th and the mid-20th centuries. Artists, writers and musicians flocked here too, as did gangsters and prostitutes, and the area retained an edgy, alternative air until the late 1980s. In contrast, Trafalgar Square, with its grandiose buildings and proximity to Whitehall, has always had closer ties to the establishment, though it has also long been a place of protest. For centuries the site of the royal stables (or mews), the square itself is a 19th-century construct, given its name in 1830.

BLOOMSBURY AND FITZROVIA
p146

REGENT'S PARK AND MARYLEBONE
p274

CAVENDISH SQUARE

John Lewis

PORTLAND PLACE

GREAT PORTLAND STREET

HOLLES ST

PRINCES ST

REGENT STREET

ARGYLL STREET

OXFORD STREET

WELLS STREET

MORTIMER STREET

RATHBONE PLACE

GREAT CHAPEL ST

DEAN STREET

SOHO

⊖ Oxford Circus

The Photographers' Gallery ⑪

POLAND STREET

BERWICK ST

NOEL STREET

WARDOUR STREET

D'ARBLAY STREET

GREAT MARLBOROUGH ST

HANOVER SQUARE

Handel & Hendrix in London

KINGLY STREET

FOUBERT'S PLACE

NEWBURGH STREET

CARNABY STREET

MARSHALL STREET

BROADWICK STREET

HOPKINS ST

INGESTRE PL

BERWICK ST

PETER ST

⑩ Berwick Street Market

⑥ GANTON ST

⑤

BEAK STREET

LEXINGTON ST

GREAT PULTENEY ST

STREET

RUPERT ST

ARCHER ST

NEW BOND STREET

CONDUIT STREET

MAYFAIR AND ST JAMES'S
p86

WARWICK STREET

REGENT STREET

GOLDEN SQUARE

BREWER STREET

SHERWOOD

③ GREAT WINDMILL

SHAFTESBUR

BRUTON STREET

DENMAN ST ④

GLASSHOUSE ST

AIR ST

Piccadilly Circus ⑥

BERKELEY SQUARE

Faraday Museum

BURLINGTON GARDENS

DOVER STREET

OLD BOND ST

STREET

⊖ Piccadilly Circus

REGENT STREET

MAYFAIR

Royal Academy of Arts

St James's Church

PICCADILLY

JERMYN STREET

JERMYN ST

ST ALBAN'S

STREET

SOHO AND TRAFALGAR SQUARE

ST JAMES'S STREET

DUKE STREET

ST JAMES'S STREET

ST JAMES'S SQUARE

ST JAMES'S

PALL MALL

0 metres 200
0 yards 200

N ↑

SOHO AND TRAFALGAR SQUARE

Must Sees
1. National Gallery
2. National Portrait Gallery
3. Chinatown

Experience More
4. Trafalgar Square
5. St Martin-in-the-Fields
6. Piccadilly Circus
7. Leicester Square
8. Charing Cross Road
9. Shaftesbury Avenue
10. Berwick Street Market
11. The Photographers' Gallery

Eat
1. Café in the Crypt
2. Barrafina
3. Casita Andina
4. Kricket
5. Pastaio

Drink
6. Ain't Nothin' But

① ⊗ 🍴 🍵 🛍

NATIONAL GALLERY

📍S3 🏛Trafalgar Square WC2 ⊖Charing Cross, Leicester Sq, Piccadilly Circus 🚆Charing Cross ⏰10am–6pm daily (till 9pm Fri) 🚫24–26 Dec, 1 Jan 🌐nationalgallery.org.uk

Erected in the heart of the West End in order to be accessible by all, the National Gallery houses some of the most famous paintings in the world, by masters such as Rubens, Velázquez, Monet and Van Gogh.

The National Gallery has flourished since its inception. In 1824 the House of Commons was persuaded to buy 38 major paintings, including works by Raphael and Rubens, and these became the start of a national collection. Today the gallery has more than 2,300 paintings produced in the Western European painting tradition. The main gallery building, designed in Greek Revival style by William Wilkins, was built between 1833 and 1838. It was subsequently enlarged and the dome added in 1876. To its left lies the Sainsbury Wing, financed by the grocery family and completed in 1991.

The Collection

The National Gallery's paintings are mostly kept on permanent display. The collection spans late-medieval times to the early 20th century, covering Renaissance Italy and the French Impressionists. There are works by artists such as Botticelli, Leonardo, Monet and Goya, and highlights include Van Eyck's *Arnolfini Portrait*, Velázquez's *Rokeby Venus*, Raphael's *The Madonna of the Pinks* and Van Gogh's *Sunflowers*.

→
The National Gallery, overlooking Trafalgar Square

←
Groups of visitors studying works by the masters in the airy galleries

---

GALLERY GUIDE

Most of the collection is housed on one floor divided into four wings. The paintings hang chronologically, with the earliest works (1250–1500) in the Sainsbury Wing. The West, North and East Wings cover 1500–1600, 1600–1700 and 1700–1930. Lesser paintings from all periods are on the lower floor.

Did You Know?

Close examination of the *Madonna of the Veil* showed it was a 19th-century fake, and not by Botticelli.

↑ Pausing for thought in front of some of the gallery's masterpieces

↑ Dating from 1437, Piero della Francesca's *The Baptism of Christ*

The Sainsbury Wing: 1250–1500

Three lustrous panels from the *Maestà*, Duccio's great altarpiece in Siena cathedral and his outstanding *Virgin and Child with Saints Dominic and Aurea* are among the earliest paintings here. The fine *Wilton Diptych* portraying England's Richard II may be by a French artist. It displays the lyrical elegance of the

---

International Gothic style. Italian masters of this style include Pisanello and Gentile da Fabriano, whose *Madonna* hangs beside another, by Masaccio – both from the 1420s. Also shown are works by Masaccio's pupil, Fra Filippo Lippi, Botticelli and Uccello. Raphaels include the famous *Madonna of the Pinks*, displayed near Piero della Francesca's *Nativity* and *Baptism*. There is also a fine collection of Mantegna, Bellini and other great works from the Venetian, Paduan and Ferrarese schools. Antonello da Messina's *Saint Jerome in his Study* has been mistaken for a Van Eyck; it is not hard to see why when you compare it with Van Eyck's *Arnolfini Portrait*. Other Netherlandish artists on display include Rogier van der Weyden and his followers. There is also a Hieronymus Bosch of *Christ Mocked* (sometimes known as *The Crowning with Thorns*). Room 66 is largely devoted to Leonardo da Vinci's second *Virgin of the Rocks*, which is hung alongside the preparatory charcoal *Virgin and Child*.

The West Wing: 1500–1600

Sebastiano del Piombo's *The Raising of Lazarus* was painted, with Michelangelo's help, to rival Raphael's *Transfiguration*, which hangs in the Vatican in

---

Rome. Other well-known names of the High (or Late) Renaissance include Agnolo Bronzino's mysterious, erotic *Venus and Cupid*, Raphael's original portrait of Pope Julius II and several Titians, including *Bacchus and Ariadne* – which the public found too garish when it was cleaned in the 1840s. The Netherlandish and German collections include *The Ambassadors*, a fine double portrait by Holbein; and Altdorfer's superb *Christ Taking Leave of his Mother*. There are also several Bruegels, including *The Adoration of the Kings*.

The North Wing: 1600–1700

The superb Dutch collection includes the largest number of works by Rembrandt outside of Amsterdam, including his poignant *Self-Portrait at the Age of 63*. Van Dyck and the prolific Rubens, too, are each amply represented, and there are also

↑ Turner's *Dido Building Carthage*, found next to Claude's *Seaport with the Embarkation of the Queen of Sheba*

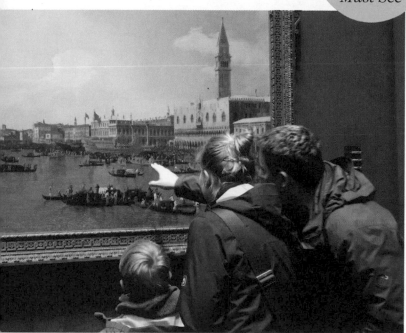

works by Vermeer and Franz Hals. French works include a grand portrait of Cardinal Richelieu by Philippe de Champaigne. Claude's seascape *Seaport with the Embarkation of the Queen of Sheba* hangs beside Turner's rival painting *Dido Building Carthage*. The glorious Spanish collection has works by Murillo, Velázquez and Zurbarán, and Italians Caravaggio and Carracci are well represented, though Guido Reni's vast *Adoration of the Shepherds* dominates all else.

The East Wing: 1700–1930

One of the gallery's most famous 18th-century works is Canaletto's *The Stonemason's Yard*, which shows a traditional Venetian view, and was thought to have been commissioned by a local patron. Other Venetians here are Longhi and Tiepolo. The French collection includes Rococo masters Chardin, Watteau and Boucher. Gainsborough's early work

Mr and Mrs Andrews and *The Morning Walk* are popular; his rival, Sir Joshua Reynolds, is represented by several of his portraits. Hogarth's satirical *Marriage à-la-mode* series is another highlight.

The great age of 19th-century landscape painting is amply represented as well, with fine works by Constable and Turner, including Constable's moody *The Hay Wain* and Turner's late-career painting *The Fighting Temeraire*. There are also works by the French artists Corot and Daubigny, often displayed downstairs.

Of Romantic art, there is Géricault's vivid work, *Horse Frightened by Lightning* and *A Shipwreck*, which possibly prefigures his *The Raft of the Medusa*. In contrast, the society portrait of *Madame Moitessier* by Ingres, though

↑ Examining Canaletto's famous work, *The Stonemason's Yard*

Romantic, is restrained and Classical. Impressionists and other French avant-garde artists are well represented. Among the highlights are *The Water-Lily Pond* by Monet, Renoir's *At the Theatre*, Van Gogh's *Sunflowers*, and Rousseau's *Surprised!* In Seurat's *Bathers at Asnières* he did not originally use his pointillist technique, but only later reworked areas of the picture using dots of colour.

→
One of the highlights of the collection, Van Gogh's *Sunflowers*

NATIONAL PORTRAIT GALLERY

⑨ S3 **⌂** 2 St Martin's Place WC2 **⊜** Leicester Sq, Charing Cross **⇄** Charing Cross
⏱ 10am-6pm daily (till 9pm Fri) **⏱** 24-26 Dec **ⓦ** npg.org.uk

Somewhat unfairly in the shadow of the National Gallery next door, the National Portrait Gallery, with over 210,000 separate works spanning six centuries, holds the world's greatest collection of portraits.

The gallery tells the story of Britain since the 16th century through the portraits of a wide cast of the nation's main characters, giving faces to the names familiar from history books. Founded in 1856, the gallery's first acquisition was one of the most famous depictions of William Shakespeare, known as the "Chandos portrait", after its former owner the Duke of Chandos. That portrait still hangs in the gallery today along with pictures of kings, queens, musicians, artists, thinkers, heroes and villains from every period since the time of Henry VII. Another of the gallery's oldest works is a Hans Holbein cartoon of Henry VIII, while there are Victorian portraits of key figures such as Charles Darwin, Charles Dickens and the Brontë Sisters.

Examining the portraits of key figures in Britain's long and varied history ↑

← Entrance to the National Portrait Gallery on St Martin's Place

GALLERY GUIDE

The main collection runs chronologically from the early Tudors in the first room on the second floor down to the contemporary portraits on the ground floor, most of which change regularly. Much of the space on the ground floor is taken up with temporary exhibitions. Arranged initially by the royal dynasties, progressing along the timeline brings up themes that overlap with time periods so that, for example, the Romantics are given their own room in the late-18th to early-19th century section.

→ A visitor admiring one of the more modern portraits housed at the fantastic National Portrait Gallery

3 🍴 🖥 🛍

CHINATOWN

📍R2 🏠Gerrard St and around W1 🚇Leicester Sq, Piccadilly Circus 🌐chinatown.co.uk

Though much smaller than its equivalents in New York City and San Francisco, London's Chinatown packs a punch. There are restaurants aplenty and a constant buzz that attracts countless locals and visitors.

Chinatown occupies the small network of pedestrianized streets north of Leicester Square and revolves around the main drag, Gerrard Street. Historically the Chinese community in London, who total more than 120,000, came predominantly from Hong Kong and were concentrated initially in Limehouse, in the East End. The current base in Soho was established in the 1960s, though the Chinese population is now widely dispersed across the city. Today, Chinatown is an intense little precinct marked by ornamental archways and, more often than not, strewn with paper lanterns. It is packed overwhelmingly with authentic restaurants and Chinese supermarkets, with bakeries and bubble tea shops, and herbal medicine, acupuncture and massage centres filling the gaps.

CHINESE NEW YEAR

Based on lunar cycles, Chinese New Year falls between 21 January and 20 February. It is raucously celebrated in Chinatown in a sea of red paper lanterns, to the noise of firecrackers and the aromas of Chinese street food. Though celebrations last for a fortnight, the main event usually falls on a Sunday when a parade makes its way through Chinatown. Shaftesbury Avenue is closed to traffic and stages are erected there and in Trafalgar Square for dance and martial arts shows.

Gerrard Street, at the heart of Chinatown, during Chinese New Year ↑

① Ornate Chinese arches stand over the area of Chinatown in Soho.

② There are many authentic places to try a variety of Chinese cuisines from all over China.

③ Traditional Chinese goods are on sale in the shops around Chinatown.

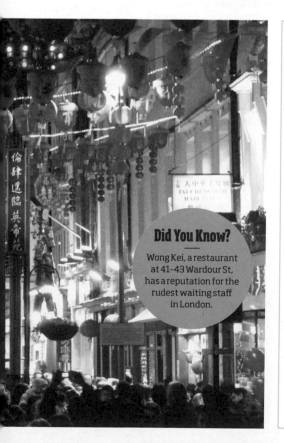

Did You Know?

Wong Kei, a restaurant at 41–43 Wardour St, has a reputation for the rudest waiting staff in London.

EAT

Shu Xiangge
Specialists in traditional Sichuan hotpots, with 80 different ingredients to add to their fragrant, communal broths. The authentic interior has a hand-painted mural.

⌂ 10 Gerrard St W1

£ £ £

XU
Atmospheric Taiwanese restaurant which re-creates the look of a 1930s Taipei social club, with wood panelling, hand-painted murals and a tea room on the ground floor. The food is modern, a fusion of Taiwanese and Cantonese cuisine.

⌂ 30 Rupert St W1
🌐 xulondon.com

£ £ £

EXPERIENCE MORE

④
Trafalgar Square

📍S3 🏛WC2 🚇Charing Cross

London's main venue for rallies and outdoor public meetings was conceived by John Nash and was mostly constructed during the 1830s. The 52-m (169-ft) column commemorates Admiral Lord Nelson, Britain's most famous sea lord, who died heroically at the Battle of Trafalgar in 1805. It dates from 1842; 14 stonemasons held a dinner on its flat top before the statue of Nelson was finally installed. Edwin Landseer's four lions guard its base. The north side of the square is now taken up by the National Gallery (p106), with Canada House on the west side and South Africa House on the east. Three plinths support statues of the great and the good; funds ran out before the fourth plinth, on the northwest corner, could be filled. It now hosts one of London's most idiosyncratic art displays, as artworks are commissioned specially for it, and change every year or so.

---

⑤
St Martin-in-the-Fields

📍S3 🏛Trafalgar Sq WC2 🚇Charing Cross 🕐8:30am-6pm Mon-Fri, 9am-6pm Sat & Sun 🌐stmartin-in-the-fields.org

There has been a church on this site since the 13th century. Famous people buried here include Charles II's mistress Nell Gwyn, and the painters William Hogarth and Joshua Reynolds. The present church was designed by James Gibbs and completed in 1726. In architectural terms it was one of the most influential ever built; it was much copied in the US, where it became a model for the Colonial style of church architecture. An unusual feature of the interior is the royal box at gallery level to the left of the altar.

From 1914 until 1927, the crypt was used as a shelter for homeless soldiers and others; during World War II it was an air-raid shelter. It is still today well-known for its work on behalf of the homeless and vulnerable. The crypt also contains a café, a gift shop and a brass rubbing centre, which is open daily. Lunchtime (free) and evening concerts (tickets required) are held in the church and weekly jazz evenings in the café. All are welcome at the daily services; check the website for times.

---

⑥
Piccadilly Circus

📍Q3 🏛W1 🚇Piccadilly Circus

For years people have been drawn to gather beneath Piccadilly Circus's centrepiece, the statue of Eros, originally intended as an angel of mercy but renamed in the public imagination after the Greek god of love. Poised delicately

Looking across Trafalgar Square to St-Martin-in-the-Fields ↓

↑ The bustling pavements of Piccadilly Circus, overseen by the statue of Eros

with his bow, Eros has become almost a trademark of the capital. It was erected in 1892 as a memorial to the Earl of Shaftesbury, the Victorian philanthropist. Part of Nash's master plan for Regent Street, Piccadilly Circus has been considerably altered over the years and consists for the most part of shops selling souvenirs for visitors and high-street chains. It has London's gaudiest array of neon advertising signs, marking the entrance to the city's lively entertainment district with its cinemas, theatres, nightclubs, restaurants and pubs.

7 ⑭ ⑫ 🏚

Leicester Square

🚇 R2 🏠 WC2 🚇 Leicester Sq, Piccadilly Circus

It is hard to imagine that this, the perpetually animated heart of the West End entertainment district, was once a fashionable place to live. Laid out in 1670 south of Leicester House, a long-gone royal residence, the square's occupants included the scientist Sir Isaac Newton and the

artists Joshua Reynolds and William Hogarth.

In Victorian times, several popular music halls were established here, including the Empire (today the cinema on the same site perpetuates the name) and the Alhambra, replaced in 1937 by the Art Deco Odeon. The TKTS booth, sat in the square, is a must-visit for cut-price theatre tickets. There is also a statue of Charlie Chaplin, which was unveiled in 1981. The statue of William Shakespeare dates from 1874.

Often crowded with visitors, the area around the Tube station here can be very congested at times; the streets of Soho and China-town to the north (p112) can be a better bet for a meal or drink.

← Statue of William Shakespeare in Leicester Square

EAT

Café in the Crypt
Popular, licensed canteen with simple food under the arches of a church crypt.

🚇 S3 🏠 St Martin-in-the-Fields, Trafalgar Sq WC2 🌐 stmartin-in-the-fields.org

£££

Barrafina
Ultracool Spanish joint with industrial modern decor.

🚇 R2 🏠 Dean St W1 🌐 barrafina.co.uk

£££

Casita Andina
Stylish Peruvian restaurant: try ceviche, octopus or tamales.

🚇 Q2 🏠 31 Great Windmill St W1 🌐 andinalondon.com

£££

Kricket
Gourmet Indian food served in tapas-style portions.

🚇 Q2 🏠 12 Denman St W1 🌐 kricket.co.uk

£££

Pastaio
Trendy pasta specialist with communal seating.

🚇 Q2 🏠 19 Ganton St W1 🌐 pastaio.london

£££

Shaftesbury Avenue, the heart of London's theatre district ↑

Charing Cross Road

📍 S2 🚇 WC2 🚊 Leicester Sq

Once London's favourite street with book lovers, with a clutch of shops able to supply just about any recent volume, many of Charing Cross Road's independent bookshops have been forced to shut due to rising rents. Several smaller, second-hand bookshops remain, however, including Quinto & Francis Edwards, which specializes in antiquarian books, and a handful in nearby Cecil Court. At the junction with New Oxford Street rises the 1960s Centre Point tower. This junction is one of the key sites for the huge Crossrail underground rail project, so expect traffic disruption.

Shaftesbury Avenue

📍 R2 🚇 W1 🚊 Piccadilly Circus, Leicester Sq

The main artery of London's theatreland, Shaftesbury Avenue has six theatres and three cinemas, all but one on its north side. It is also packed with restaurants, bars and clubs, making it a go-to destination of an evening. This street was cut through an area of terrible slums between 1877 and 1886 in order to improve communications across the city's busy West End; it follows the route of a much earlier highway. It is named after the Earl of Shaftesbury (1801–85), whose attempts to improve housing conditions had helped some of the local poor. The earl is also commemorated by the Eros statue in Piccadilly Circus (p114). The Lyric Theatre, designed by C J Phipps, has been open for almost as long as the avenue.

→

Installation images from Deutsche Börse Photography Foundation Prize 2018 at the Photographers' Gallery

Berwick Street Market

📍 R2 🚇 W1 🚊 Piccadilly Circus 🕗 8am–6pm Mon-Sat 🌐 thisissoho.co.uk/the-market

There has been a market here since the late 18th century. It was a Berwick Street trader, Jack Smith, who introduced

---

DRINK

Ain't Nothin' But
Popularly referred to simply as the Blues Bar, this London stalwart squeezes an always-enthusiastic crowd into its dimly lit single room, rarely failing to get the party cookin'.

📍 Q2 🏠 20 Kingly St W1 🌐 aintnothinbut.co.uk

---

grapefruit to London in 1890. Today this remains the West End's best street market, despite the encroachment of development on its western side. Today you'll find sizzling street food alongside the fresh produce and flowers. Long a destination for vinyl lovers – with Reckless Records at No 30, and Sister Ray at No 75 – it also has a growing number of cafés and restaurants. At its southern end the street narrows into an alley on which the famous strip club Raymond Revuebar (once the comparatively respectable face of Soho sleaze) presented its "festival of erotica" from 1958 to 2004.

THE HEART OF SOHO

Beating a path through Soho is Old Compton Street, a busy thoroughfare of restaurants, bars, clubs and shops. Home for centuries to poets, writers and musicians, it's now an LGBT+ hub, the Admiral Duncan pub leading a pack of popular bars and clubs. Turn off on Frith Street to see iconic jazz club Ronnie Scott's and Bar Italia; above the latter, John Logic Baird first demonstrated TV in 1926.

Did You Know?

In the 1960s, four out of five Soho strip clubs were controlled by Maltese crime gang, the Syndicate.

The Photographers' Gallery

📍 Q1 🏠 16-18 Ramillies St W1 🚇 Oxford Circus 🕐 10am–6pm Mon-Sat; 11am–6pm Sun 🌐 thephotographersgallery.org.uk

This fore-running gallery exhibits work from both new and well-known photographers, as well as staging regular talks, workshops (especially for young photographers) and film screenings. Entry is free before noon, and when exhibitions are staged, the gallery stays open late (until 8pm) on Thursdays. There's a bar-café, and the bookshop also sells cameras and prints.

COVENT GARDEN AND THE STRAND

The site of a convent garden in medieval times, Covent Garden was laid out as an Italianate piazza in the 1630s by Inigo Jones, whose St Paul's Church still dominates the west side. Initially among the city's most fashionable addresses, coffee houses, then brothels and an increasing number of market stalls transformed the area's reputation and the wealthier residents trickled away. To accommodate the expansion of the market a permanent market building was commissioned and constructed in the 1830s, the elegant Neo-Classical structure dominating the centre of the piazza today. It housed a produce market until 1974 when the market moved to a larger site in Nine Elms, between Vauxhall and Battersea, better able to cope with its inflated size. Traders still occupy the building in Covent Garden but cater mostly to tourists now, operating from shops, craft stalls and restaurants.

COVENT GARDEN AND THE STRAND

Must Sees
1 Covent Garden Piazza and Central Market
2 Somerset House

Experience More
3 Royal Opera House
4 St Paul's Church
5 Neal Street and Neal's Yard
6 Savoy Hotel
7 London Transport Museum
8 Museum of Freemasonry
9 St Mary-le-Strand
10 Cleopatra's Needle
11 Victoria Embankment Gardens
12 London Coliseum
13 London Film Museum

Eat
① Opera Tavern
② Chick 'n' Sours
③ Dishoom

Drink
④ The Lamb & Flag

HOLBORN AND THE INNS OF COURT p132

SOUTH BANK p216

COVENT GARDEN AND THE STRAND

0 metres 200
0 yards 200

N

Strolling and snacking under the iron and glass roof of the Apple Market ↑

COVENT GARDEN PIAZZA AND CENTRAL MARKET

S2 **Covent Garden WC2** **Covent Garden, Leicester Sq** **Charing Cross** **coventgarden.london**

One of London's most distinct and animated squares, Covent Garden comprises a bustling piazza filled with street performers and a market alive with shops, cafés and the occasional opera singer. It is a must-visit – a claim substantiated by the crowds who flock here.

The central, covered Apple Market, designed in 1833 for fruit and vegetable wholesalers, today houses an array of stalls and small shops selling designer clothes, books, arts and crafts, decorative items and antiques. The 17th-century architect Inigo Jones planned this area to be an elegant residential square, modelled on the piazza of Livorno in northern Italy, but the Victorian buildings on and around the piazza now, including the Royal Opera

House, are almost entirely commercial. The market stalls continue south into the neighbouring Jubilee Hall, which was built in 1903. The colonnaded Bedford Chambers on the north side give a hint of Inigo Jones's plan, although these buildings are not original either, having been rebuilt and partially modified in 1879. Despite the renovations, the tradition of street entertainers in the piazza has endured since at least the 17th century.

EAT

The Ivy Market Grill
The first of the the once-exclusive Ivy restaurant's offshoots. Smart Art Deco interior and a menu heavy on seafood and steaks.

🏠 1a Henrietta St WC2
🌐 theivymarket grill.com

£££

Tuttons
Sit out on the piazza or in the refined dining area in this Covent Garden stalwart. Serves classic English food.

🏠 11/12 Russell St WC2
🌐 tuttons.com

£££

1 The Punch & Judy is a popular market pub with tables inside the Apple Market and outside on the terrace overlooking the piazza.

2 Street entertainers are a much-loved tradition in the piazza. These days musicians, circus performers and magicians must pass an audition in order to perform here.

3 Jubilee Market offers mainly souvenirs, jewellery and cheaper items, though on Mondays here and in the Apple Market antiques and vintage collectables are on sale.

Courtyard of Somerset House with fountains and café tables ↑

2 (Ⓜ) (Ⓨ) (💻) (🏛)

SOMERSET HOUSE

📍 T2 🏠 Strand WC2 🚇 Temple, Charing Cross
🚆 Charing Cross ⛴ Embankment Pier 🕐 8am–11pm daily
📷 Courtauld Gallery: until 2020 🌐 Somerset House:
somersethouse.org.uk; Courtauld Gallery: courtauld.ac.uk

This grand Georgian building, with four Neo-Classical wings around a huge stone courtyard, is an innovative arts and cultural centre offering a range of events and exhibitions in a marvellous riverside location.

Somerset House is best known as the home of the Courtauld Gallery, the city's premiere collection of Impressionist paintings. It is also a unique and popular venue for outdoor summer cinema and eclectic festivals, art fairs and installations.

Built in the 1770s, its first resident was the Royal Academy of Arts. Later tenants included the Navy Board at the end of the 1780s. The building retains some striking architectural features, including the classical grandeur of the Seamen's Waiting Hall and the spectacular five-storey rotunda staircase called Nelson's Stair, both in the South Wing. Strolling through the wing from the courtyard leads to a riverside terrace featuring an open-air summer café and a restaurant, perfect for a sundowner. Below are the modern Embankment Galleries with a range of contemporary arts exhibitions, including photography, design and fashion.

EAT

Bryn Williams at Somerset House
Top-notch modern seasonal British cuisine with an emphasis on salads and grilled vegetables.

🏠 South Wing
🌐 bryn-somerset house.co.uk

£££

Fernandez & Wells
This light-filled café, part of a respected London chain, serves quality breakfasts and light lunch dishes, plus cakes, tea and coffee.

🏠 East Wing
🌐 fernandez andwells.com

£££

EXPERIENCE MORE

 ③

Royal Opera House

T2 **Bow St WC2**
Covent Garden
roh.org.uk

Built in 1732, the first theatre on this site served as more of a playhouse, although many of Handel's operas and oratorios were premiered here. Like its neighbour, the Theatre Royal Drury Lane, the building proved prone to fire and burned down in 1808 and again in 1856. The present opera house was designed in 1858 by E M Barry. John Flaxman's portico frieze, depicting tragedy and comedy, survived from the previous building of 1809.

The Opera House has had both high and low points during its history. In 1892, the first British performance of Wagner's *Ring* cycle was conducted here by Gustav Mahler. Later, during World War I, the building was used as a storehouse by the government. Today, it is home to the Royal Opera and Royal Ballet companies – the best tickets can cost over £200

(though restricted-view tickets up in the "slips" can be had for as little as £12). Backstage tours are available.

④

St Paul's Church

S2 **Bedford St WC2**
Covent Garden **8:30am-5pm Mon-Fri, 9am-1pm Sun**
actorschurch.org

St Paul's is the "Actors' Church" and plaques commemorate famed men and women of the theatre. Inigo Jones designed the altar at the west end to allow his grand portico to face east into Covent Garden Piazza. When clerics objected to this unorthodox placement, the altar was moved to its conventional position at the east end, but Jones went ahead with his original exterior design. Thus the church is entered from the west, and the east portico is a fake door.

The church grounds are a particularly pleasant place to pause – and surprisingly quiet in contrast to the hustle and bustle of neighbouring Covent Garden.

Courtauld Gallery

Closed until at least autumn 2020 for an ambitious expansion programme, the Courtauld is most famous for its exquisite collection of Impressionist and Post-Impressionist paintings but also has works by Botticelli, Bruegel, Bellini and Rubens. World-famous paintings by Monet, Gauguin, Pissarro, Modigliani and Renoir are here, as are Manet's *A Bar at the Folies-Bergères*, Van Gogh's *Self-Portrait with Bandaged Ear*, Cézanne's *The Card Players* and studies of dancers by Degas. While the gallery is shut its works are on display across the UK and further afield; check the website for details.

↑ The Floral Hall - now the Paul Hamlyn Hall - at the Royal Opera House

↑ The brightly painted former warehouses of Neal's Yard and the original branch of Neal's Yard Remedies

 PICTURE PERFECT
Neal's Yard

A riot of rainbow-coloured walls, window frames and flower baskets, Neal's Yard - secreted in the triangle between Monmouth St, Neal St and Shorts Gardens - is the perfect subject to brighten any photo album.

5

Neal Street and Neal's Yard

S1 **WC2** **Covent Garden**

In this attractive street, former warehouses dating from the 19th century can be identified by the hoisting mechanisms high on their exterior walls. Most buildings have been converted into shops and restaurants. Off Neal Street is Neal's Yard, a bright and cheerful courtyard of independent restaurants and shops, most displaying vividly painted façades. Seek out Homeslice for a 20" pizza or try veggie delights at Wild Food Café; either will set you up for an afternoon of shopping. Neal's Yard Remedies offers potions and lotions, while Neal's Yard Dairy is one of London's best cheese shops.

6

Savoy Hotel

T2 **Strand WC2** **Charing Cross, Embankment** **fairmont.com/savoy**

Pioneer of en-suite bathrooms and electric lighting, the grand Savoy was built in 1889 on the site of the medieval Savoy Palace. A lavish £220 million refurbishment took place between 2008 and 2010, incorporating both the original Edwardian and the later Art Deco styles. The Gatsbyesque forecourt is the only street in Britain where traffic drives on the right.

Attached to the hotel are the Savoy Theatre, built for the D'Oyly Carte opera and famed for performing the operas of Gilbert and Sullivan, and the Simpson's in the Strand English restaurant, where traditional roasts are served ceremoniously from silver carving trolleys.

SEVEN DIALS

The pillar at this junction of seven streets features six sundials, the central spike forming the seventh. In the 19th century this was a slum area and a nexus for street thieves; with a choice of seven escape routes, pickpockets often evaded their pursuers. Today Seven Dials is a vibrant shopping and dining area that's perfect for strolling, its cobbled streets and charming hidden courtyards filled with one-off shops, boutiques, high-end cosmetics stores, bars and restaurants.

London Transport Museum

Q T2 **A** The Piazza WC2
@ Covent Garden **C** 10am–
6pm daily (last adm: 5:15pm)
W ltmuseum.co.uk

You don't have to be a train spotter to enjoy this museum. The intriguing collection is housed in the picturesque Victorian Flower Market and features public transport from the past and present. The history of London's transport is in essence a social history of the capital, reflecting the city's growth and then promoting it.

The museum houses a fine collection of 20th-century commercial art. London's bus and train companies have long been prolific patrons of contemporary artists, and copies of some of the finest posters on display can be bought at the museum shop. They include the innovative Art Deco designs of E McKnight Kauffer, as well as work by renowned artists of the 1930s, such as Graham Sutherland and Paul Nash.

This museum is excellent for children (and they can enter free of charge). There are plenty of engagingly hands-on exhibits, including a London bus and an Underground train that children can climb aboard and pretend to drive.

The museum also offers Hidden London, a programme of events and tours in disused stations across the city; check the website for more.

Museum of Freemasonry

Q T1 **A** Freemasons' Hall,
60 Great Queen St WC2
@ Covent Garden **C** 10am–
5pm Mon–Sat **W** free
masonry.london.museum

Looming over a corner on Great Queen Street, the Art Deco Freemasons' Hall was built in 1933 as a memorial to some 3,000 freemasons who died in active service in World War I. The headquarters of English freemasonry, the cultish traditions of this secretive organization are in evidence in the building's museum. Ceremonial objects are displayed around the main exhibit, a huge Grand Master's throne made for George I in 1791, topped with a crown and still used today. Peek into one of the lodge rooms where masons meet; it looks like a courtroom, and is hung with portraits of previous Grand Secretaries (leaders of this Masonic lodge).

EAT

Opera Tavern
Succulent braised pork cheeks are among the flavoursome tapas here.

Q S2 **A** 23 Catherine St
WC2 **W** saltyard
group.co.uk

£ £ £

Chick 'n' Sours
Deep-fried chicken, cocktails and a thumping soundtrack. This is fried chicken, but not as you know it.

Q T2 **A** 1a Earlham St
WC2 **W** chickn
sours.co.uk

£ £ £

Dishoom
Bombay brasserie serving Irani delights.

Q T2 **A** 12 Upper St
Martin's Lane WC2
W dishoom.com

£ £ £

Early motor buses on show in the London Transport Museum

⑨ St Mary-le-Strand

📍 T2 🏠 Strand WC2
🚇 Temple 🕐 For services; check website for times
🌐 stmarylestrand.org

Now beached on a road island at the east end of the Strand, this pleasing church was consecrated in 1724. It was the first public building by James Gibbs, who also designed the church of St Martin-in-the-Fields on Trafalgar Square *(p114)*.

Gibbs was influenced by one of his early supporters, Sir Christopher Wren, but the exuberant external decorative detail here was inspired by the Baroque churches of Rome, where Gibbs studied. Its multi-arched tower is layered like a wedding cake, and culminates in a cupola and lantern. St Mary-le-Strand is now the official church of the Women's Royal Naval Service.

⑩ Cleopatra's Needle

📍 T3 🏠 Embankment WC2
🚇 Embankment, Charing Cross

Erected in Heliopolis in about 1500 BC, this incongruous pink granite monument is much older than London itself. Its inscriptions celebrate the deeds of the pharaohs of ancient Egypt. It was presented to Britain by the then Viceroy of Egypt, Mohammed Ali, in 1819 and erected in 1878. It has a twin in New York's Central Park.

---

⑪ Victoria Embankment Gardens

📍 T3 🏠 WC2 🚇 Embankment, Charing Cross
🕐 7:30am–dusk daily

This narrow sliver of a public park, which was created when the Embankment was built, boasts well-kept flowerbeds, a

clutch of statues of British worthies (including the renowned Scottish poet Robert Burns) and, in summer, a season of concerts.

Its main historical feature is the York water gate at its northwest corner, which was built as a triumphal entry to the Thames for the Duke of Buckingham in 1626.

← Greenery by the Thames at Victoria Embankment Gardens

Aston Martin V12
from *Die Another Day*,
London Film Museum

London Coliseum

**◎ S3 ☐ St Martin's Lane
WC2 ☻ Leicester Sq, Charing
Cross ☐ For guided tours;
check website ☒ eno.org**

London's largest theatre and
one of its most elaborate, this
flamboyant building, topped
with a large globe, was
designed in 1904 by Frank
Matcham and was equipped
with London's first revolving
stage. It was also the first
theatre in Europe to have lifts.
A former variety house, today
it is the home of the English
National Opera, and well
worth visiting, if only for the
Edwardian interior with its
gilded cherubs and heavy
purple curtains. In 2003,
the original glass roof was
restored, providing dramatic
views over Trafalgar Square.

London Film Museum

**◎ T2 ☐ 45 Wellington St
WC2 ☻ Covent Garden
⏰ 10am–6pm daily; last
entry 1 hr before closing
☒ londonfilmmuseum.com**

Though previously an actual
museum of film, this now
misleadingly named place is
really a James Bond museum,

the Bond in Motion exhibition
having effectively become the
permanent and only display.
The Bond memorabilia on
show includes outfits and
posters, but the exhibition
revolves around an impressive
collection of the original
vehicles featured in the films.
There are aircraft, boats, sleds
and motorcycles, but it's the

cars, many of them set against
a moving backdrop from their
respective movie, that usually
attract the most excitement.
Among the highlights are the
unmistakable submersible
white Lotus Esprit S1 from *The
Spy Who Loved Me* and the
quintessential Bond car, the
Aston Martin DB5, first seen in
1964's *Goldfinger*.

THEATRELAND

So choc-a-bloc with theatres is the West End that it has
earned the moniker Theatreland, which you will see
written on street signs, particularly around Soho and
Covent Garden. Theatre first took off in London in the
late 16th century, and in 1663 the West End had its first
playhouse, the Theatre Royal, a previous incarnation of
the theatre that stands on Drury Lane, Covent Garden,
today. The present structure was completed in 1812, in
a century when Theatreland really began to boom; the
nearby Adelphi, on the Strand, had been built in 1806
and then, after the Theatres Act of 1843, dozens more
followed to cater for the Victorian appetite for music hall.
Today the West End has around 50 working theatres.

A SHORT WALK
COVENT GARDEN

Distance 1.5 km (1 mile) **Nearest Tube**
Leicester Square **Time** 25 minutes

Although no longer alive with the calls of fruit
and vegetable market traders going about their
business, visitors, residents and street entertainers
throng Covent Garden Piazza, much as they would
have done centuries ago. Pause to people-
watch as you stroll through this buzzing
area, popping into vibrant boutiques
and historic pubs along the way.

Bright and colourful
Neal Street and Neal's
Yard are home to lots of
charming shops and
cafés (p126).

A replica of a 17th-century
monument marks the junction
at Seven Dials.

The airy Thomas Neal's complex
houses designer shops and the
Donmar Warehouse Theatre.

Ching Court is a Post-
Modernist courtyard by
architect Terry Farrell.

St Martin's Theatre is home to
the world's longest-running
play: The Mousetrap.

Stanfords, established in 1852,
is the largest map and guide
retailer in the world.

Parts of the Lamb &
Flag, one of London's
oldest pubs, date
from 1623 (p128).

The exclusive Garrick
Club is one of the oldest
in the world.

START

New Row is lined
with little shops
and cafés.

Goodwin's Court is a
charming, albeit small,
alley lined with former
Georgian-era shops.

Did You Know?

Eliza Doolittle, of
George Bernard Shaw's
Pygmalion (1913),
was a flower seller
in Covent Garden.

Locator Map
For more detail see p120

↑ Plants in a wooden market
barrow in Covent Garden

Covent Garden
station

Many of the world's greatest
classical singers and dancers
have appeared on the Royal
Opera House's stage (p125).

Bow Street Police Station housed
London's first police force, the Bow
Street Runners, in the 18th century.
It is being converted into a hotel.

A theatre has stood on the site of
the Theatre Royal Drury Lane since
1663, making it London's oldest
theatre. It is owned by composer
Andrew Lloyd Webber and stages
popular musicals.

8 Russell Street, now
a French bakery, is
where Dr Johnson first
met his biographer,
James Boswell.

The history of the city's
historic public transport
system is brought to life
in the London Transport
Museum (p127).

FINISH

Performers of all kinds – jugglers, clowns,
acrobats and musicians – entertain
the crowds in Covent Garden Piazza and
under cover in the Central Market (p122).

Jubilee Market sells
clothes and bric-a-brac.

Despite appearances, St Paul's
Church faces away from the
Piazza. Its grand portico serves
as a stage for a colourful cast
of street performers (p125).

Rules restaurant is
frequented by the
rich and famous for its
typically English food.

JAMES ST

FLORAL STREET

BOW STREET

RUSSELL STREET

WELLINGTON ST

COVENT GARDEN

REET

REET

HENRIETTA ST

SOUTHAMPTON ST

MAIDEN LANE

0 metres   100
0 yards   100

N ↑

HOLBORN AND THE INNS OF COURT

Holborn has been the home of the legal profession in London since the 13th century. The sprawling Royal Courts of Justice, the country's central civil courts, were built here, where the Strand meets Fleet Street, between 1873 and 1882. Much older are the Inns of Court, dating from the medieval period, which supply the courts here and elsewhere with their barristers and judges. Though the exact foundation dates for all four Inns of Court are uncertain, the reason for their location can be traced to a decree of Henry III, from 1234.
It stated that no body providing legal education could be located in the City of London, forcing the legal profession to move just outside the boundary of the City to Holborn. Though student barristers can now study elsewhere, to graduate they must still belong to one of the Inns.

Charles Dickens Museum

GUILFORD STREET

LAMB'S CONDUIT STREET

GRAY'S INN ROAD

HOLBORN AND THE INNS OF COURT

OLD GLOUCESTER STREET

SOUTHAMPTON ROW

BLOOMSBURY AND FITZROVIA
p146

THEOBALD'S ROAD

Gray's I. Fields

BEDFORD ROW

JOCKEY'S FIELDS

RAYMOND BUILDINGS

PRINCETON STREET

WARWICK C

British Museum

BLOOMSBURY SQUARE

BLOOMSBURY WAY

RED LION SQUARE

RED LION STREET

SANDLAND STREET

BROWNLOW ST

EAGLE STREET

PROCTOR ST

HAND CT

MUSEUM STREET

SOUTHAMPTON ROW

HIGH HOLBORN

HOLBORN

NEW OXFORD STREET

COVENT GARDEN AND THE STRAND
p118

KINGSWAY

Holborn ⊖

THEOBALD'S ROAD

LINCOLN'S INN FIELDS

2 Sir John Soane's Museum

3 Lincoln's Inn Fields

The Old Curiosity Shop **4**

5 Hunterian Museum

LINCOLN'S INN FIELDS

Lincoln's Inn Garden

NEWMAN'S ROW

SERLE STREET

Linco Inr

Great Hall **1**

N SQ

CAREY STREET

STF

PORTUGAL STREET

London School of Economics

COVENT GARDEN

HOUGHTON STREET

KINGSWAY

ALDWYCH

St Cleme Danes **7**

Theatre Royal

Bush House

ARI

STRAND

Courtauld Gallery

LANCASTER PL

Somerset House

STRAND

VICTORIA EMBANKME

Victoria Embankment Gardens

Waterloo Bridge

Cleopatra's Needle

HOLBORN AND THE INNS OF COURT

Must Sees

1 Inns of Court (Lincoln's Inn; Inner Temple; Middle Temple; Gray's Inn)
2 Sir John Soane's Museum

Experience More

3 Lincoln's Inn Fields
4 The Old Curiosity Shop
5 Hunterian Museum
6 Fleet Street
7 St Clement Danes
8 Temple Bar Memorial
9 Royal Courts of Justice
10 St Bride's
11 Dr Johnson's House
12 Ye Olde Cheshire Cheese
13 St Etheldreda's Church
14 The London Silver Vaults
15 St Andrew, Holborn
16 Leather Lane Market

Drink

① El Vino

Shop

② Twinings

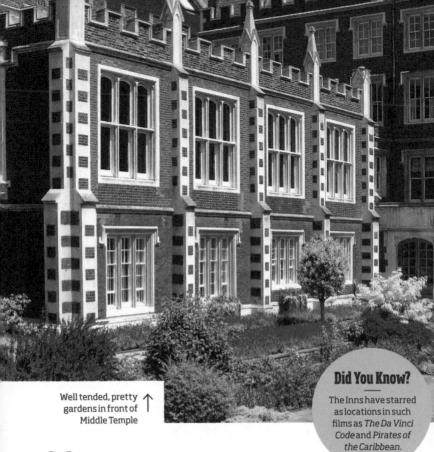

Well tended, pretty gardens in front of Middle Temple ↑

1

INNS OF COURT

Resembling the colleges of Oxford or Cambridge University, the four Inns of Court – Lincoln's Inn, Gray's Inn, Inner Temple and Middle Temple – are oases of calm in the middle of London and perfect sites for a relaxing and intriguing wander through history.

The Inns of Court are the centuries-old homes of the Bar in England and Wales, and every barrister must belong to one of the four Inns. Established in the late medieval period, barristers have long used the Inns for training and study and as accommodation. The leafy precincts, each with their own chapel, historic hall and landscaped gardens, make great places for a lunchtime picnic, and their jumble of passageways, hidden corners and courtyards are well worth exploring. Temple, the joint campus of Inner and Middle Temples, was first home to the Knights Templar, who were based here in the 13th century, and a rebuilt version of their church is a highlight of all four Inns.

It is among the most historic churches in London and one of only four medieval "round churches" in England.

→ A perfect place to relax, on the grass of Lincoln's Inn Fields

Lincoln's Inn

◎ J4 ⬡ Lincoln's Inn Fields WC2 ⊜ Holborn, Chancery Lane ⏱ 7am-7pm Mon-Fri [tour] ⧉ lincolnsinn.org.uk

Some of the buildings in Lincoln's Inn, the most well preserved of London's Inns of Court, date back to the late 15th century. The coat of arms above the arch of the Chancery Lane gatehouse is Henry VIII's, and the heavy oak door is from the same time. Shakespeare's contemporary, Ben Jonson, is believed to have laid some of the bricks of Lincoln's Inn during the reign of Elizabeth I. The chapel is early 17th-century Gothic. Lincoln's Inn has its share of famous alumni; Oliver Cromwell, John Donne, the 17th-century poet, and William Penn, founder of the US state of Pennsylvania, were all students here.

Inner Temple and Middle Temple

◎ K5 ⬡ Inner Temple: King's Bench Walk EC4; Middle Temple: Temple Lane EC4 ⊜ Temple ⏱ Inner Temple: 8am-7pm Mon-Fri ⧉ innertemple.org.uk; middletemple.org.uk

Temple's series of courtyards and buildings comprise two of the four Inns of Court: Middle Temple and Inner Temple. The name derives from the Knights Templar, a chivalrous order based here in medieval times, whose initiations probably took place in the crypt of Temple Church. Built in the 12th century, and maintained by the Inns since 1608, the circular Temple Church boasts an impressive Elizabethan organ and 13th-century effigies of the Knights Templar in its nave.

Among Temple's other ancient buildings is Middle Temple Hall. Completed in 1572, its fine Elizabethan interior survives. Behind Temple, peaceful lawns stretch lazily down towards the Embankment.

Gray's Inn

◎ K4 ⬡ High Holborn WC1 ⊜ Holborn, Chancery Lane ⏱ 6am-8pm Mon-Fri, by prior arrangement ⧉ graysinn.org.uk

This ancient legal centre and law school dates to the 14th century, though it was largely rebuilt after damage inflicted during World War II. The Shakespeare play *A Comedy of Errors* was first performed in Gray's Inn Hall in 1594. The hall's 16th-century interior screen still survives. The young Charles Dickens was employed as a clerk here between 1827 and 1828. This lovely garden, known as "the Walks", once a convenient site for staging duels, is open to lunchtime strollers, except for public holidays.

THE KNIGHTS TEMPLAR

The Knights Templar, who founded Temple and built Temple Church, was a religious order established to protect pilgrims on their way to and from Jerusalem in the 12th century. The Holy City had been seized in the late 11th century by Christian crusaders but pilgrimage routes were fraught with danger. The order was dissolved in 1312.

💬 **INSIDER TIP**
Summer Spot

The best time to visit the Inns of Court are when the gardens are open: on weekdays between noon and 3pm. Middle Temple Gardens are only open in summer.

② Ⓜ 🛍

SIR JOHN SOANE'S MUSEUM

📍 J4 🏠 13 Lincoln's Inn Fields WC2 🚇 Holborn 🕐 10am–5pm Wed–Sun 🔒 24–26 & 31 Dec, 1 Jan & a week in Jan for conservation 🌐 soane.org

One of the most delightful and unusual museums in London, this extraordinary house, filled to bursting with an eclectic gathering of beautiful and peculiar objects, was left to the nation by the architect Sir John Soane in 1837.

Though laden with Classical statuary and other eye-catching and unusual artifacts, it is the interior design of the building itself that makes this place unlike any other museum. The house abounds with architectural surprises and illusions. Cunningly placed mirrors play tricks with light and space, and in the centre of the basement an atrium stretches up to the roof, the glass dome of which illuminates the galleries on every floor. In the picture gallery on the ground floor, walls turn out to be folding panels which knowledgeable curators open to reveal further paintings and, most unexpectedly, a floorless extension to the room itself, hung with yet more pictures.

↑ The museum, made up of three houses that Soane bought one by one

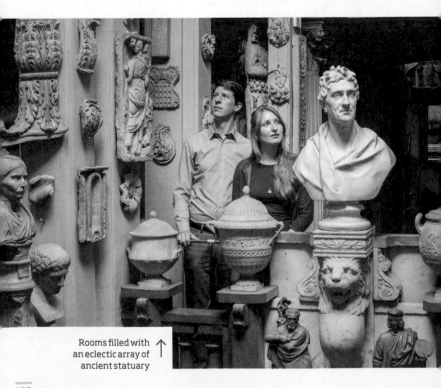

← Rooms filled with an eclectic array of ancient statuary

WHO WAS SIR JOHN SOANE?

Born in 1753, the son of a bricklayer, John Soane eventually became one of Britain's leading architects of the 19th century. Most of his buildings were Neo-Classical in style and he was responsible for designing Dulwich Picture Gallery (p325), Pitzhanger Manor (p330) and the Bank of England (p184).

EXPERIENCE MORE

3

Lincoln's Inn Fields

🗺 J4 🏠 WC2 🚇 Holborn
🕐 Dawn-dusk daily

A former public execution site, many religious martyrs and those suspected of treachery to the Crown perished here under the Tudors and Stuarts. When the developer William Newton wanted to build on this site in the 1640s, students at Lincoln's Inn and other residents made him undertake that it would remain a public area forever. Thanks to this early protest, tennis is played on the public courts here year-round, while lawyers read their briefs in the fresh air.

4

The Old Curiosity Shop

🗺 J4 🏠 13-14 Portsmouth St WC2 🚇 Holborn 🌐 the-old-curiosity-shop.com

Whether it inspired Charles Dickens's 19th-century novel of the same name or not, the Old Curiosity Shop is a genuine 16th-century building. With its wooden beams and overhanging first floor, it gives a rare impression of a London streetscape from before the Great Fire of 1666. The shop is still trading, currently as a handmade-shoe shop.

5

Hunterian Museum

🗺 J4 🏠 35-43 Lincoln's Inn Fields WC2 🚇 Holborn, Chancery Lane 🕐 For refurbishment until 2021 🌐 hunterianmuseum.org

Inside the Royal College of Surgeons, the Hunterian Museum started life as the personal collection of John Hunter (1728–93), one of the leading teachers of surgery in his day, who amassed a large collection of human and animal anatomical specimens to aid his teaching. Most famously the skeleton of Charles Byrne, the "Irish Giant" at 2.31 m (7 ft 7 in) tall, is here. It is not a museum for the squeamish, but the surgical instruments and interactive displays on modern surgery are fascinating for those with an interest in the subject.

↑ The Old Curiosity Shop provides a glimpse of London as it looked before 1666

↑ Fleet Street, one of the oldest streets in the City of London, which once rang with the sounds of printing presses

Fleet Street

K5 EC4 Temple, Blackfriars, St Paul's

England's first printing press was set up by William Caxton in the late 15th century. In around 1500, his assistant began his own business in Fleet Street, and the area grew to become the centre of London's publishing industry. Playwrights Shakespeare and Ben Jonson were patrons of the old Mitre Tavern, now No 37 Fleet Street. In 1702, England's first daily newspaper, *The Daily Courant*, was issued from Fleet Street – conveniently placed for the City and Westminster, which were the main sources of news. Later the street became synonymous with the Press. The grand Art Deco building with Egyptian-style detail at No 135 is the former headquarters of the *Daily Telegraph*.

Did You Know?

Sweeney Todd, the "Demon Barber of Fleet Street", is said to have had his parlour at 152 Fleet St.

Next to the church of St-Dunstan-in-the-West (which largely dates from the 1830s) is a building adorned with the names of former newspapers.

The printing presses underneath the newspaper offices were abandoned in 1987, when new technology made it easy to produce papers away from the centre of town in areas such as Wapping and the Docklands. Today the newspaper offices have also left Fleet Street, even though some of the journalists' traditional watering holes remain, such as Ye Olde Cheshire Cheese public house (*p142*), and the legendary El Vino wine bar (*p141*), found at the western end opposite Fetter Lane.

St Clement Danes

J5 Strand WC2 Temple 9am-4pm Mon-Fri, 10am-3pm Sat, 9:30am- 3pm Sun 26 Dec-1 Jan, public hols raf.mod.uk

Sitting proudly isolated on a traffic island, this wonderful church was designed by Christopher Wren in 1680. Its name derives from an earlier church built here by the descendants of Danish

invaders, whom Alfred the Great had allowed to remain in London in the 9th century. From the 17th to the 19th centuries many people were buried here, and their memorial plaques are now in the crypt. Outside, to the east, is a statue (1910) of Dr Johnson (*p142*), who often came to services here.

Nearly destroyed during World War II, the church was rebuilt and became the central church of the Royal Air Force (RAF). The interior is dominated by RAF symbols, memorials and monuments. Housed in elaborate glass cabinets along the aisles, remembrance books record the names of over 150,000 men and women who died while serving the RAF.

The church bells ring to various tunes, including that of the old nursery rhyme *Oranges and Lemons*, in whose lyrics the church features.

Temple Bar Memorial

K5 Fleet St EC4 Temple, Chancery Lane

In the middle of Fleet Street stands a monument looking somewhat like a giant sentry box, with Queen Victoria and her son, the Prince of Wales,

DRINK

El Vino

Immortalized as "Pomeroys" in John Mortimer's Rumpole of the Bailey stories, wood-panelled wine bar El Vino is famous for the lengthy lunches enjoyed here by both barristers and, in the past, journalists.

📍K5 🏠47 Fleet St EC
🌐elvino.co.uk

standing guard on either side. Dating from 1880, it marks the spot where Temple Bar, a magnificent gateway by Sir Christopher Wren, used to stand. This was the principal entrance to the City of London, where by tradition the monarch, when in State procession to the Tower of London or St Paul's Cathedral, had to pause and ask permission of the Lord Mayor to enter. The original gateway was dismantled when it began to cause traffic congestion, and spent over a century in the grounds of a country estate in Hertfordshire before being erected at the entrance of Paternoster Square near St Paul's (p174) in 2004.

Royal Courts of Justice (the Law Courts)

📍K5 🏠Strand WC2
🚇Holborn, Temple, Chancery Lane ⏰9:30am-4:30pm Mon-Fri 🚫Public hols 🌐theroyalcourtsof justice.com

Knots of demonstrators and television cameras can often be seen outside this sprawling and fanciful Victorian Gothic building, waiting for the verdict of a contentious case. These are the nation's main civil courts, dealing with such matters as divorce, libel, civil liability and appeals. Cases involving criminal offences are dealt with at the Old Bailey (p187), ten minutes' walk to the east. The public are admitted to all the courtrooms and a list details which case is being heard in which

one. The massive building was completed in 1882 and is said to contain 1,000 rooms and 5.6 km (3.5 miles) of corridors.

St Bride's

📍K5 🏠Fleet St EC4
🚇Blackfriars ⏰8am-6pm Mon-Fri, 10am-3:30pm Sat, 10am-6:30pm Sun 🚫Public hols 🌐stbrides.com

St Bride's is one of Wren's best-loved churches. Its position just off Fleet Street has made it the traditional venue for memorial services to departed journalists, and wall plaques commemorate notable pressmen and women and printers. The marvellous octagonal layered spire has been the model for tiered wedding cakes since shortly after it was added in 1703. The church was bombed during World War II, but its interior had been faithfully restored by 1957. The crypt contains remnants of earlier churches on the site, and a section of Roman pavement. Tours lasting 90 minutes are led at 2:15pm on Tuesdays.

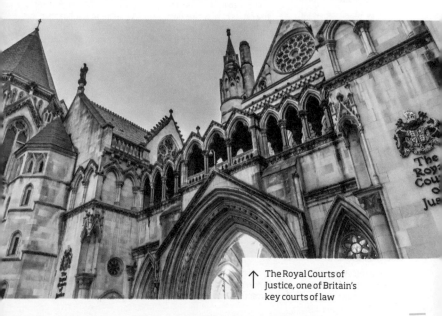

↑ The Royal Courts of Justice, one of Britain's key courts of law

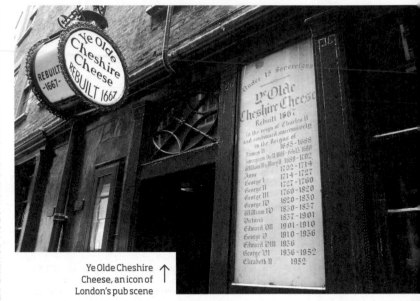

Ye Olde Cheshire
Cheese, an icon of ↑
London's pub scene

Dr Johnson's House

Q K4 **⌂** 17 Gough Sq EC4
⊜ Blackfriars, Chancery
Lane, Temple **⏰** May-Sep:
11am-5:30pm Mon-Sat;
Oct-Apr: 11am-5pm
Mon-Sat **⊘** Public hols
w drjohnsonshouse.org

The oft-quoted Dr Samuel
Johnson was an 18th-century
scholar famous for the many
witty (and often contentious)
remarks that his biographer,
James Boswell, recorded and
published. Johnson lived at
17 Gough Square from 1748 to
1759. He compiled the first
definitive English dictionary
(published in 1755) in the attic,
where six scribes and assistants
stood all day at high desks.

The house, built before
1700, retains some period
features and is furnished with
18th-century pieces. There is
a small collection of exhibits
relating to Dr Johnson and
the times in which he lived,
including a tea set belonging
to his friend Mrs Thrale and
pictures of Johnson and his
contemporaries. There are
also replica Georgian costumes
for children to try on. A statue
of one of Johnson's favourite
cats, Hodge, stands outside.

↑ Hodge looking out
towards the famed
Dr Johnson's House

⑫
Ye Olde Cheshire Cheese

Q K4 **⌂** 145 Fleet St EC4
⊜ Blackfriars **⏰** 11am-
11pm Mon-Fri, noon-
11pm Sat

There has been an inn here
for centuries and parts of this
building date back to 1667,
when rebuilding took place
after the Great Fire of 1666.

The diarist Samuel Pepys
often drank here in the 17th
century, but it was Dr Samuel
Johnson's association with
"the Cheese" that made it a
place of pilgrimage for the
19th-century literati. Novelists
Mark Twain and Charles
Dickens were frequent visitors.
In recent years it has been
argued that there is no real
evidence that Johnson actually
drank here; nevertheless, this
is a great old pub, one of few
to have kept the 18th-century

SHOP

Twinings
The oldest tea shop
in London. Learn
about the history
of Britain's favourite
drink, and try (and buy)
a variety of brews
from the world-
famous brand.

Q K5 **⌂** 216 Strand
WC2 **w** twinings.co.uk

↑ The stained-glass west window of St Etheldreda's Church

The HATTON GARDEN box is a sidebar.

HATTON GARDEN

Named for Sir Christopher Hatton, Hatton Garden is the centre of London's diamond and jewellery district. Millions of pounds change hands daily in scores of small shops with sparkling window displays. In April 2015, an underground safe deposit facility was robbed of upwards of £25 million, in what has been described as the "largest burglary in English legal history".

arrangement of small rooms with fireplaces, tables and benches, rather than knocking through the walls to make larger bars.

---

⑬

St Etheldreda's Church

📍K4 🏠14 Ely Place EC1 ⊖Farringdon ⏰8am-5pm Mon-Sat, 8am-12:30pm Sun 🌐stetheldreda.com

Built in 1290, this rare survivor is the oldest Catholic church in England. First the town chapel of the Bishops of Ely, it passed through various hands over the centuries, including those of Sir Christopher Hatton, an Elizabethan courtier, who built Hatton House in the grounds and used the church crypt as a tavern. Rebuilt and restored several times, the church has some stunning stained glass.

---

⑭

The London Silver Vaults

📍K4 🏠53-64 Chancery Lane WC2 ⊖Chancery Lane ⏰9am-5:30pm Mon-Fri, 9am-1pm Sat 🌐silver vaultslondon.com

These silver vaults began life as the 19th-century Chancery Lane Safe Deposit Company.

Visitors are led downstairs, then through steel security doors to reach a nest of underground shops shining with antique and modern silverware. Prices range from modest to eye-watering.

---

⑮

St Andrew, Holborn

📍K4 🏠5 St Andrew St EC4 ⊖Chancery Lane, Farringdon ⏰9am-5pm Mon-Fri 🌐standrewholborn.org.uk

This has been a site of worship for over 1,000 years. The medieval church that stood here survived the Great Fire, but in 1668 renowned architect Christopher Wren was asked to redesign it. The lower part of the tower is virtually all that remains of the earlier church. One of Wren's most spacious churches, it was gutted during World War II but faithfully restored as the church of the London trade guilds.

Benjamin Disraeli, the Jewish-born prime minister, was baptized here in 1817, at the age of 12. In the 19th century, a charity school was attached to the church.

---

⑯

Leather Lane Market

📍K4 🏠Leather Lane ⊖Farringdon, Chancery Lane ⏰10am-2pm Mon-Fri

Running parallel to Hatton Garden is Leather Lane Market. A traditional London market, it sells a bit of everything, including some tasty street food, and is a perfect place to pick up a treat or two.

↑ The impressive silverware and antiques in the London Silver Vaults

A SHORT WALK
INNS OF COURT

Distance 2 km (1.25 miles) **Nearest Tube** Holborn **Time** 30 minutes

This is calm, dignified, legal London, packed with history and interest. Lincoln's Inn, adjoining one of the city's first residential squares, has buildings dating back to the late 15th century. Suited lawyers carry bundles of briefs between their offices here and the Neo-Gothic Law Courts. Nearby is Temple, another historic legal district, which has a famous 13th-century round church.

The Sir John Soane's Museum was the home of the Georgian architect. It was left, with his collection, to the nation (p138).

LINCOLN'S INN FIELDS

LINCOLN'S INN FIELDS

Lincoln's Inn (p137)

The mock-Tudor archway, leading to Lincoln's Inn and built in 1845, overlooks the Lincoln's Inn Fields (p139).

START

The Old Curiosity Shop is a rare 16th-century, pre-Great Fire building (p139).

PORTSMOUTH ST

PORTUGAL STREET

C A

0 metres 100
0 yards 100
N ↑

FINISH

The Gladstone statue was erected in 1905 to commemorate William Gladstone, the Victorian statesman who served four terms as prime minister.

↑ The peaceful green haven of the Lincoln's Inn Fields public square

↑ The imposing façade of the Royal Courts of Justice, the nation's main civil courts

Locator Map
For more detail see p134

HOLBORN AND THE INNS OF COURT

The opening scene of *Charles Dickens' Bleak House* was set in the Old Hall, which dates back to 1490.

Did You Know?

Lincoln's Inn Fields is the largest public square in London.

Look for the gold lions on the railings of the Law Society's headquarters.

For two centuries Fleet Street was the centre of the national press. The newspaper offices left in the 1980s (p140).

El Vino is a wine bar where Fleet Street's journalists once mingled with barristers (p141).

No 17 Fleet Street has a superb half-timbered façade (1610) that survived the Fire. James I's eldest son, Prince Henry, had a room on the first floor of this former tavern.

Temple was first home to the Knights Templar, who were based here in the 13th century.

A dragon marks where the City of London meets Westminster at the Temple Bar Memorial (p140).

Designed by Wren (1679), St Clement Danes is the Royal Air Force's church (p140).

The Royal Courts of Justice, the country's main court for civil cases and appeals, was built in 1882. It is made out of 35 million bricks faced with Portland stone (p141).

CHANCERY LANE

BELL YARD

FETTER LANE

FLEET STREET

STRAND

MIDDLE TEMPLE LANE

REET

The Reading Room at the British Museum

BLOOMSBURY AND FITZROVIA

The handsome garden squares of Fitzrovia and Bloomsbury date mainly from the late 18th and early 19th centuries, but it wasn't until the early 20th century that the area became inseparably connected with the cultural and intellectual elite of London. By that time Bloomsbury was already established as a place of learning, home to the British Museum, founded in 1753, and the University of London, founded in 1826. Along with Fitzrovia it was an apt location, therefore, for the homes and haunts of the avant-garde set known as the Bloomsbury Group, a network of mostly upper-middle-class, learned and artistic friends and associates. Since the Bloomsbury Group's heyday the university has expanded significantly, adding the monolithic Senate House – now home to the School of Oriental and African Studies and central library – to its collection of campuses, and cementing the area's place as the student capital of central London.

LIDLINGTON PLACE

POLYGON RD

OSSULSTON STREET

ALBANY STREET

REDHILL STREET

CHESTER TERRACE

OUTER

EVERSHOLT STREET

CIRCLE

KING'S CROSS, CAMDEN AND ISLINGTON
p160

Regent's Park

CARDINGTON STREET

ROBERT   STREET

NASH STREET

ALBANY   STREET

STANHOPE STREET

WILLIAM   ROAD

CLARENCE GARDENS

HAMPSTEAD ROAD

STARCROSS STREET

NORTH GOWER STREET

EUSTON STREET

STEPHENSON WAY

Euston

EUSTON SQUARE

UPPER WOBURN PL

ENDSLEIGH GDNS

ENDSLEIGH STREET

TAVITON STREET

TAVIS
SQUARE

DRUMMOND   STREET

ST

Wellcome Collection ⑥

GOWER PLACE

GORDON ST

GORDON SQUARE

Park Square Gardens

LONGFORD ST

TRITON SQUARE

Euston Square

University College London

WOBURN SQUARE

TORRINGTON SQUARE

MALET STREET

Regent's Park

EUSTON ROAD

OSNABURGH STREET

WARREN STREET

Warren Street

GRAFTON WAY

PARK CRESCENT

Great Portland Street

WARREN STREET

Fitzroy Square ⑧

Grant Museum of Zoology ⑪

GOWER

CHENIES MEWS

HUNTLEY

TORRINGTON PLACE

RIDGMOUNT GDNS

STREET

PLACE

PORTLAND PLACE

GREAT PORTLAND STREET

CLEVELAND   STREET

WHITFIELD   STREET

FITZROY STREET

STREET

TOTTENHAM

RIDGMOUNT STREET

CHENIES ST

BT Tower

MAPLE   STREET

HOWLAND   STREET

CHARLOTTE   STREET

ALFRED PLACE

STORE STREET

BLOOMS

BEDFORD SQUARE

HANSON   STREET

Pollock's Toy Museum ⑦

SCALA ST

COURT

REGENT'S PARK AND MARYLEBONE
p274

WEYMOUTH   STREET

RIDING HOUSE ST

TOTTENHAM ST

GOODGE ST

③

Goodge Street

② ⑤

PERCY ST

STEPHEN ST

MORWELL ST

BEDFORD AVE

GREAT RUSS

NEW CAVENDISH STREET

HARLEY   STREET

CAVENDISH PLACE

GREAT TITCHFIELD   ST

MORTIMER STREET

WELLS STREET

BERNERS STREET

①

GOODGE ST

RATHBONE ST

NEWMAN   STREET

RATHBONE PL

Tottenham Court Road

N

CHARING CROSS ROAD

EAST CASTLE STREET

Oxford Circus

OXFORD   STREET

SOHO AND TRAFALGAR SQUARE
p102

SOHO

BLOOMSBURY AND FITZROVIA

BROADWICK   STREET

WARDOUR   ST

OLD COMPTON ST

LEXINGTON STREET

BEAK   STREET

GERRARD STREET

Leicester Square

0 metres   300

0 yards   300

N ↑

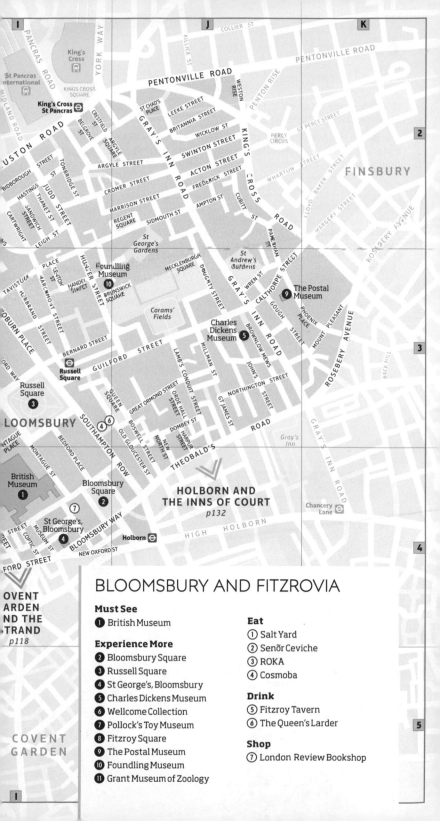

BLOOMSBURY AND FITZROVIA

Must See
1. British Museum

Experience More
2. Bloomsbury Square
3. Russell Square
4. St George's, Bloomsbury
5. Charles Dickens Museum
6. Wellcome Collection
7. Pollock's Toy Museum
8. Fitzroy Square
9. The Postal Museum
10. Foundling Museum
11. Grant Museum of Zoology

Eat
1. Salt Yard
2. Senőr Ceviche
3. ROKA
4. Cosmoba

Drink
5. Fitzroy Tavern
6. The Queen's Larder

Shop
7. London Review Bookshop

HOLBORN AND
THE INNS OF COURT
p132

COVENT
GARDEN
AND THE
STRAND
p118

1

BRITISH MUSEUM

📍 I4 🏠 Great Russell St WC1 🚇 Tottenham Court Road, Holborn, Russell Square 🚆 Euston 🕐 10am–5:30pm daily, till 8:30pm Fri 🌐 britishmuseum.org

The British Museum holds one of the world's greatest collections of historical and cultural artifacts. This immense hoard of treasure comprises over eight million objects spanning the history of mankind, from prehistoric times to today.

INSIDER TIP
Eye Openers

The museum offers an excellent set of free tours. There are over a dozen daily "eye-opener tours" of individual rooms; and on Friday evenings the "spotlight tours" focus on specific exhibits such as the Rosetta Stone. There's no need to book, simply check the website for where and when to meet.

The oldest public museum in the world, the British Museum was established in 1753 to house the books, antiquities, and plant and animal specimens of the physician Sir Hans Sloane (1660–1753). The collection expanded rapidly and during the 19th century the museum acquired a mass of Classical and Middle Eastern antiquities, some of which still make up the top attractions here, such as the Rosetta Stone and the Parthenon sculptures. You can now see items drawn from a dizzying number of cultures and civilizations, from Stone Age Europe and Ancient Egypt to modern Japan and contemporary North America. There are sculptures and statues, mummies and murals, coins and medals, ceramics, gold and silver, prints, drawings and innumerable other man-made objects from every corner of the globe and every period of history.

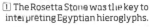

1 The Rosetta Stone was the key to interpreting Egyptian hieroglyphs.

2 The museum holds the largest collection of Egyptian mummies outside of Egypt.

3 Beautiful statues from the Parthenon in Ancient Greece.

The Greek Revival-style main entrance to the British Museum on Great Russell Street ↓

A World of Treasures

There are 95 galleries covering 4 km (2.5 miles) over three floors and eight levels of the museum, though the majority of exhibits are on the ground and upper floors. Ancient Egyptian artifacts are on the upper floor in Rooms 61 to 66 and in Room 4, beside the Great Court. The Greece, Rome and Middle East collections are also spread across the two main floors, though major items such as the Parthenon sculptures are in the large rooms of the ground floor to the west of the Great Court. The Africa collection is on the lower floor, while Asia exhibits are on the ground and upper floors on the north side. The Americas collection is located in the northeast corner of the main floor. The Sainsbury Gallery hosts major temporary exhibitions.

The world-famous Reading Room, designed by Sir Norman Foster, at the centre of the museum's Great Court

Did You Know?

The Portland Vase, made before the birth of Christ, was reassembled after it was smashed by a visitor in 1845.

Inside the Enlightenment gallery, formerly the library of King George III ↑

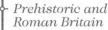

GREAT COURT AND READING ROOM

The architectural highlight of the building is the Great Court, a breathtaking conversion of the original 19th-century inner courtyard. Opened in 2000, the court is now covered by a tessellated glass roof, creating Europe's largest indoor public square. At the centre of the Great Court is the glorious dome-roofed Reading Room of the former British Library where figures such as Mahatma Gandhi and Karl Marx studied.

Top Collections

Prehistoric and Roman Britain

▶ Highlights among the relics of ancient Britain on display include the gold "Mold Cape", a ceremonial Bronze Age cape found in Wales; an antlered headdress worn by hunter-gatherers 9,000 years ago; and "Lindow Man", a 1st-century AD victim of sacrifice who was preserved in a bog until 1984.

Europe

Sutton Hoo's treasure, the burial hoard of a 7th-century Anglo-Saxon king, is in Room 41. The artifacts include a helmet and shield, Celtic bowls, and gold and garnet jewellery. Exquisite timepieces include a 400-year-old clock from Germany, designed as a model galleon; in its day it pitched, played music and even fired a cannon. Nearby are the famous 12th-century Lewis chessmen. Baron Ferdinand Rothschild's (1839–98) Renaissance treasures are in Room 2a.

Middle East

Galleries devoted to the Middle East collections cover 7,000 years of history, with famous items such as 7th-century BC Assyrian reliefs from King Ashurbanipal's palace at Nineveh, two large human-headed bulls from 7th-century BC Khorsabad and the Black Obelisk of Shalmaneser III, an Assyrian king. The upper floors contain pieces from ancient Sumeria, part of the Oxus Treasure (which lay buried for over 2,000 years) and the diverse new Islamic World galleries.

Egypt

Egyptian sculptures in Room 4 include a fine red granite head of a king, thought to be Amenhotep III, and a huge statue of King Rameses II. Here too is the Rosetta Stone, used as a key for deciphering Egyptian hieroglyphs. An array of mummies, jewellery and Coptic art is upstairs.

Greece and Rome

◀ The Greek and Roman collections include the controversial Parthenon sculptures. These 5th-century BC reliefs decorated the temple to Athena on the Acropolis, Athens. Much of it was ruined, and what survived was removed by the British diplomat Lord Elgin. There is also the Nereid Monument and sculptures from the Mausoleum at Halicarnassus.

Asia

Fine porcelain, Shang bronzes (c 1500–1050 BC) and ceremonial bronze vessels are in the Chinese Collection. In the Sir Percival David gallery the Chinese ceramics date from the 10th to early 20th centuries. There is a fine collection of sculpture from the Indian subcontinent, including sculpted reliefs that once covered the walls of the Buddhist temple at Amaravati. A Korean section contains works of Buddhist art, and there is a traditional Japanese teahouse in Room 92.

Africa

African sculptures, textiles and graphic art are in Room 25. Famous bronzes from the Kingdom of Benin, set in due course to return to Nigeria, stand alongside modern African prints, paintings, drawings and colourful fabrics.

EXPERIENCE MORE

THE BLOOMSBURY GROUP

The Bloomsbury Group was an informal set of writers, artists and intellectuals who lived in and around Bloomsbury at the beginning of the 20th century. The group, with its passionate belief in the "aesthetic experience and the pursuit of knowledge", and modern attitudes towards feminism, sexuality and politics, first gathered at No 46 Gordon Square, home of the Stephen sisters, Virginia (later Woolf) and Vanessa (later Bell). Other key members included novelist E M Forster, economist John Maynard Keynes, the biographer Lytton Strachey and artists Duncan Grant and Dora Carrington.

Bloomsbury Square

📍 I4 🏠 WC1 🚇 Holborn

This is the oldest of the Bloomsbury squares. It was laid out in 1661 by the 4th Earl of Southampton, who owned the land. None of the original buildings survive and the square's shaded garden is encircled by a busy one-way traffic system. (There is a car park below the square that, unusually for central London, nearly always has a free space or two.)

From this square, the entire Bloomsbury area was gradually developed. Noted for the brilliance of many of its inhabitants, it gave its name most famously to the avant-garde Bloomsbury Group. Look out for their individual plaques throughout the area.

→

The austere but bright interior of St George's, Bloomsbury

Russell Square

📍 I3 🏠 WC1 🚇 Russell Sq

One of London's largest squares, Russell Square is a lively place, with a fountain, café and traffic roaring around its perimeter. The east side boasts perhaps the best of the Victorian grand hotels to survive in the capital. Designed by Charles Doll and opened in 1898, the former Russell Hotel – now the Kimpton Fitzroy – remains a wondrous

↑ Russell Square, an oasis in a whirl of busy traffic

confection of red terracotta, with colonnaded balconies and prancing cherubs beneath the main columns.

The poet T S Eliot worked at the west corner of the square from 1925 until 1965, in what were the offices of publisher Faber & Faber.

4 St George's, Bloomsbury

📍 I4 🏛 Bloomsbury Way WC1 🚇 Holborn, Tottenham Court Rd, Russell Sq ⏰ Hours vary, check website 🌐 stgeorges bloomsbury.org.uk

St George's was designed by Nicholas Hawksmoor, a pupil of Christopher Wren, and completed in 1730. It was built as a place of worship for the residents of fashionable Bloomsbury. In 1913, the funeral of Emily Davison, the suffragette killed by King George V's racehorse at the Epsom Derby, was held here. The crypt is the unlikely home

of the **Museum of Comedy**, the first of its kind in the UK. Attached is a venue that hosts stand-up comedy performances in the evenings.

Museum of Comedy
⏰ 1–5pm daily; check website for performances 🌐 museumofcomedy.com

5 Charles Dickens Museum

📍 J3 🏛 48 Doughty St WC1 🚇 Chancery Lane, Russell Sq ⏰ 10am–5pm Tue–Sun (last adm 4pm) ⏰ 1 Jan, 25 & 26 Dec, and occasionally Sat & Sun for events 🌐 dickensmuseum.com

The novelist Charles Dickens lived in this early-19th-century terraced house for three of his most productive years (from 1837 to 1839). *Oliver Twist* and *Nicholas Nickleby* were entirely written here, and the *Pickwick Papers* was finished. Although Dickens had a number of London homes throughout his lifetime, this is the only one to have survived.

In 1923, it was acquired by the Dickens Fellowship and it is now a well-conceived museum with some of the principal rooms laid out exactly as they were in Dickens's time. Others have been adapted to display a varied collection of articles associated with him.

The museum houses over 100,000 exhibits, including manuscripts, paintings and personal items, papers and pieces of furniture from his other homes, and first editions of many of his best-known works. As well as its permanent collection, the museum puts on special exhibitions and events, and

→ A bust of the great chronicler of London, at the Charles Dickens Museum

runs a monthly "Housemaid's Tour". The garden café (no entry fee required) provides respite from the busy city centre and has a decent selection of drinks and treats.

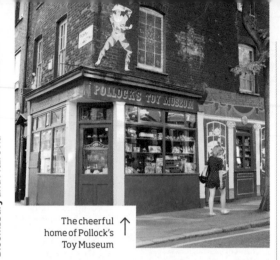

The cheerful home of Pollock's Toy Museum ↑

6 Wellcome Collection

📍H3 🏠183 Euston Rd NW1 🚇Euston, King's Cross, Warren St ⏰10am–6pm Tue–Sat (to 10pm Thu), 11am–6pm Sun, noon–6pm public hols 🚫1 Jan, 24–26 Dec 🌐wellcome collection.org

Sir Henry Wellcome (1853–1936) was a pharmacist, entrepreneur and collector. His passionate interest in medicine and its history, as well as archaeology and ethnography, led him to gather more than one million objects from around the world, now housed in this building.

The museum's permanent exhibition, Medicine Man, includes more than 900 diverse objects, spanning from Napoleon's toothbrush to Florence Nightingale's moccasins. Changing displays cover a range of engaging topics exploring medicine, art and the human condition. Visitors can also discover the reimagined Reading Room – a hybrid area bridging library, exhibition and event space – relax in the café or enjoy after-noon tea in the restaurant.

The Wellcome Library, which occupies the upper floors, is the world's largest collection of books devoted to the history of medicine.

7 Pollock's Toy Museum

📍H4 🏠1 Scala St W1 (entrance on Whitfield St) 🚇Goodge St, Warren St, Tottenham Court Rd ⏰10am–5pm Mon–Sat 🚫Public hols 🌐pollocks toys.com

Named for Benjamin Pollock, a renowned maker of toy theatres in the late 19th and early 20th centuries, this is a child-sized museum created in two 18th- and 19th-century houses. The small rooms have been filled with a fascinating assortment of historic toys from all over the world. There are dolls, puppets, trains, cars, construction sets, a fine rocking horse and a splendid collection of mainly Victorian doll's houses. Parents beware – the exit leads you through a toyshop.

8 Fitzroy Square

📍H3 🏠W1 🚇Warren St, Great Portland St

Designed by Robert Adam in 1794, the square's south and east sides survive in their original form, built in dignified Portland stone. Blue plaques record the homes of many artists, writers and statesmen:

writers George Bernard Shaw and Virginia Woolf both lived at No 29 – although not at the same time. Shaw gave money to the artist Roger Fry to establish the Omega workshop at No 33 in 1913. Here young artists were paid a fixed wage to produce Post-Impressionist furniture, pottery, carpets and paintings for sale to the public.

9 The Postal Museum

📍J3 🏠15–20 Phoenix Place WC1 🚇Farringdon ⏰10am–5pm daily 🌐postalmuseum.org

Just over the road from the Mount Pleasant Royal Mail Sorting Office, once the largest sorting office in the world, the Postal Museum charts the 500 years of Britain's postal service in a series of engaging and interactive exhibits. The star attraction is Mail Rail, a 15-minute miniature train ride through tunnels that once formed part of the postal service's underground railway. The at-times pitch-black, narrow, atmospheric tunnels feature audiovisual displays along the way and deposit you in the original engineering depot. The museum itself contains exhibits spanning the full life of the oldest postal service in the world.

10 Foundling Museum

📍I3 🏠40 Brunswick Square WC1 🚇Russell Sq ⏰10am–5pm Tue–Sat, 11am–5pm Sun 🚫1 Jan, 24–26 & 31 Dec 🌐foundling museum.org.uk

In 1722, Captain Thomas Coram, a retired sailor and shipbuilder recently returned from the Americas and quite horrified by the poverty on London's streets, vowed to set up a refuge for abandoned children. Assisted by two friends, the artist William Hogarth and the composer George Frideric Handel, Coram worked tirelessly to raise funds. Hogarth donated paintings to the hospital and other artists followed suit. The wealthy were encouraged to view the works of art and visit the children, in the hope that they would donate money to the cause.

On the ground floor, the story of the many children cared for here is told. The collection of 18th-century paintings, sculpture, furniture and interiors is displayed, with one room dedicated to Handel, on the upper floors.

Next to the museum, with its entrance on Guilford Street, is Coram's Fields, a unique park for children and youngsters (all adults must be accompanied by children). It includes a youth centre, a city farm and a café.

Grant Museum of Zoology

📍H3 🏛21 University St WC1 🚇Warren St, Euston Square, Russell Square 🕐1–5pm Mon–Sat 🌐ucl.ac.uk/culture/grant-museum-zoology

The heart of Bloomsbury's university district is Gower Street: on one side is the Neo-Classical main building of University College London, designed by William Wilkins in 1826, and opposite is the original terracotta building of University College Hospital. UCL owns several museum collections, including the Grant Museum of Zoology, established in 1828. It houses around 68,000 specimens – animal skeletons, taxidermy, mounted insects and other creatures preserved in jars (including one containing 18 preserved moles) – in crowded wooden cases, making it an atmospheric, occasionally gruesome, insight into the world of 19th-century science and collecting.

Unusual exhibits at the Grant Museum of Zoology *(inset and below)*

EAT & DRINK

Salt Yard
Excellent tapas combining Spanish and Italian cuisines.

📍H4 🏛54 Goodge St W1 🌐saltyard group.co.uk

£££

Señor Ceviche
Peruvian street food.
📍H4 🏛18 Charlotte St W1
🌐senor-ceviche.com

£££

ROKA
Japanese *robatayaki* (barbecue) specialist.

📍H4 🏛37 Charlotte St W1 🌐roka restaurant.com

£££

Cosmoba
Classic Italian restaurant, serving pizza, pasta, meat and fish.

📍I3 🏛9 Cosmo Pl WC1 🌐cosmoba.co.uk

£££

The Queen's Larder
Olde-worlde Bloomsbury pub with decent ales.

📍I3 🏛1 Queen Square WC1
🌐queenslarder.co.uk

Fitzroy Tavern
Award-winning, beautifully restored Victorian pub.

📍H4 🏛16 Charlotte St W1

A SHORT WALK
BLOOMSBURY

Distance 2 km (1.25 miles) **Nearest Tube**
Holborn **Time** 25 minutes

This so-called "brainy quarter" is dominated by the grand
British Museum and, to its north, the main campus of
University College London. A walk through the area will
take you past Georgian buildings (formerly the homes
of some of London's most prolific writers and greatest
minds) and pretty squares, as well as a good handful of
bookshops to browse.

*Senate House (1932), the
administrative headquarters
of the University of London,
holds a priceless library.*

↑ Bedford Square, one of
London's best-preserved
Georgian squares

| 0 metres | 100 | N |
| 0 yards | 100 | ↑ |

Bedford Square

*An embarrassment of riches,,
the vast British Museum
(p150) attracts some six
million visitors a year.*

Did You Know?

Bloomsbury is older than
you think – the area is
mentioned in the 1086
Domesday Book as a
"wood for 100 pigs".

*Museum Street is lined
with small cafés and
shops selling old books,
prints and antiques.*

*Pizza Express occupies a
charming and little-
altered Victorian dairy.*

Russell Square (p154), once part of the Duke of Bedford's estate, is now a shady retreat on a hot day.

The Duke of Bedford's statue commemorates the fifth duke, Francis Russell (1765–1805). An avid farmer, he is shown with sheep and a plough.

Locator Map
For more detail see p148

BLOOMSBURY AND FITZROVIA

↑ Bloomsbury Square, laid out in 1661

Bloomsbury Square

SOUTHAMPTON ROW

BEDFORD PLACE

MONTAGUE ST

...SSELL STREET

BURY PLACE

...LE RUSSELL STREET

BLOOMSBURY SQUARE

BLOOMSBURY WAY

● FINISH

● START

Sicilian Avenue is a small and unexpected pedestrian precinct dating from 1905, with colonnades that evoke Roman architecture.

The tower on the typically flamboyant Hawksmoor church of St George's (p155) is modelled on the tomb of 4th-century Greek king Mausolus.

KING'S CROSS, CAMDEN AND ISLINGTON

King's Cross was predominantly rural until the late 18th century. Commonly referred to as Battle Bridge, after a mythical battle said to have taken place here between Boudicca and the Romans, the new name was adopted following the erection of a memorial to George IV in 1830 at the local crossroads. By this time King's Cross was becoming increasingly industrial, driven partly by the completion of the Regent's Canal in 1820, connecting it to the manufacturing cities of the north of England, and then by the construction of train depots, goods stations and passenger service termini. Decades of decline followed World War II but were reversed in the first years of this century when St Pancras Station became the terminus for international train routes to the rest of Europe, kick-starting a multi-billion-pound investment in the area. The urbanization of neighbouring Camden and Islington, connected to King's Cross by the canal, did not set in until the 19th century. Since then they have both undergone periods of boom and decline but, in keeping with King's Cross, are currently on an upward curve.

KING'S CROSS, CAMDEN AND ISLINGTON

Experience

1. British Library
2. St Pancras International
3. St Pancras Old Church and Graveyard
4. Granary Square
5. Camley Street Natural Park
6. Kings Place
7. Camden Market
8. Estorick Collection of Modern Italian Art
9. The Jewish Museum
10. The Angel, Islington and Upper Street

Eat

1. The Lighterman
2. Rotunda
3. German Gymnasium
4. Caravan

EXPERIENCE

①

British Library

📍 I2 🏠 96 Euston Rd NW1
🚇 King's Cross St Pancras
🕐 9:30am–8pm Mon–Thu, 9:30am–6pm Fri, 9:30am–5pm Sat, 11am–5pm Sun 🌐 bl.uk

This modern building houses the national collection of books, manuscripts and maps, as well as the British Library Sound Archive. Designed in red brick by Sir Colin St John Wilson, it opened in 1997 after nearly 20 years of construction. A copy of nearly every printed book in the UK is held here – more than 14 million – and can be consulted by those with a Reader Pass (you can pre-register for one online). The real highlight, though, is the Treasures Gallery, which holds some extraordinary items, such as a Gutenberg Bible, Shakespeare's First Folio and lyrics by the Beatles. There are other free exhibitions, which change regularly (these often close earlier than the main building during the week), plus talks, discussions and workshops. Occasionally, the special exhibitions have an entry charge. Tours are highly recommended; it's advisable to book at least two weeks in advance.

②

St Pancras International

📍 I2 🏠 Euston Rd NW1
🚇 King's Cross St Pancras
🌐 stpancras.com

St Pancras, London's terminus for Eurostar rail services to continental Europe, is hard to miss, thanks to the extravagant frontage, in red-brick gingerbread Gothic, of the former Midland Grand Hotel. Opened in 1874 it was one of the most sumptuous hotels of its time. Threatened with demolition in the 1960s, it was saved by a campaign led by the poet John Betjeman (there is a statue of him on the upper level of the station concourse). The hotel has since been magnificently restored and has a swish cocktail bar.

---

③

St Pancras Old Church and Graveyard

📍 I1 🏠 Pancras Rd NW1
🚇 King's Cross St Pancras
🕐 9am–dusk daily (church usually closes around 3pm)
🌐 posp.co.uk

This site is thought to have been a place of Christian worship since the 4th century – there are fragments of Roman tiles embedded in one of the walls, and some Norman masonry – though much of the church building dates to 1847. There are lunchtime recitals here on Thursdays. The graveyard, now a green space with a few monuments dotted around, was until the 1850s one of the largest burial sites in London.

←

Café tables set below towering shelves of books at the British Library

With the arrival of the railways, half the site was built over, and gravestones were moved – hence the remarkable sight of closely packed gravestones embedded into the base of a tree. This is the Hardy Tree, named after author Thomas Hardy, who worked as an archi-

---

EAT

The Lighterman
British pub-style food in a first-floor dining room with a spacious terrace.

📍 I1 🏠 3 Granary Sq N1 🌐 thelighterman.co.uk

£ £ £

Rotunda
Enjoy the plant-filled terrace on the canal, perfect on a sunny day.

📍 J1 🏠 Kings Pl, 90 York Way N1
🌐 rotundabarandrestaurant.co.uk

£ £ £

German Gymnasium
Hearty German food in a modern continental grand café.

📍 I1 🏠 1 King's Blvd N1 🌐 germangymnasium.com

£ £ £

Caravan
Good veggie options in a hip, busy industrial warehouse setting.

📍 I1 🏠 1 Granary Sq N1 🌐 caravanrestaurants.co.uk

£ £ £

←
Visitors admiring the sparkling fountains of Granary Square at night

graphic design, animation, scientific drawings, picture books and political cartoons.

House of Illustration

 2 Granary Sq N1
King's Cross St Pancras
10am-6pm Tue-Sun
houseofillustration.org.uk

tectural technician on the site. Sir John Soane *(p138)* designed his own family mausoleum, which is said to have inspired Sir Giles Gilbert Scott's design of London's famous red telephone box.

Granary Square

I1 King's Cross St Pancras kingscross.co.uk

Urban regeneration has transformed this area behind King's Cross station into a cultural and social hub, with major building projects still ongoing. The focus of the area is attractive Granary Square, which leads down to Regent's Canal. It is dominated by magnificent fountains that dance to an ever-changing pattern of lights, a magnet for small children on hot days. There are also a number of good restaurants and bars, and a popular food market.

Occupying the former King's Cross Goods Yards offices, built in 1850, is the **House of Illustration**. These three small rooms form the UK's only gallery dedicated to illustration. Founded by Sir Quentin Blake, best known for his illustrations of Roald Dahl's children's books, the gallery stages an eclectic programme of exhibitions, past examples featuring work from Soviet Russia, Japan, Thailand and North Korea. Displays cover a broad range of techniques and mediums, including

Camley Street Natural Park

I1 12 Camley St N1 King's Cross St Pancras For renovation; reopening in early 2020 wildlondon.org.uk

Occupying land on the Regent's Canal once used as a coal drop for the nearby railways, this is a lovable little nature reserve run by the London Wildlife Trust. It packs in grassland, woodland and wetland habitats for birds, butterflies, bats and frogs in a small space. There is a visitor centre, paths around the reserve and some lovely places to sit and picnic.

Kings Place

J1 90 York Way N1 King's Cross St Pancras Galleries: 10am-6pm Mon-Sat kingsplace.co.uk

This concert and arts venue is perched on the edge of the Battlebridge Basin and Regent's Canal, a small wharf whose moorings are usually full of attractive narrowboats. Performances of classical, jazz, folk or world music are regularly staged, and there are two commercial art galleries. The open spaces are dotted with sculpture and art.

PLATFORM 9¾

Wannabe witches and wizards flock to King's Cross station to find the elusive Platform 9¾, from where Harry Potter and his fellow students catch the Hogwarts Express. Though there's little to be found between platforms 9 and 10, a luggage trolley embedded into a concourse wall (conveniently, next to the Harry Potter Shop) provides a perfect photo op for those waiting for their owl from Hogwarts.

The bright lights of Granary Square, King's Cross

7 Camden Market

G1 ⬛NW1 ⊜Camden Town, Chalk Farm ⓒ10am-6pm daily; some cafés and bars open later
⬛camdenmarket.com

The huge Camden Market is really a series of interconnected markets running along Chalk Farm Road and Camden High Street. Packed at the weekends, most of the shops and some of the stalls are also open on weekdays.

The first market here was a small crafts market set up at Camden Lock in 1975, and today the lock, crossing the Regent's Canal, is the focus of this sprawling agglomeration.

Independently trading on an industrial scale, the warren of hundreds of stalls, units and shops occupy a network of restored and converted Victorian warehouses.

The market has been at the forefront of alternative fashion since the days of punk, and the current jumble of handmade and vintage clothes and jewellery, arts and crafts, records and music memorabilia, and all kinds of quirky one-offs maintain the market's place among the most original shopping destinations in the city. This is also street food heaven, with scores of stalls, cafés and wonderfully inelegant restaurants dishing out authentic nosh from all over the world.

Some of the more interesting stalls are in the Stables Market towards the Chalk Farm end, where you will also find a statue of Camden habituée, the late singer-songwriter Amy Winehouse.

8 Estorick Collection of Modern Italian Art

L1 ⬛39a Canonbury Sq N1 ⊜Highbury & Islington ⓒ11am-6pm Wed-Sat, noon-5pm Sun
⬛estorickcollection.com

Based on American and Anglo-German couple Eric and Salome Estorick's collection of modern Italian art, this is one of the more surprising of Islington's assets. It is housed in an unpretentious Georgian building with a delightful garden, partly occupied by an inviting café. At the core of the collection are important works of the Italian Futurism movement: paintings and drawings by the likes of Umberto Boccioni, Carlo Carrà, Luigi Russolo and Gino Severini. Spread over six galleries on three floors, there is plenty of striking modern Italian art of other genres, including sculpture.

←

Bronze statue of the late Amy Winehouse

←
Victorian industrial
heritage buildings
at Camden Lock

The Jewish Museum

🅚 G1 🏠 129-131 Albert
St NW1 🚇 Camden Town
🕑 10am–5pm Sat–Thu,
10am–2pm Fri 🚫 Jewish
hols, 25 & 26 Dec, 1 Jan
🌐 jewishmuseum.org.uk

London's Jewish Museum
was founded in 1932 in
Bloomsbury, and it has
occupied several locations –
at one point it was split
between two sites, in Finchley
and Camden. In 2007 the
museum celebrated its 75th
anniversary by starting work
to bring the two collections
together in a single building.
Reopened in 2010, the
museum today has large
galleries, education facilities
and displays for children.

Celebrating Jewish life in
Britain from the Middle Ages
onwards, the museum is
packed with memorabilia.

It has important collections of
Jewish ceremonial objects and
some illuminated marriage
contracts. The highlight is
a 17th- or 18th-century
Venetian synagogue ark.
There is also an exhibition
on the Holocaust.

The Angel, Islington
and Upper Street

🅚 K1 🏠 Islington N1
🚇 Angel, Highbury &
Islington

One of the destination high
streets in north London,
Upper Street runs for 1.5 km
(1 mile) between Angel and
Highbury & Islington tube
stations. Lively day and night,
the street is one long parade
of restaurants, cafés, pubs,
bars, fashion boutiques and
a contrasting mix of civic
buildings, churches, an
arthouse cinema and a live
music and clubbing venue.

Parallel to the main drag is
Camden Passage, an alleyway
even more densely packed
with shops, cafés and covered
markets. It's a popular place

GREAT VIEW
Primrose Hill

A 15-minute walk from
Camden Market or the
Jewish Museum is the
delightful Primrose Hill.
Climb to the top of this
grassy promontory for
spectacular views of
the city skyline – look
out for the London Eye
and St Paul's Cathedral.

for antiques hunters looking
for the latest bargain.

The area to the south
of the high street known as
Angel takes its name from
a 17th-century coaching inn
on the corner of Pentonville
Road, since replaced by the
current sand-coloured
structure, crowned with
an elegant domed cupola.
Built in 1903 as the Angel
Hotel it now houses a bank
and offices.

Shops and restaurants
(inset and below) line
popular Upper Street ↓

THE CITY

The capital's financial district, the City, built on the
site of the original Roman settlement, was, for
many centuries, London in its entirety – its full
name remains the "City of London". Royal government was moved from the City of London to the
City of Westminster by Edward the Confessor in
the 11th century, but the area's importance as a
centre of trade remained and indeed grew. In the
12th century, the City was granted autonomous
self-government, a privilege it has retained, and
dozens of tradesmen's guilds, known as livery
companies, were set up. Much of the early City,
including many of the grand halls of the liveries,
was obliterated by the Great Fire of 1666, but the
jumbled street plan, with names like Cheapside
and Poultry, stand as testament to the City's
medieval past. After the fire, Christopher Wren
rebuilt dozens of the city's churches, with his
magnificent dome for St Paul's Cathedral rising
above them all. Now the spires and financial institutions stand alongside dour postwar office blocks
and an ever-expanding array of skyscrapers.

K　**L**　**M**

CITY ROAD

NORTHAMPTON SQUARE

GOSWELL ROAD

LEVER STREET

CENTRAL STREET

PERCIVAL STREET

BATH STREET

Old Street

FEATHERSTONE STREET

ST JOHN STREET

COMPTON STREET

OLD STREET

GARRETT ST

BANNER STREET

Bunhill Fields

GREAT SUTTON ST

BALTIC STREET

GOLDEN LANE

WHITE CROSS STREET

DUFFERIN ST

BUNHILL ROW

3

CLERKENWELL CLOSE

CLERKENWELL ROAD

CLERKENWELL

ERROL ST

FARRINGDON ROAD

TURNMILL ST

BRITTON ST

ST JOHN'S LANE

22 Museum of the Order of St John

Charterhouse **21**

ALDERSGATE STREET

FANN STREET

CHISWELL STREET

LAMB'S PASSAGE

2

FINSBURY STREET

ROPEMAKER ST

SAFFRON HILL

BENJAMIN ST

EAGLE COURT

CHARTERHOUSE SQUARE

Barbican

BEECH STREET

SILK STREET

Moorgate

GREVILLE ST

COWCROSS ST

Farringdon

CHARTERHOUSE STREET

Barbican Centre **3**

St Giles, Cripplegate

MOOR LANE

FORE STREET

Smithfield Market **13**

LONG LANE

CLOTH FAIR **14**

St Bartholomew-the-Great

Museum of London **4**

LONDON WALL

4

FARRINGDON ROAD

HOLBORN VIADUCT

SNOW HILL

HOSIER LANE

GILTSPUR STREET

LITTLE BRITAIN

ALDERMANBURY SQUARE

BASINGHALL AVE

MOORGATE

St Botolph

NEWGATE STREET

NOBLE ST

WOOD ST

LOVE LANE

BASINGHALL ST

TELEGRAPH STREET

Old Bailey **16**

Central Criminal Court

ANGEL STREET

ST MARTIN'S LE GRAND

GRESHAM ST

Guildhall **18**

COLEMAN STREET

City Thameslink

OLD BAILEY

PATERNOSTER SQUARE

St Paul's

FOSTER LANE

GUTTER LANE

WOOD STREET

MILK ST

KING ST

IRONMONGER LANE

OLD JEWRY

LOTHBURY

Bank England Muse **7**

FLEET STREET

LUDGATE CIRCUS

LUDGATE HILL

Temple Bar

WARWICK LA

ST PAUL'S CHURCHYARD

NEW CHANGE

CHEAPSIDE

St Mary-le-Bow **8**

BOW LANE

POULTRY

PRINCES ST

Mansion House **6**

Bar

5

NEW BRIDGE ST

PILGRIM ST

BLACKFRIARS LA

CARTER LANE

KNIGHTRIDER ST

St Paul's Cathedral **1**

i

ST PAUL'S CHURCHYARD

WATLING ST

3

CANNON STREET

QUEEN STREET

St Stephen Walbrook **9**

ST SWITHIN'S LANE

Apothecaries Hall

HOLBORN AND THE INNS OF COURT
p132

QUEEN VICTORIA STREET

Mansion House

UPPER THAMES STREET

COLLEGE STREET

Cannon Street

ALLHALLOWS LANE

SUFFOLK LANE

Blackfriars

HIGH TIMBER ST

QUEENHITHE

QUEEN ST PLACE

BELL WHARF LA

COUSIN LA

ANGEL LANE

LAUREL LANE

Blackfriars Bridge

Blackfriars Pier

Millennium Bridge

Bankside Pier

Southwark Bridge

Cannon St Rail Bridge

6

Blackfriars Bridge

THE CITY

Shakespeare's Globe

Tate Modern

SOUTHWARK AND BANKSID
p202

PARK STREET

0 metres　300
0 yards　300

N ↓

K　**L**　**M**

THE CITY

Must Sees

① St Paul's Cathedral
② Tower of London
③ Barbican Centre

Experience More

④ Museum of London
⑤ The Royal Exchange
⑥ Mansion House
⑦ Bank of England Museum
⑧ St Mary-le-Bow
⑨ St Stephen Walbrook
⑩ Monument
⑪ All Hallows by the Tower
⑫ Tower Bridge
⑬ Smithfield Market
⑭ St Bartholomew-the-Great
⑮ The Sky Garden
⑯ Old Bailey
⑰ Leadenhall Market
⑱ Guildhall
⑲ St Katharine Docks
⑳ St Katharine Cree
㉑ Charterhouse
㉒ Museum of the Order of St John

Eat

① José Pizarro
② The Jugged Hare

Drink

③ Merchant House

SHOREDITCH AND SPITALFIELDS
p192

1 🛡️ Ⓜ️ 🖼️ 🏛️

ST PAUL'S CATHEDRAL

📍L5 🏠Ludgate Hill EC4 🚇St Paul's, Mansion House 🚆City Thameslink, Blackfriars 🕐Cathedral: 8:30am–4:30pm (last adm: 4pm) Mon–Sat; Galleries: 9:30am–4:15pm Mon–Sat 🌐stpauls.co.uk

Holding its own against the towering skyscrapers of the City, the enormous dome of St Paul's Cathedral stands out as the star of the area's churches. Completed in 1711, Sir Christopher Wren's Baroque masterpiece was England's first purpose-built Protestant cathedral, and has many similarities with St Peter's in Rome, notably in its ornate dome.

Following the Great Fire of London in 1666, the medieval cathedral of St Paul's was left in ruins. The authorities turned to Christopher Wren to rebuild it, but his ideas met with considerable resistance from the conservative Dean and Chapter. Wren's 1672 Great Model plan was rejected and a watered-down plan was finally agreed in 1675. Wren's determination paid off, though: the cathedral is considered his greatest masterpiece. Its dome is one of the largest in the world, standing 111 m (365 ft) high and weighing 65,000 tonnes.

The cathedral has a strong choral tradition and is famed for its music, with regular concerts and organ recitals.

The cathedral's imposing west front, dominated by its two huge towers

CHRISTOPHER WREN

Sir Christopher Wren (1632–1723) played an integral part in the restoration of London after the Great Fire of 1666. He devised a new city plan, replacing the narrow streets with wide avenues radiating from piazzas. His plan was rejected, but he was commissioned to build 52 new churches; 31 have survived various threats of demolition and the bombs of World War II, although six have only partial remains. Wren's great masterpiece is the massive St Paul's, while nearly as splendid is St Stephen Walbrook, his domed church of 1672–7. Other landmarks are St Bride's, off Fleet Street, said to have inspired the traditional shape of wedding cakes, and St Mary-le-Bow in Cheapside.

GREAT VIEW
Vista of St Paul's

Cross the Millennium Bridge to Bankside and look back to capture a great view of the famous cathedral.

↑ The elegant dome of St Paul's, viewed from the Millennium Bridge

Majestic Interior

Visitors to St Paul's will be immediately impressed by its cool, beautifully ordered and extremely spacious interior. The nave, transepts and choir are arranged in the shape of a cross, as in a medieval cathedral, but Wren's Classical vision shines through this conservative floorplan, which was forced

on him by the cathedral authorities. Aided by some of the finest craftsmen of his day, he created an interior of grand majesty and Baroque splendour, a worthy setting for the many great ceremonial events that have taken place here. These include the funeral of Sir Winston Churchill in 1965 and the wedding of Prince Charles and Lady Diana Spencer in 1981.

→ Illustration of St Paul's Cathedral and its interior (below)

The lantern weighs a massive 700 tonnes.

The Golden Gallery is at the highest point of the dome.

The brick cone located inside the outer dome supports the heavy lantern.

Windows at the top of the cone are visible through the oculus.

The Stone Gallery offers a splendid view over London.

The balustrade was added against Wren's wishes.

Carvings on the pediment depict the Conversion of St Paul.

Flying buttresses support the nave walls and the dome.

The main entrance is through the West Portico, approached from Ludgate Hill.

Wren intended a single colonnade along the West Portico, but it now has two tiers of columns.

The North and South Transepts cross the nave in a medieval style that contrasts with Wren's original plan.

Timeline

604
△ Bishop Mellitus builds the first St Paul's; it burns down in 1087

1087
△ Bishop Maurice begins Old St Paul's: a Norman cathedral built of stone

1708
△ Wren's son Christopher lays the last stone on the lantern

2011
△ Extensive restorations finished

1 The Whispering Gallery allows views down to the wide expanse of the crossing, the area under the dome.

2 Much of the fine wrought ironwork such as the screens, were made by Jean Tijou, a Huguenot refugee.

3 Intricate carvings of cherubs, fruit and garlands adorn the cathedral.

4 In the crypt are the tombs of famous figures and popular heroes, such as Lord Nelson.

The imposing walls ↑
of the historic
Tower of London

② ⬡ ⬡ ⑂ ⬡ 🛍

TOWER OF LONDON

📍 05 🏰 Tower Hill EC3 🚇 Tower Hill, DLR Tower Gateway
🚆 Fenchurch Street 🕐 9am–5:30pm Tue–Sat; 10am–
5:30pm Sun & Mon (till 4:30pm Nov–Feb) 🌐 hrp.org.uk

A former fortress, palace and prison, the Tower of London attracts nearly three million visitors a year, who come to see the Crown Jewels and to hear tales of its dark and intriguing history.

For much of its 900-year history, the Tower was somewhere to be feared. Those who had committed treason or threatened the throne were held within its dank walls – many did not get out alive, and some were tortured before meeting violent deaths on nearby Tower Hill.

The Tower has been a tourist attraction since the reign of Charles II (1660–85), when both the Crown Jewels and the collection of armour were first shown to the public, and it remains popular today. Come to discover the brutality of royal regimes, the curious menagerie that once called the Tower home and the regalia of Britain's kings and queens.

💬 INSIDER TIP
Tour with a Beefeater

Join a Yeoman Warder, or Beefeater, on a tour of the Tower. A lively retelling of tales of executions, plots and prisoners, it's an entertaining way to explore the Tower's history. Tours are included in the entry fee and set off every 30 minutes from near the main entrance, lasting for an hour.

Timeline

1066
△ William I erects a temporary castle

1534–5
△ Thomas More imprisoned and executed

Did You Know?
—
The Tower has a colony of ravens. Legend has it that if they leave the Tower, the kingdom will fall.

↑ Yeoman Warders guarding the Tower

↑ King Edward I's bedchamber inside St Thomas's Tower

1553–4
△ Lady Jane Grey held and executed

1603–16
△ Walter Raleigh imprisoned in Tower

1671
△ "Colonel Blood" tries to steal Crown Jewels

1941
△ Prominent Nazi Rudolf Hess held in Queen's House

Life Within the Tower

The area within the mighty walls houses the remaining parts of the Medieval Palace built by Henry III, as well as several towers that held prisoners, including Anne Boleyn, Thomas Cromwell and Catherine Howard. High-ranking prisoners could live in some comfort with their own servants but the rest suffered hardship, torture and, ultimately, death.

The White Tower

The Crown Jewels are kept in the Jewel House.

The aristocratic prisoners were executed on Tower Green.

Beauchamp Tower held high-ranking prisoners.

Edward V and his brother, Richard, are said to have been murdered in the Bloody Tower.

Main entrance

Did You Know?

In 1952, London gangsters the Kray twins were among the last to be held at the Tower.

[1] A sentry from the Tower Guard stands on duty outside the Jewel House.

[2] Many were imprisoned in the Tower, some tortured or held in solitary confinement.

[3] The Tower of London enclosure is in the centre of the city, beside the Thames and the iconic Tower Bridge. There are several towers, a palace, residences and a chapel.

The beautiful Chapel of St John is made from stone brought from France.

The Crown Jewels

Comprising crowns, sceptres and orbs used at coronations and other state occasions, the priceless Crown Jewels *(below)* have enormous historical significance. They mostly date from 1661 when a new set was created for the coronation of Charles II.

Wakefield Tower was part of the Medieval Palace.

Prisoners entered the Tower by boat through Traitors' Gate.

Henry III created the Medieval Palace in 1220. His son Edward I enlarged it.

← The walls enclose towers, residences and open areas

Coronation Regalia

Apart from the crowns, other items used during coronation ceremonies *(left)* include the Orb, the jewelled State Sword and the Sceptre with the Cross containing the world's biggest cut diamond.

Royal Armouries and the Line of Kings

On the ground floor of the White Tower, admire suits of armour from Tudor and Stuart times *(right)*, including a gargantuan set made for Henry VIII, famed for its impressive codpiece. The armour collection incorporates the Line of Kings.

THE PRINCES IN THE TOWER

One of the Tower's darkest mysteries concerns two boy princes, sons and heirs of Edward IV. They were put into the Tower by their uncle, Richard of Gloucester, when their father died in 1483. Neither was seen again and Richard was crowned later that year. In 1674, the skeletons of two children were found nearby.

Graffiti in the Beauchamp Tower

Surprisingly elaborate carvings grace the walls of this tower, poignant messages from 16th- and 17th-century prisoners facing execution. One shows the family crest of Lord Dudley, teenage husband of the ill-fated Lady Jane Grey, imprisoned with his three brothers.

↑ The Barbican's concrete Brutalist architecture with lake and fountains

3 (ᴍ) (ᵞ) (▢) (🖰)

BARBICAN CENTRE

📍 M4 🏠 Barbican Estate EC2 🚇 Barbican, Moorgate 🚉 Moorgate, Liverpool Street 🕐 9am–11pm Mon–Sat, from 11am Sun, from noon public hols; Art gallery: 10am–6pm daily (till 9pm Thu & Fri); Conservatory: noon–5pm Sun (but check website for days) 🌐 barbican.org.uk

A Brutalist masterpiece, this residential, commercial and cultural complex is a formidable, fabulous anomaly in the City: an oasis of culture and community in London's largest financial district. Look out for world-class theatrical performances and concerts here.

The soul at the concrete heart of the Barbican Estate, the Barbican Centre is one of London's largest and most complete arts institutions, with two cinemas, a concert hall, two theatres and gallery spaces all celebrating the arts. The centre is also home to a public library, three restaurants, several cafés and bars and a tropical conservatory. A dynamic programme of events typically includes seasons of plays by the Royal Shakespeare Company, concerts by the resident London Symphony Orchestra, and plenty of independent cinema. The centre has always made room for experimental, genre-defying performers and artists, so expect anything from multimedia art exhibitions to street dance operas. Jazz and world music also feature frequently, with musicians and singers from Latin American and Africa often on the bill, but at any time you will find a broad range of one-off shows and events.

↑ The Barbican Hall, well known for its world music performances

EXPERIENCE MORE

Museum of London

📍 L4 🏠 150 London Wall EC2 🚇 Barbican, St Paul's, Moorgate ⏰ 10am–6pm daily 🌐 museumoflondon.org.uk

Opened in 1976 on the edge of the Barbican Estate, this museum provides a lively account of London life from prehistoric times to the present day The eclectic set of displays, which are laid out chronologically, range from detailed models and life-sized sets to items recovered from archaeological digs, photographs and recordings of Londoners talking about their lives.

Prehistory exhibits, such as flint hand axes found in the gravels under the modern city, begin on the entrance level and visitors can walk through Roman and medieval London galleries to the War, Plague and Fire exhibit, which includes a display on the Great Fire of 1666.

On the lowest level, the history of London after the disastrous fire up to the present day is explored. The Lord Mayor of London's spectacular State Coach is on show here. Finely carved and painted, this gilded coach from c 1757 is paraded once a year during the Lord Mayor's Show. The Victorian Walk uses several original shopfronts to re-create the atmosphere of late-19th-century London. There are also the bronze and cast-iron Brandt Edgar lifts from Selfridges department store on Oxford Street and unusual items such as a 1964 Beatles dress printed with the faces of the Fab Four.

One of the newest permanent galleries is the London 2012 Cauldron, the centrepiece of the opening and closing ceremonies at the London Olympics. Photographs, videos, diagrams and the copper petal elements which rose together to form the Olympic Flame combine to describe the spectacle and the ingenuity of the design.

THE BARBICAN ESTATE

Housing over 4,000 residents in its Brutalist tower and terrace blocks, this ambitious piece of postwar city planning was designed by Chamberlin, Powell & Bon and built on a site devastated by World War II bombs. It is a maze of concrete pavements, overhead walkways, stone staircases and looming tower blocks, but it is softened considerably by islands of green – small gardens dotted around the estate – and by an ornamental lake and fountains.

↑ Visitors examining exhibits at the fascinating Museum of London

⑤

The Royal Exchange

📍 N5 **🚇 EC3** **🚉 Bank**
🌐 theroyalexchange.co.uk

Sir Thomas Gresham, an Elizabethan merchant and courtier, founded the Royal Exchange in 1565 as a centre for commerce of all kinds. The original building was centred on a vast courtyard where merchants and tradesmen did business. Queen Elizabeth I gave it its royal title and it is still one of the sites from which a new monarch is announced. Dating from 1844, this is the third splendid building on the site since Gresham's. The building is now a luxurious shopping centre with designer stores and a branch of Fortnum and Mason (p95) with an elegant bar and café.

⑥

Mansion House

📍 M5 **🏛 Walbrook EC4**
🚉 Bank, Mansion House
🕐 To group tours by appt only **🌐 cityoflondon.gov.uk**

The official residence of the Lord Mayor was designed by George Dance the Elder and completed in 1758. The Palladian front with its six Corinthian columns is one of the most familiar City landmarks. The state rooms have a dignity appropriate to the office of mayor, one of the most spectacular being the 27-m (90-ft) Egyptian Hall. An impressive collection of 17th-century Dutch art includes works by Frans Hals.

The cellars once housed 11 holding cells, a reminder of the building's other function as a magistrate's court; the mayor is chief magistrate of the City during his time in office. Emmeline Pankhurst, who campaigned for women's suffrage in the early 20th century, was once held here.

---

⑦

Bank of England Museum

📍 M5 **🏛 Bartholomew Lane EC2** **🚉 Bank** **🕐 10am–5pm Mon–Fri** **🚫 Public hols**
🌐 bankofengland.co.uk

The Bank of England was set up in 1694 to raise money for foreign wars. It grew to become Britain's central bank, and also issues currency notes. Sir John Soane (p138) was the architect of the 1788 bank building on this site, but only the exterior wall of his design has survived. The rest was destroyed in the 1920s and

↑ Gold bar that visitors can try to lift in the Bank of England Museum

1930s when the building was enlarged by Sir Herbert Baker. The only part of Soane's design left today is the curtain wall around the outside of the building. There is now a reconstruction of Soane's stock office of 1793 in the museum. As well as images illustrating the architectural history of the building, the museum reveals the work of the Bank and financial system, and there is an interactive exhibit where visitors can set monetary policy.

Glittering gold bars (which you can touch), silver-plated decorations and a Roman mosaic floor, which was discovered during the rebuilding, are among the items on display, along with a unique collection of banknotes.

↓ The Neo-Classical façade of the Royal Exchange

↑ St Mary-le-Bow's steeple, housing Bow bells

> **Bow bells have significance for Londoners: traditionally only those born within their sound can claim to be true Cockneys.**

⑧

St Mary-le-Bow

🗺 M5 🏠 Cheapside EC2 🚇 St Paul's, Mansion House 🕐 7:30am–6pm Mon–Wed, 7:30am–6:30pm Thu, 7:30am–4pm Fri 🌐 stmarylebow.co.uk

The church takes its name from the bow arches in the Norman crypt. When Wren rebuilt the church (in 1670–80) after the Great Fire, he continued this pattern through the arches on the steeple. The weathervane is an enormous dragon.

The church was bombed in 1941, leaving only the steeple and two walls standing. It was restored in 1956–62, when the bells were recast and rehung. Bow bells have significance for Londoners: traditionally only those born within their sound can claim to be true Cockneys. Tours of the church are offered by arrangement.

⑨

St Stephen Walbrook

🗺 M5 🏠 39 Walbrook EC4 🚇 Bank, Cannon St 🕐 10am–4pm Mon, Tue & Thu, 11am–3pm Wed, 10am–3:30pm Fri 🌐 ststephenwalbrook.net

The Lord Mayor's parish church was built by architect Christoper Wren in 1672–9 and it is considered the finest of his City churches. The deep, coffered dome, with its ornate plasterwork, was a forerunner of St Paul's Cathedral.

St Stephen's airy columned interior comes as a surprise after its plain exterior. The font cover and pulpit canopy are decorated with exquisite carved figures that contrast strongly with the stark simplicity of Henry Moore's massive white stone altar (1972), installed in 1987.

However, perhaps the most moving monument of all is a telephone in a glass box. This is a tribute to Rector Chad Varah who, in 1953, founded the Samaritans, a volunteer-staffed telephone helpline for people in emotional need.

The church is also the home of the London Internet Church, which brings together people from all over the world to worship and discuss Christianity. There are free lunchtime music recitals on Tuesdays (1pm) and Fridays (12:30pm), to which you are welcome to bring and eat a packed lunch.

> ### THE CITY'S LIVERY HALLS
>
> There are around 110 livery companies in London, each traditionally representing a specific profession or trade. They were first created by groups of medieval tradesmen who formed associations, or guilds, to protect, promote and regulate their trades, setting up headquarters in large houses or halls around the City. Though many did not survive the Great Fire, several dozen companies maintain their own hall to this day, while blue plaques mark former halls. Some have grand, ornate interiors worthy of a palace, but they are difficult places to visit - a few allow group tours, others are not publicly accessible.

🔟

Monument

📍 N5 🏠 Monument St EC3
🚇 Monument 🕐 Platform:
9:30am–5:30pm daily (to
6pm Apr–Sep) 🚫 24–26 Dec
🌐 themonument.info

The column designed by Wren to commemorate the Great Fire of London of 1666 is the tallest isolated stone column in the world. It is 61.5 m (202 ft) high and is said to be 61.5 m west of where the fire started, in Pudding Lane. Reliefs around the column's base show Charles II restoring the city. It's a tough climb up 311 steps to the top of the column, but the views from the viewing platform are spectacular.

1️⃣1️⃣

All Hallows by the Tower

📍 N5 🏠 Byward St EC3
🚇 Tower Hill 🕐 8am–6pm
Mon–Fri (till 5pm Nov–Mar),
10am–5pm Sat & Sun 🚫 26
Dec–2 Jan 🌐 ahbtt.org.uk

The oldest church in the city retains some original Saxon features and a Roman pavement, discovered in 1926, on display in the Crypt Museum, along with other Roman and Saxon artifacts. The church carried out the temporary burials of those executed on nearby Tower Hill, including Thomas More, and it was from the church tower that Samuel Pepys watched the Great Fire consume London in 1666.

1️⃣2️⃣

Tower Bridge

📍 O6 🏠 SE1 🚇 Tower Hill
🕐 Exhibition: Apr–Sep:
10am–5:30pm daily; Oct–
Mar: 9:30am–5pm daily
🚫 24–26 Dec 🌐 tower
bridge.org.uk

Completed in 1894, this flamboyant piece of Victorian engineering is a symbol of London. Its pinnacled towers and linking catwalk support the mechanism for raising the roadway when big ships have to pass through, or for special occasions; check the website for details. When raised, the bridge is 40 m (135 ft) high.

Walking across the bridge is free but access to the elevated walkways requires a ticket. This includes entry to the exhibition in the North Tower and the Engine Rooms, reached via the South Tower, a look at the steam engine that powered the lifting machinery until 1976, when the system was electrified.

1️⃣3️⃣

Smithfield Market

📍 L4 🏠 Charterhouse
St EC1 🚇 Farringdon,
Barbican 🕐 2–9am
Mon–Fri 🚫 Public hols
🌐 smithfield market.com

Animals have been traded here since the 12th century, but the site was granted its first official charter in 1400.

In 1648, Smithfield was officially established as a cattle market, and live cattle continued to be sold here until the mid-19th century. It now confines itself to wholesale trading in meat and poultry. It was originally sited in Smithfield, outside the City walls and, although moved to its present location in Charterhouse Street in the 1850s and called the London Central Meat Market, the original name stuck. The old buildings are by Victorian architect Horace Jones, but there are 20th-century additions. Some pubs in the area keep market hours, serving hearty breakfasts from dawn. Now modernized, the market is one of the best-equipped meat markets in the world. Visitors should aim to arrive by 7am.

 14

St Bartholomew-the-Great

☑ L4 ◪ West Smithfield EC1 ◉ Barbican ◷ 8:30am–5pm Mon–Fri (to 4pm mid-Nov–mid-Feb), 10:30am–4pm Sat, 8:30am–8pm Sun ◫ greatstbarts.com

One of London's oldest churches, St Bart's was founded in 1123 by the monk Rahere, whose tomb is inside. A courtier of Henry I, he dreamed that the saint saved him from a winged monster.

The 13th-century arch used to be the door; the gatehouse above it is from a later period. The crossing and chancel are original, with fine Norman detailing. There are also some Tudor monuments. In the south transept is a gilded statue of St Bartholomew by Damien Hirst. In 1725, US

 ←

Tower Bridge, an enduring symbol of London, at sunset

↑ The Sky Garden, top deck of the "Walkie-Talkie" building

statesman Benjamin Franklin worked for a printer in the Lady Chapel. The church also featured in the films *Four Weddings and a Funeral*, *Shakespeare in Love* and *The Other Boleyn Girl*.

15

The Sky Garden

☑ N5 ◪ 20 Fenchurch St EC3 ◉ Bank, Monument ◷ 10am–6pm Mon–Fri (last adm: 5pm), 11am–9pm Sat & Sun (last adm: 8pm) ◫ skygarden.london

The Rafael Viñoly-designed 20 Fenchurch Street is commonly known as the "Walkie-Talkie", thanks to its unusual shape. Not without controversy (its shape and position make it particularly obtrusive on the city skyline), it is one of few skyscrapers with free public access, provided that you book ahead for the Sky Garden, a three-level viewing deck. Tickets are released each Monday for the following week and go quickly. There are also bars and restaurants.

This is a perfect place from which to view London's other mega-structures. To the south is the Shard *(p212)*; north are Tower 42, the "Gherkin" and the Leadenhall Building, aka the "Cheesegrater", "The Scalpel" and 22 Bishopsgate, the city's tallest skyscraper.

16

Old Bailey

☑ L4 ◪ EC4 ◉ St Paul's ◷ 9:55am–12:40pm & 1:55–3:40pm Mon–Fri (reduced times Aug; hours vary from court to court) ◷ Public hols ◫ cityoflondon.gov.uk

The new Central Criminal Courts opened here in 1907 on the site of the infamous and malodorous Newgate prison. Across the road, the Magpie and Stump pub served "execution breakfasts" until 1868, when mass public hangings outside the gates were stopped. Today, the courts are open to the public when in session.

DRINK

Merchant House
Hidden away down an alley, this basement bar and lounge serves up exceptional cocktails, which evoke the Empire. The Brig, a private bar inside seating just 2–4 people, can be hired.

☑ M5 ◪ 13 Well Court, off Bow Lane EC4 ◫ merchanthouse.bar

→ Elegant wrought-iron and glass vaulting at Leadenhall Market

17

Leadenhall Market

📍 N5 🏛 Gracechurch St EC3
🚇 Bank, Monument
🕐 Times vary; check website
🌐 leadenhallmarket.co.uk

There has been a food market here, on the site of a Roman forum, since the Middle Ages. Today's ornate Victorian covered shopping arcade was designed in 1881 by Sir Horace Jones. Leadenhall is now home to boutique wine shops, cheesemongers, florists and fine food shops, along with several traditional pubs and wine bars. At Christmas the decorated stores are an attractive sight.

18

Guildhall

📍 M4 🏛 Guildhall Yard EC2
🚇 St Paul's 🕐 Great Hall: 10am–4.30pm Mon–Sat, (daily May–Sep) 🚫 1 Jan, 25 & 26 Dec, occasionally for events 🌐 guildhall. cityoflondon.gov.uk

Guildhall has been the administrative centre of the City for at least 800 years. For centuries its Great Hall was used for trials, and many people were condemned to death here, including Henry Garnet, one of the Gunpowder Plot conspirators.

Overlooking the Great Hall at one end are the figures of legendary giants Gog and Magog, the guardians of the City, while statues of notable figures such as Churchill and Nelson line its 46-m- (150-ft-) long sides. Each year, a few days after the Lord Mayor's parade, the prime minister addresses a banquet here.

On the south side of Guildhall Yard is a Wren-designed church, St Lawrence Jewry, while on the east side is the **Guildhall Art Gallery**. It houses the studio collection of 20th-century artist Sir Matthew Smith, portraits from the 16th century to the present day, 18th-century works including John Singleton Copley's *Defeat of the Floating Batteries at Gibraltar*, and numerous Victorian works.

In 1988, the foundations of a Roman amphitheatre were discovered beneath the gallery. Built in AD 70 and with a capacity of about 6,000 spectators, the arena would have hosted animal hunts, executions and gladiatorial combat. Public access to the atmospheric ruins is through the art gallery.

Guildhall Art Gallery and Roman Amphitheatre

🕐 10am–5pm Mon–Fri, noon–4pm Sun 🚫 1 Jan, 24–26 Dec
🌐 cityoflondon.gov.uk

19

St Katharine Docks

📍 O6 🏛 E1 🚇 Tower Hill
🌐 skdocks.co.uk

This most central of all London's docks was designed by Thomas Telford and opened in 1828 on the site of St Katharine's Hospital. Commodities as diverse as tea, marble and live turtles (turtle soup was a Victorian delicacy) were unloaded here.

During the 19th and early 20th centuries, the docks flourished, but by the mid-20th century, cargo ships were delivering their wares in massive containers. The old docks became too small and closed in 1968.

The redevelopment of St Katharine's has been one of the City's most successful – the old warehouse buildings have shops and restaurants on their ground floors, and offices above. In front is a marina, and there are other entertainment facilities.

The dock is well worth wandering through after visiting the Tower (p178) or Tower Bridge (p186). A weekly street food market is held here on Saturdays from 11am to 3pm.

 20

St Katharine Cree

◉N5 ⬛86 Leadenhall St EC3 ⊜Aldgate, Tower Hill ◷9:30am-4pm Mon-Fri ◔Aug ⬤sanctuaryinthecity.net

A rare pre-Wren 17th-century church with a medieval tower, this was one of only eight churches in the City to survive the fire of 1666. Some of the elaborate plasterwork on and beneath the high ceiling of the nave portrays the coats of arms of the guilds, with which the church has special links. The 17th-century organ, supported by magnificent carved wooden columns, has in the past been played by both Purcell and Handel.

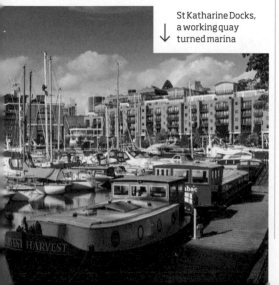

St Katharine Docks, a working quay
↓ turned marina

21

Charterhouse

◉L3 ⬛Charterhouse Sq EC1 ⊜Barbican ◷Museum: 11am-5:20pm Tue-Sun ◔1 Jan, 24-26 Dec ⬤thecharterhouse.org

The Tudor gateway on the north side of Charterhouse square leads to the site of a former Carthusian monastery, which was dissolved under Henry VIII. In 1611, the buildings were converted into a hospital for poor pensioners, and a charity school – called Charterhouse – whose pupils included Methodism founder John Wesley, writer William Thackeray and Robert Baden-Powell, founder of the Boy Scouts.

In 1872, the school relocated to Godalming in Surrey. Part of the original site was subsequently taken over by St Bartholomew's Hospital medical school. Some of the old buildings remain, including the chapel and part of the cloisters. Today Charterhouse is still home to more than 40 pensioners supported by the charitable foundation. There is a small museum open to all, but access to the rest of the site is by guided tour only, conducted every day except Monday; book online.

EAT

José Pizarro

Classic Spanish tapas and inventive dishes .

◉N4 ⬛36 Broadgate Circle EC2 ⬤jose pizarro.com

£ £ £

The Jugged Hare

Gastropub serving excellent game dishes

◉M3 ⬛49 Chiswell St EC1 ⬤thejuggedhare.com

£ £ £

22

Museum of the Order of St John

◉L3 ⬛St John's Lane EC1 ⊜Farringdon ◷10am-5pm Mon-Sat (daily Jul-Sep) ◔Christmas week, bank holiday weekends ⬤museumstjohn.org.uk

The Tudor gatehouse and parts of the 12th-century church are all that remain of the priory of the Knights of St John, which flourished here for 400 years and was the precursor of the St John Ambulance. Over the years, the priory buildings have had many uses, such as offices for Elizabeth I's Master of the Revels and a coffee shop run by the artist William Hogarth's father.

The museum contains hundreds of treasures from the order's history, including illuminated manuscripts and a bronze cannon donated by Henry VIII. The rest of the building, including the priory church with its 12th-century crypt, can be seen on free guided tours at 11am and 2:30pm on Tuesdays, Fridays and Saturdays.

A SHORT WALK
THE CITY

Distance 1.5 km (1 mile) **Nearest Tube**
St Paul's **Time** 25 minutes

This route through the business centre of London
unsurprisingly takes in vast institutions, such as the
the Bank of England and Bloomberg's European
headquarters. Alongside these 20th- and 21st-
century buildings stand the majestic architectural
visions of Christopher Wren, England's most sublime
and probably most prolific architect (p174). Marvel
at his genius as you pass some of his churches.

Did You Know?

Bread Street was
named for the bread
market located here in
medieval times.

St Paul's
station

START

Anyone born within
earshot of the bells of
Wren's St Mary-le-Bow
(the historic Bow Bells) is
said to be a true Londoner
or Cockney (p185).

N E W   C H A N G E

W A T L I N G   S T R E E T

B R E A D   S T R E E T

B O W   L A N E

ST PAUL'S CHURCHYARD

C A N N O N   S T R E E T

G O D L I M A N   S T R E E T

F R I D A Y   S T

Q U E E N   V I C T O R I A

Mansion
House
station

Wren's master-
piece – St Paul's
Cathedral – still
dominates the
City skyline
(p174).

The College
of Arms assesses
who has a legiti-
mate claim to
a British family
coat of arms.

St Nicholas Cole Abbey
was the first church
Wren built in the City (in
1677). Like many others,
it had to be restored
after World War II
bomb damage.

St James Garlickhythe's
name refers to a medieval
Thames wharf where
garlic was landed.

St Mary Aldermary was
rebuilt in Gothic style by
Wren after the Great Fire.

Buses driving past the beautiful St Paul's Cathedral

Locator Map
For more detail see p172

THE CITY

Mansion House is the official home of the City of London's Lord Mayor and has some fine artworks (p184).

The intriguing story of England's financial system is explored at the Bank of England Museum (p184).

Bank station

KING ST

IRONMONGER LANE

OLD JEWRY

PRINCE'S STREET

THREAD NEEDLE STREET

REET

FINISH

CORNHILL

LOMBARD ST

KING WILLIAM STREET

CANNON STREET

ST SWITHIN'S

Since its foundation in Tudor times, the Royal Exchange has been at

Lombard Street is named after Italian bankers who settled here from Lombardy in the 13th century. It is still a banking

St Mary Woolnoth is a characteristically powerful work by Wren's pupil, Nicholas Hawksmoor.

The dome of St Stephen Walbrook (p185) is a forerunner to that atop St Paul's.

St Mary Abchurch owes its unusually spacious feel to the large dome designed by Wren. Admire the altar carving by Grinling Gibbons.

0 metres 100
0 yards 100
N ↑

SHOREDITCH AND SPITALFIELDS

Just outside the boundaries of the City, Spitalfields has long rotated around its market, which first emerged in the late 17th century after traders had begun operating outside the city gates. As the market expanded people began to settle in its vicinity, notably Huguenots fleeing religious persecution in France. The Huguenots also moved to nearby Shoreditch and their skilled weavers soon dominated the textile industry in the area. Waves of Irish, then Jewish and most recently Bangladeshi immigrants followed. The market survived, was given its own building in the late 19th century and flourished for decades as a wholesale market. It was saved from destruction in the early years of this century and reborn as a market for vintage clothing, antiques, arts and crafts, in keeping with the recent gentrification of the area, extending across Shoreditch and beyond.

SHOREDITCH AND SPITALFIELDS

Experience
1. Old Spitalfields Market
2. Wesley's Chapel and Leysian Mission
3. Petticoat Lane
4. Bunhill Fields
5. Brick Lane
6. Hoxton
7. Dennis Severs' House
8. Whitechapel Gallery
9. 19 Princelet Street
10. Christ Church, Spitalfields
11. St Leonard's Church
12. Columbia Road Market
13. Rich Mix
14. Geffrye Museum
15. V&A Museum of Childhood

Eat
1. Dinerama
2. The Brick Lane Food Hall
3. Sunday Upmarket
4. Ely's Yard

Shop
5. Boxpark

↑ Independent traders with their wares on display at Old Spitalfields Market

EXPERIENCE

❶
Old Spitalfields Market

📍 O3 🏠 16 Horner Sq E1
🚇 Liverpool St, Aldgate
🕐 Market stalls: 10am–6pm daily (till 5pm Sun), 7am–6pm Thu 🌐 oldspitalfields market.com

Produce has been traded at Spitalfields Market since 1682, though the original covered market buildings date to 1887. The vegetable market finally moved out in 1991, after which today's version of the market – known for antiques, fashion, bric-a-brac and crafts stalls – started to take shape. Today the market space is a mix of restaurants, shops and traditional market stalls. It is open every day; Thursdays are good for antiques and collectibles, and every other Friday for vinyl records, but it is on Sundays that the crowds really arrive, in search of vintage clothing and unique

items. This is also a major foodie destination, with superb street food from top names, both global and local – from Pacific pokè and Burmese tea leaf salad to East Anglian oysters and the unrivalled Reuben sandwich from the iconic Monty's Deli.

---

❷
Wesley's Chapel and Leysian Mission

📍 M3 🏠 49 City Rd EC1
🚇 Old Street, Moorgate
🕐 10am–4pm Mon–Sat
🌐 wesleyschapel.org.uk

John Wesley, the founder of the Methodist Church, laid this chapel's foundation stone in 1777. He preached here until his death in 1791 and is buried behind the chapel. Next door is the house where he lived, in which some of his furniture, books and other possessions can be seen. The chapel is more ornate than in Wesley's day, with stained-glass

windows and French jasper pillars, which replaced the original ones made from ships' masts. Margaret Thatcher, Britain's first female prime minister, was married here. Beneath the chapel is a small museum devoted to the history of Methodism. There are free lunchtime recitals most Tuesdays.

---

❸
Petticoat Lane

📍 O4 🏠 Middlesex St E1
🚇 Aldgate East, Aldgate, Liverpool St 🕐 9am–2pm Sun (main market); (smaller market on Wentworth St)

During the prudish Victorian era, the name of this street, long famous for its market, was changed to the more respectable but colourless Middlesex Street. That is still its official designation, but the old name, derived from the petticoats and lace sold here by the Huguenots who came from France, has stuck, and is now applied to the market held every Sunday morning in this and the surrounding streets. Though the street is not particularly attractive, the

> **Thursdays are good for antiques and collectibles, and every other Friday for vinyl records, but it is on Sundays that the crowds really arrive, in search of vintage clothing and unique items.**

lively market creates plenty of atmosphere. A great variety of goods are sold, but there is still a bias towards clothing, especially leather coats. It's a noisy and cheerful scene, with Cockney stallholders making use of their wit to attract custom. There are scores of snack bars for pitstops.

4

Bunhill Fields

M3 **City Rd EC1** **Old Street** **8am-7pm or dusk Mon-Fri, 9:30am-7pm or dusk Sat, Sun & public hols** **1 Jan, 25 & 26 Dec** **cityoflondon.gov.uk**

This burial ground was first designated a cemetery after the Great Plague of 1665, when it was enclosed by a brick wall and gates. Twenty years later it was allocated to Nonconformists, who were banned from being buried in churchyards because of their refusal to use the Church of England prayer book.

The cemetery is situated on the edge of the City, and shaded by large plane trees. There are monuments to the well-known writers Daniel Defoe, John Bunyan and William Blake, as well as to members of the Cromwell family. John Milton wrote his epic poem *Paradise Lost* while he lived in Bunhill Row, located on the west side of the cemetery. In summertime (Apr–Oct), there are guided walks of the cemetery on Wednesdays at 12:30pm.

↑ Taking a selfie in front of street art by Alexis Diaz and Elian

5

Brick Lane

O3 **E1** **Liverpool St, Aldgate East** **Shoreditch High St** **Market: 10am-5pm Sun** **visitbrick lane.org**

Once a lane running through brickfields, Brick Lane has long been synonymous with the area's British-Bangladeshi community. Now their curry houses sit next to hip galleries and quirky boutiques. Shops and houses, some dating from the 18th century, have seen immigrants of many nationalities, and ethnic foods, spices, silks and saris are all on sale here. In the 19th century this was mainly a Jewish quarter, and some Jewish shops remain, most famously a 24-hour bagel shop at No 159. On Sundays, a large market is held here and in the surrounding streets.

Towards the northern end of Brick Lane is the Old Truman Brewery, home to a mix of bars, shops and stalls: separate markets at weekends sell food, vintage clothes and new fashion.

←

A monument to William Blake and his wife in Bunhill Fields

EAT

Dinerama
Best spot for street food after dark, this old truck depot offers craft beer and cocktails.

N3 **19 Great Eastern St EC2** **Wed-Sat**

£££

The Brick Lane Food Hall
Treats from Poland, Ethiopia, Japan, Korea and more inside a redbrick warehouse.

O3 **Old Truman Brewery, Brick Lane E1** **Sat & Sun**

£££

Sunday Upmarket
International street food is found among artsy stalls.

O3 **Old Truman Brewery, Brick Lane E1** **Sun**

£££

Ely's Yard
The food trucks and stalls are here all week.

O3 **Old Truman Brewery, Dray Walk, E1**

£££

6

Hoxton

📍 N2 🚇 N1, E2
🚉 Old St

Hoxton, at the heart of hipster London, is a loosely defined district that revolves around its two main streets: Old Street and Kingsland Road. This once-gritty landscape of Victorian warehouses is now home to trendy places to eat, increasingly pricey clothes stores and a significant percentage of the city's newer street art. The converted warehouses house some of the city's most rambunctious nightlife, with clubs and bars radiating out from the Shoreditch High Street and Old Street junction, some of them on neatly proportioned Hoxton Square, just behind Old Street.

 7

Dennis Severs' House

📍 O3 🏠 18 Folgate St E1
🚇 Liverpool St ⏰ Noon-2pm & 5-9pm Mon, 5-9pm Wed & Fri, noon-4pm Sun
🌐 dennissevershouse.co.uk

At No 18 Folgate Street, built in 1724, the late designer and performer Dennis Severs re-created a historical interior that takes you on a journey from the 17th to the 19th centuries. It offers what he called "an adventure of the imagination… a visit to a time-mode rather than… merely a look at a house".

The rooms are like a series of *tableaux vivants*, as if the occupants had simply left for a moment. There is bread on the plates, wine in the glasses, fruit in the bowl; the candles flicker and horses' hooves are heard clattering on the cobbles outside.

This highly theatrical experience is far removed from the usual museum re-creations, and the house is particularly atmospheric on the regular "Silent Night" evenings (book ahead) and at Christmas. Praised by many, including artist David

↑ The immaculately re-created interior of Dennis Severs' House

Hockney, it is truly unique. The house's motto is "You either see it or you don't."

↗ Around the corner on Elder Street are two of London's earliest surviving terraces, where several Georgian red-brick houses have been carefully restored.

 8

Whitechapel Gallery

📍 O4 🏠 77-82 Whitechapel High St E1 🚇 Aldgate East, Aldgate ⏰ 11am-6pm Tue-Sun (to 9pm Thu)
🗓 1 Jan, 24-26 Dec
🌐 whitechapelgallery.org

A striking Art Nouveau façade by C Harrison Townsend

→ Industrial chic in the gentrified Hoxton district

fronts this light, airy gallery, founded in 1901 and later expanded in the 1980s and again in 2007–9. Situated close to Brick Lane and the area's burgeoning art scene, this independent gallery was founded with the aim of bringing great art to the people of east London. Today it enjoys an international reputation for high-quality shows of major contemporary artists and for events, talks, live performances, films and art-themed evenings (especially on the first Thursday of each month, when many galleries in the area open late).

In the 1950s and 1960s, the likes of Jackson Pollock, Anthony Caro, Mark Rothko, Robert Rauschenberg and John Hoyland all displayed their work in the gallery. In 1970 David Hockney's first exhibition was held here.

The gallery has a well-stocked arts bookshop and a relaxed café which on Thursday evenings becomes a popular wine bar. There is an entry charge for some special exhibitions.

 9

19 Princelet Street

📍03 🏠19 Princelet St E1 🚇Liverpool St 🕐 Check website for dates 🌐19princeletstreet.org.uk

This 1719 Huguenot silk merchant's house, with a Victorian synagogue hidden within, epitomizes the area's multicultural history as a refuge for the dispossessed. Now it exists as a museum of immigration, with exhibitions celebrating the people who have arrived and settled in London's East End. It is hoped that, with funding, this historic gem can be further developed into a permanent centre. For now, one-off group visits can be booked in advance via the website (booking at least four weeks ahead is advisable).

↑ Standing proudly over the streets of Spitalfields, Christ Church is an iconic sight

 10

Christ Church, Spitalfields

📍04 🏠Commercial St E1 🚇Liverpool St 🕐10am–4pm Mon–Fri (unless in use as venue), 1–4pm Sun 🌐ccspits.org

Christopher Wren's pupil Nicholas Hawksmoor built six London churches, and this is his finest. Christ Church was commissioned by parliament in the Fifty New Churches Act of 1711, which was aimed at combating the threat of Nonconformism and intended to make a powerful statement in an area fast becoming a Huguenot stronghold.

Completed in 1729, the building was mauled by alterations in the 1850s. By 1960 it had become derelict, narrowly escaping demolition. After a lengthy programme of restoration promoted by the Friends of Christ Church Spitalfields, the church was returned to its former glory by 2004. The superb organ was restored to full working order in 2015, and the renovated crypt revealed much of the original walls. The impression of size and strength created by its portico and spire is continued inside by such features as the high ceiling and the gallery. Tours are for groups, and should be booked at least two weeks ahead.

HUGUENOTS IN LONDON

Among the first really significant waves of immigration into east London was the influx of tens of thousands of Huguenots from France in the late 17th century. These were Protestant refugees, fleeing persecution in their home country, and their numbers were highest in Spitalfields. Many were weavers by trade and they came to dominate the silk and textile industry that already existed in this part of the city. Spitalfields became known as "Weaver Town".

Beautiful blooms at
the Columbia Road
flower market ↑

⑪ St Leonard's Church

📍 O2 🏠 Shoreditch High St
E1 🚇 Old St, Shoreditch
High St 🕐 Mar–Sep: noon–
2pm Mon–Fri, 9:30am–
1:30pm Sun year-round
🌐 shoreditchchurch.org.uk

Standing as it does on the
spot where several major
Roman roads converged, this
has been a site of worship for
millennia. The Norman-era
St Leonard's was the original
"Actors' Church" *(p125)* and
many famous names of Tudor
theatre are buried in the
crypt, including Richard
Burbage, who played the first

Hamlet, Macbeth and Romeo,
and his brother Cuthbert,
founder of the Globe Theatre.
    Erected in 1736–40, the
current Palladian-style church
is the oldest building in
Shoreditch. Its fine acoustics
make it still popular today as a
performance space for actors
and musicians. Sunday service
is at 10:30am.

⑫ Columbia Road Market

📍 O2 🏠 Columbia Rd
E2 🚋 Hoxton 🕐 8am–3pm
Sun 🌐 columbiaroad.info

A visit to this flower and plant
market is one of the most
delightful things to do on a
Sunday morning in London,
whether you want to take
advantage of the exotic
species on offer or not –
though it's hard to resist, as
prices are competitive and the
range impressive. Set in a
well-preserved street of small
Victorian shops, it is a lively,
sweet-smelling and colourful
affair. Apart from the stalls,
there are several shops
selling, among other things,
home-made bread and
farmhouse cheeses, antiques
and interesting objects, many
flower related. There are also
cafés, a tapas bar and pubs
to refuel at along the street.
Visit early to miss the crowds.

⑬ Rich Mix

📍 O3 🏠 35–47 Bethnal
Green Rd E1 🚇 Shoreditch
High St 🕐 10am–late
🌐 richmix.org.uk

This hip independent cultural
centre spread over five floors
offers a diverse programme
of live music, theatre, dance,
spoken word, comedy and

SHOP

Boxpark
Independent clothing
brands, accessories,
cosmetics, homewares
and kooky gifts are
traded from repurposed
shipping containers in
this fun, pop-up-style
retail park.
📍 O3 🏠 Bethnal
Green Rd E1 🌐 boxpark.
co.uk

film. There's an emphasis on both multiculturalism and local talent, with a marked international outlook reflected in the African, Brazilian and other film festivals for which its three-screen cinema has become a major venue. The building is a converted leather factory with an unusual mishmash of performance and exhibition spaces giving off an industrial chic vibe. There are three bars buried within its straight-edged interior, but the Indian street food café facing the street is much easier to find.

Geffrye Museum

◎ 01 ⌂ 136 Kingsland Rd E2 ◉ Hoxton ◐ Museum and gardens closed until 2020; restored almshouse open for tours (see website) ⓦ geffrye-museum.org.uk

This delightful museum is housed in a set of restored almshouses that were built in 1715 on land bequeathed by Sir Robert Geffrye, a 17th-century Lord Mayor of London. Inside, you take a trip through historical room settings, each providing an insight into the domestic interiors of the urban middle classes from 1600 to the present day, reflecting changes in society, behaviour, style and taste. Each room contains superb examples of British furniture of the period. Outside, a series of period garden "rooms" show designs and planting schemes popular in urban gardens between the 16th and 20th centuries.

The museum is currently closed until 2020 for a £18m redevelopment, which will open up two previously unseen floors and a new café. One of the almshouses remains open for tours, and there are often events in the green space in front of the buildings, such as an outdoor cinema or a wacky cocktail garden: check the website for more details.

V&A Museum of Childhood

◎ 02 ⌂ Cambridge Heath Rd E2 ◉ Bethnal Green ◐ 10am–5:45pm daily ⓦ vam.ac.uk/moc

With an amazing array of toys, games, puzzles, lavish dolls' houses, model train sets, furniture and costumes, dating from the 16th century up to the present day, this museum has the largest collection of childhood-related objects in the UK.

There are plenty of activities to keep children amused, including story-telling, arts and crafts workshops, and fun trails.

↑ Five centuries of fun and games *(inset)* at the V&A Museum of Childhood

SOUTHWARK AND BANKSIDE

Southwark and its stretch of riverbank, known as Bankside, once offered an escape from the City, a place to indulge in the many forms of entertainment that were banned across the river. Among the illicit pleasures that thrived here from the late 16th century were brothels, theatres, and bear and cock pits. Even today, the streets leading off Borough High Street are lined with a remarkable number of pubs, and the George survives as the only galleried inn in London. Shakespeare's company was famously based at the Globe Theatre, which has been reconstructed close to its original site. Docks, wharves and warehouses were built along Bankside in the 18th and 19th centuries as the area industrialized, but a century later, bomb damage during World War II, and the decline in river trade that followed, ushered in a period of decline. Southwark's riverside renaissance as one of the capital's top visitor destinations began in the 1990s and since the turn of the millennium Tate Modern, the Millennium Bridge and the Shard have all opened, accompanied by a sweeping regeneration of the whole area.

SOUTHWARK AND BANKSIDE

Must Sees
1. Tate Modern
2. Shakespeare's Globe

Experience More
3. Southwark Cathedral
4. The Old Operating Theatre
5. Bankside Gallery
6. Borough Market
7. The Rose Playhouse
8. Clink Prison Museum
9. The Shard
10. Bermondsey Street

11. City Hall
12. HMS *Belfast*

Eat
1. Roast
2. Flat Iron Square
3. The Garrison

Drink
4. The George
5. The Anchor

1

TATE MODERN

⑨ L6 **⚐ Bankside SE1** **⊜ Pimlico** **⊜ Blackfriars, Southwark** **⊟ Blackfriars**
🕐 10am-6pm Sun-Thu, 10am-10pm Fri & Sat **🔒 24-26 Dec** **⬛ tate.org.uk**

Looming over the southern bank of the Thames, Tate Modern, housed in the converted Bankside power station, holds one of the world's premier collections of contemporary art. With an ever-changing roster of exhibitions, it is London's most visited gallery.

Opened to coincide with the new millennium, this Goliath of a gallery boasts a collection of over 70,000 works of modern art, featuring paintings and sculptures by some of the most significant artists of the 20th and 21st centuries, Pablo Picasso, Salvador Dalí, Mark Rothko and Francis Bacon among them. Lesser known artists and less mainstream media also abound, with pieces composed of bottle tops or, most famously, a porcelain urinal, in the guise of Marcel Duchamp's notorious *Fountain*. The focal point of the building is the awesome Turbine Hall, which is often filled by a specially commissioned work. Other exhibition spaces, including the galleries of the towering Blavatnik Building, feature collections on a single theme or hugely popular temporary shows.

INTERACTIVE ART

Tate Modern has created a series of interactive activities and experiences under its Bloomberg Connects umbrella. These products, including the Tate app, the digital Drawing Bar and the digital gallery, in which you can immerse yourself in the studios and cities of artists, enable members of the public to actively connect with art, artists and other visitors. The award-winning handheld multimedia guides present audio commentary alongside images, film clips and games.

One Two Three Swing! by SUPERFLEX, an installation in the Turbine Hall ↓

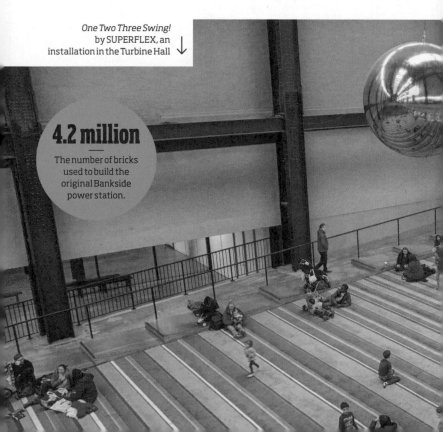

4.2 million
—
The number of bricks used to build the original Bankside power station.

⓵ The striking 99-m- (325-ft-) high chimney of Tate Modern reveals the building's former role as a power station.

② The Tate Modern has an excellent and extensive permanent collection displayed across the site, spanning photographs, paintings, sculptures and video art.

③ The cool interior of the Blavatnik Building extension has added a large number of galleries and performance spaces to the Tate.

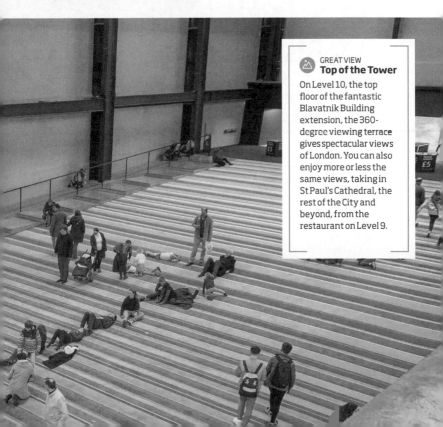

> △ GREAT VIEW
> ### Top of the Tower
>
> On Level 10, the top floor of the fantastic Blavatnik Building extension, the 360-degree viewing terrace gives spectacular views of London. You can also enjoy more or less the same views, taking in St Paul's Cathedral, the rest of the City and beyond, from the restaurant on Level 9.

2

SHAKESPEARE'S GLOBE

⊙ L5 **⌂ New Globe Walk SE1** **⊖ Blackfriars, London Bridge, Mansion House** **⊙ Tours & exhibition: 9am–5pm** **⊙ 24 & 26 Dec** **Ⓦ shakespearesglobe.com**

To see a Shakespeare play at the reconstructed Globe is a magical experience. Time-travel to the 1600s and watch Romeo woo Juliet, Beatrice and Benedick squabble, and Hamlet seek revenge.

Built along the south bank of the Thames, Shakespeare's Globe is a fine reconstruction of the Elizabethan theatre where many of the famous playwright's works were first performed. The circular wooden structure is open in the middle, leaving some of the audience exposed to the elements. Those holding seated tickets enjoy a roof over their heads. Performances (staged from late April until mid-October) are thrilling, with first-rate

acting. A second theatre, the Sam Wanamaker Playhouse, is a splendidly atmospheric, candlelit reproduction of a Jacobean indoor theatre, with performances year-round. The Globe also houses an exhibition telling the history of Elizabethan theatre in Southwark, the process of building the Globe and the exquisite costumes made for shows there. You can also listen to classic performances of speeches from Shakespeare's works.

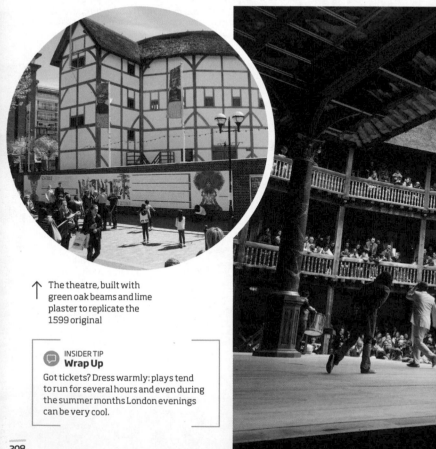

↑ The theatre, built with green oak beams and lime plaster to replicate the 1599 original

💬 INSIDER TIP
Wrap Up

Got tickets? Dress warmly: plays tend to run for several hours and even during the summer months London evenings can be very cool.

1 A performance at the Globe is always a lively experience.

2 The ornate and intimate Sam Wanamaker Playhouse is indoors.

3 The roof of the Globe is made of water reed thatch. There has been a law banning the use of thatch in the city since the Great Fire of London in 1666, so the theatre had to line the roof with fire-retardant material in order to gain special permission to use it.

Did You Know?

The Taming of the Shrew is considered Shakespeare's first play, written before 1592.

EXPERIENCE MORE

3

Southwark Cathedral

📍M6 🏠Montague Close SE1 🚇London Bridge 🕐7:30am–6pm Mon–Fri, 8:30am–6pm Sat & Sun 🌐cathedral.southwark.anglican.org

This church did not become a cathedral until 1905 – yet some parts of it date back to the 12th century, when the building was attached to a priory, and many of its medieval features remain. The memorials are quite fascinating and include a late-13th-century wooden effigy of a knight. John Harvard, the first benefactor of Harvard University, was baptized here in 1607 and there is a chapel named after him.

In 2000, the cathedral was restored in a multi-million-pound programme, which included the addition of new buildings housing a shop and a refectory. The exterior has been landscaped to create a herb garden, with the attractive Millennium Courtyard leading to the riverside.

4

The Old Operating Theatre

📍M6 🏠9a St Thomas St SE1 🚇London Bridge 🕐10:30am–5pm Tue–Sun, 2–5pm Mon 🚫24–26 & 31 Dec, 1 Jan 🌐oldoperatingtheatre.com

St Thomas' Hospital, one of the oldest in Britain, stood here from its foundation in the 12th century until it was moved west in 1862. At this time, nearly all of its buildings were demolished in order to make way for the railways. The women's operating theatre survived only because it had

↑ Surgical items forming a *memento mori* at The Old Operating Theatre

been constructed in a garret over the hospital church. The UK's oldest operating theatre, dating from 1822, it remained forgotten until the 1950s. It has now been fitted out just as it would have been in the early 19th century, before the discovery of either antiseptics or anaesthetics. Another section of the garret, which was once used by the hospital apothecary to store herbs, has a collection of traditional herbs and remedies, plus displays of antiquated medicines. As the museum is upstairs in a historic building, wheelchair access is problematic.

5

Bankside Gallery

📍L5 🏠48 Hopton St SE1 🚇Blackfriars, Southwark 🕐11am–6pm daily during exhibitions 🚫1 Jan, 24–26 Dec 🌐banksidegallery.com

This modern riverside gallery is the headquarters of two historic British societies: the

←

The tower and east end of Southwark Cathedral, built in golden sandstone and flint

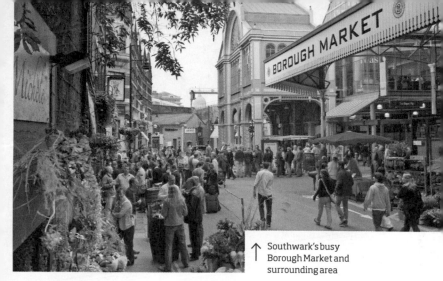

↑ Southwark's busy Borough Market and surrounding area

Royal Watercolour Society and the Royal Society of Painter-Printmakers. The members of these societies are elected by their peers in a tradition that dates back over 200 years. The exhibitions held here feature the work of both societies and many of the pieces on display are for sale. There is also a superb specialist art shop that sells both books and materials.

There is an unparalleled view of St Paul's Cathedral from the nearby pub, the Founders' Arms – built on the site of the foundry where the cathedral's bells were cast.

extremely popular fine food market (beware: the crowds can be huge, especially on Fridays and Saturdays), known for gourmet goods, as well as quality fruit and vegetables, and organic meat, fish and dairy produce. A number of hot food stalls, selling a tempting array of dishes from around the world, also share the space. Food demonstrations take place in the glass atrium on Borough High Street on Thursdays and Fridays. The specialist food shops and pubs on the streets around the market are also well worth checking out.

6
Borough Market

📍M6 🏠8 Southwark St SE1 🚇London Bridge 🕐10am–5pm Wed–Thu, 10am–6pm Fri, 8am–5pm Sat (some stalls also 10am–5pm Mon & Tue) 🌐boroughmarket.org.uk

Borough Market has existed in some form or another for over a thousand years. It moved to its current position in 1756 and became one of Britain's biggest fruit and vegetable markets after the arrival of the railways in the 19th century. Today, it's an

7 🏠
The Rose Playhouse

📍M6 🏠56 Park St SE1 🚇London Bridge 🕐Noon–4pm Sat 🌐rosetheatre.org.uk

In 1989 the remains of the Rose theatre, dating from Elizabethan times, were discovered during excavations ahead of building work for a new office block. The Rose, built in 1587, was the first of the Bankside theatres, and it staged plays by Shakespeare and Christopher Marlowe. The site of the original Globe theatre was just over the road

DRINK

The George
The only remaining galleried coaching inn in London, with seating outside in the courtyard.

📍M6 🏠75–77 Borough High St SE1 🌐greene king-pubs.co.uk

The Anchor
Ales have been quaffed here for centuries. The present 18th-century premises has a terrace by the river.

📍M6 🏠34 Park St SE1 🌐greeneking-pubs.co.uk

on Park Street (a plaque marks the spot). Preserved in a specially designed space, with a modern building overhead, the archaeological remains are submerged in water, with lights indicating the shape of the theatre. A small volunteer-run exhibition tells the story of the excavation. The atmospheric space is also sometimes used as a small theatre – check the website for details.

Scary skeletons spooking visitors at the Clink Prison Museum ↑

EAT

Roast

Traditional British food at its best in a smart dining room overlooking Borough Market.

M6 The Floral Hall, Stoney St SE1 roast-restaurant.com

£££

Flat Iron Square

A sociable hub for street food and quality independent fast-food restaurants in the railway arches near Borough Market.

M6 68 Union St SE1 flatironsquare.co.uk

£££

The Garrison

The seasonal British menu served here is a mixture of the creatively modern and the satisfyingly traditional.

N7 99-101 Bermondsey St SE1 thegarrison.co.uk

£££

8

Clink Prison Museum

M6 1 Clink St SE1 London Bridge Jul-Sep: 10am-9pm daily; Oct-Jun: 10am-6pm Mon-Fri, 10am-7:30pm Sat & Sun clink.co.uk

The prison that was once located here was founded in the 12th century. It was owned by successive Bishops of Winchester, who lived in the adjoining palace, of which all that now remains is a lovely rose window on Clink Street. During the 15th century, the prison became known as the "Clink", and this has become a British slang term for any prison or jail cell. It closed down in 1780.

The museum alongside the remains of the palace illustrates the history of the prison. Tales are told of the inmates incarcerated here, including prostitutes, debtors, and priests imprisoned by the bishopric as heretics. Visitors can handle instruments of torture that leave little to the imagination – a trip here is not for the faint-hearted.

9

The Shard

N6 London Bridge St London Bridge The View from the Shard: 10am-10pm daily; last adm 1 hour before closing theviewfromthe shard.com

Designed by Renzo Piano, the Shard is the tallest building in western Europe. At 310 m (1,016 ft) high with a crystalline façade, the 95-storey tower houses offices, restaurants – several with incredible views across the city – a five-star hotel, exclusive apartments and the country's highest observation gallery, the View from the Shard.

→

The Shard, rising up behind the visor-shaped City Hall

Take a high-speed lift from the entrance on Joiner Street to the top of the building for spectacular, unobstructed views of the capital. There are two viewing floors, the higher of which is right among the "shards" with the breeze blowing overhead.

Bermondsey Street

📍N7 🚇SE1 🚈London Bridge, Borough

Bermondsey's winding streets still hold traces of its past in the form of medieval, 18th-century and Victorian buildings. Today, Bermondsey Street is home to galleries, coffee shops and a few great restaurants. The area is also famous for its antiques market, held in Bermondsey Square at the bottom end of the street. Each Friday morning from 6am, seriously committed antiques dealers trade their latest acquisitions, and the best bargains tend to go before most people are even awake.

The **Fashion and Textile Museum** at No 83 puts on a programme of exhibitions covering all aspects of fashion and design, and also runs an education programme. Further along the street, White Cube Bermondsey is a major space for international contemporary art.

Fashion and Textile Museum
🕐11am-6pm Tue-Sat (till 8pm Thu), 11am-5pm Sun 🌐ftmlondon.org

City Hall

📍06 🏠The Queen's Walk SE1 🚈London Bridge
🕐8:30am-6pm Mon-Thu, 8:30am-5:30pm Fri
🌐london.gov.uk/about-us

The Norman Foster–designed domed glass building just by Tower Bridge is the headquarters for London's mayor and the Greater London Authority. Anyone can visit the building and head up the walkway to the second floor to look in on the assembly chamber, or sit in on Mayor's Question Time, when assembly members interrogate the mayor on London issues; this takes place ten times a year on Wednesday mornings (check website for dates). On the lower ground floor are temporary exhibitions and a café. Outside, the stone amphitheatre known as the Scoop hosts free events in summer, including plays, music and screenings.

HMS Belfast

📍N6 🏠The Queen's Walk SE1 🚈London Bridge, Tower Hill 🕐Mar-Oct: 10am-6pm daily (last adm: 5pm); Nov-Feb: 10am-5pm (last adm: 4pm) 🗓24-26 Dec 🌐iwm.org.uk/visits/hms-belfast

Launched in 1930 to serve in World War II, HMS *Belfast* was instrumental in the destruction of the German battle cruiser *Scharnhorst* in the Battle of North Cape, and also played a role in the Normandy landings. After the war, the battle cruiser was sent to work for the United Nations during the Korean War, and remained in service with the Royal Navy until 1965. The only surviving World War II cruiser, it has been used as a floating naval museum since 1971. Ideal for children and adults alike, visitors can climb down ladders to the engine room 4.5 m (15 ft) below sea level, and experience what it was like in the gun turrets during a battle. Exhibits also explore the ship's history post-World War II, including during the Cold War.

A SHORT WALK
SOUTHWARK

Distance 2 km (1.25 miles) **Nearest Tube** Southwark
Time 20 minutes

Out of the jurisdiction of the City authorities, Southwark was the place for illicit pleasures from medieval times until the 18th century. The 18th and 19th centuries brought new business, and docks, warehouses and factories were built to meet the demand. Today, a riverside walk here provides spectacular views of St Paul's and takes in the Tate Modern, a regenerated Borough Market, the recreation of Shakespeare's Globe Theatre and the Shard.

BLACKFRIARS BRIDGE

Millennium Bridge

Southwark Bridge was opened in 1912 to replace a bridge of 1819.

●**START**

HOLLAND STREET

PARK STREET

EMERSON STREET

SOUTHWARK BRIDGE ROAD

SUMNER STREET

Tate Modern, the former Bankside Power Station, is a spectacular space to show off a huge collection of contemporary art (p206).

The brilliant recreation of Shakespeare's Globe Theatre has open-air performances in the summer months and an exhibition open all year round (p208).

0 metres 100
0 yards   100

N ↑

←

One Two Three Swing! by SUPERFLEX at the Tate Modern

↑ The historic Anchor pub, a popular drinking establishment since the time of Shakespeare

Locator Map
For more detail see p204

SOUTHWARK AND BANKSIDE

Clink Prison Museum, on the site of the notorious old prison, looks back at Southwark's colourful past (p212).

The riverside pub the Anchor has been a firm favourite for centuries (p211).

14th-century rose window

The Golden Hinde II is a replica of Sir Francis Drake's galleon built in the 1970s; it sailed the globe for several decades before docking here.

London Bridge, in its various forms, was the only river crossing in London from Roman times until 1750. The present bridge, completed in 1972, replaced the one of 1831.

CLINK STREET

PARK STREET

BANK END

STONEY STREET

CATHEDRAL STREET

MONTAGUE CLOSE

LONDON BRIDGE

Despite major alterations, Southwark Cathedral still contains medieval elements (p210).

There has been a market on or near the site of Borough Market since 1276 (p211).

SOUTHWARK STREET

BOROUGH HIGH STREET

ST THOMAS STREET

● FINISH

The Hop Exchange was where hops from Kent for brewing were traded; its pediment features carved scenes of the hop harvest.

The War Memorial, commemorating soldiers who fell in World War I, was erected in 1924 on Borough High Street.

The George is London's only surviving traditional galleried inn (p211).

SOUTH BANK

It was not until the 18th century that the stretch
of marshy land over the river from Westminster,
opposite what would later become the Victoria
Embankment, was drained and developed, and
referred to as the South Bank. Pleasure gardens
gave way to industrialization, and by the late 1830s
the riverfront was dominated by the Lion Brewery,
which stood here until it was demolished in 1949,
by which time it had already been abandoned.
After World War II the land lay bomb damaged and
derelict until London County Council decided to
develop it for the 1951 Festival of Britain.
Conceived as a much-needed tonic for a war-worn
population, a large exhibition site full of cultural
and leisure venues and installations was created
for the festival. The only permanent construction
was the Royal Festival Hall, and the Southbank
Centre, which now dominates the site, grew up
around that building. It was in the spirit of the
Festival of Britain that the new millennium was
marked on the South Bank with the raising of the
London Eye, a gigantic ferris wheel.

COVENT
GARDEN

I

J

SOUTHAMPTON STREET

LANCASTER PLACE

Somerset
House

Temple

VICTORIA EMBANKMENT

STRAND

River   Thames

**COVENT GARDEN
AND THE STRAND**
p118

Waterloo
Bridge

THE QUEEN'S WALK

Gabriel's
Wharf

Charing
Cross

Embankment
Pier

Embankment

NORTHUMBERLAND AVENUE

WATERLOO ROAD

BFI
Southbank

4

National
Theatre

UPPER GROUND

CORNWALL

DOON ST

STAMFORD STREET

Hungerford
Rail Bridge

**Festival
Pier**

Queen
Elizabeth
Hall

Jubilee
Footbridges

Southbank
Centre **1**

Royal
Festival
Hall

Hayward
Gallery

6

WHITEHALL

EMBANKMENT

VICTORIA

Ministry
of Defence

*Jubilee
Gardens*

BELVEDERE ROAD

BFI Imax

MEPHAM STREET

STATION APPROACH

EXTON

Waterloo

London
Eye

**London
Eye Pier** **3**

YORK ROAD

LEAKE ST

STATION APPROACH

SPUR ROAD

PARLIAMENT STREET

Westminster
Pier

Westminster

London
Dungeon **7**

Sea Life
London Aquarium **5**

County
Hall

BELVEDERE ROAD

FORUM
MAGNUM
SQUARE

LOWER MARSH

FRAZIER

BAYLIS

BRIDGE ST

Westminster
Bridge

WESTMINSTER
BRIDGE ROAD

7

Big Ben

Houses of
Parliament

Florence
Nightingale
Museum **6**

*St Thomas's
Hospital*

UPPER MARSH

ROYAL ST

WESTMINSTER BRIDGE ROAD

**Lambeth
North**

CARLISLE LANE

HERCULES ROAD

KENNINGTON ROAD

**WHITEHALL AND
WESTMINSTER**
p68

ALBERT EMBANKMENT

LAMBETH PALACE ROAD

CARLISLE LANE

HERCULES ROAD

COSSER STREET

*Victoria
Tower
Gardens*

*Archbishop's
Park*

LAMBETH   ROAD

St John's
Smith Square

Lambeth
Palace **9**

Museum of
Garden History **10**

THORNEY ST

MILLBANK

Lambeth
Bridge

LAMBETH HIGH ST

OLD
PARADISE ST

LAMBETH WALK

WALNUT TREE WALK

FITZALAN STREET

8

I

J

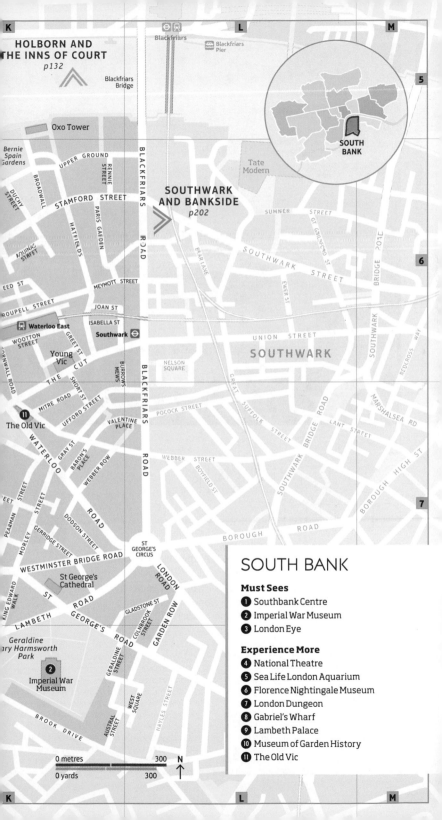

HOLBORN AND
THE INNS OF COURT
p132

Blackfriars

Blackfriars
Pier

Blackfriars
Bridge

Oxo Tower

Bernie
Spain
Gardens

UPPER GROUND

RENNIE STREET

BROADWALL

DUCHY STREET

STAMFORD STREET

PARIS GARDEN

HATFIELDS

BLACKFRIARS ROAD

SOUTHWARK
AND BANKSIDE
p202

Tate
Modern

SOUTH
BANK

SUMNER STREET

GT GUILDFORD ST

SOUTHWARK STREET

EMER ST

BRIDGE ROAD

MEYMOTT STREET

YOUNG STREET

ROUPELL STREET

JOAN ST

ISABELLA ST

BLACKFRIARS ROAD

UNION STREET

BRIAR LANE

FEED ST

Waterloo East

Southwark

WOOTTON STREET

GREET ST

SOUTHWARK

Young Vic

THE CUT

BURROWS MEWS

NELSON SQUARE

GREAT SUFFOLK STREET

SOUTHWARK WAY

REDCROSS WAY

CORNWALL ROAD

MITRE ROAD

SHORT ST

UFFORD STREET

POCOCK STREET

MARSHALSEA RD

⑪ The Old Vic

VALENTINE PLACE

LANT STREET

WATERLOO

GRAY ST

BARON'S PLACE

WEBBER ROW

WEBBER STREET

BOYFIELD ST

SOUTHWARK BRIDGE ROAD

BOROUGH HIGH ST

EET STREET

PEARMAN STREET

MORLEY STREET

GERRIDGE STREET

DODSON STREET

ROAD

WESTMINSTER BRIDGE ROAD

ST GEORGE'S CIRCUS

BOROUGH ROAD

KING EDWARD WALK

ST GEORGE'S

St George's Cathedral

ROAD

GLADSTONE ST

COLNBROOK STREET

LONDON ROAD

GARDEN ROW

LAMBETH

Geraldine
Mary Harmsworth
Park

② Imperial War Museum

GERALDINE STREET

AUSTRAL STREET

WEST SQUARE

HAYLES STREET

BROOK DRIVE

| 0 metres | 300 |
| 0 yards | 300 |

N ↑

SOUTH BANK

Must Sees

① Southbank Centre
② Imperial War Museum
③ London Eye

Experience More

④ National Theatre
⑤ Sea Life London Aquarium
⑥ Florence Nightingale Museum
⑦ London Dungeon
⑧ Gabriel's Wharf
⑨ Lambeth Palace
⑩ Museum of Garden History
⑪ The Old Vic

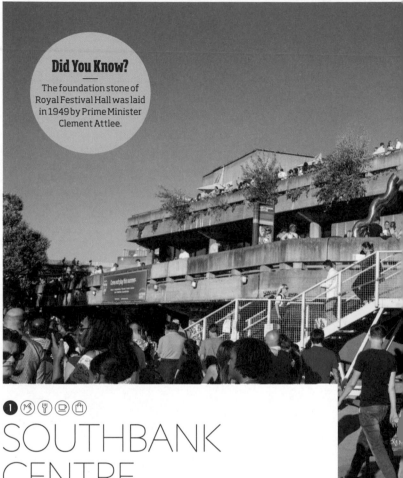

Did You Know?

The foundation stone of Royal Festival Hall was laid in 1949 by Prime Minister Clement Attlee.

SOUTHBANK CENTRE

📍 J6 🏠 **Belvedere Rd, South Bank SE1** 🚇 **Waterloo, Embankment** 🚆 **Waterloo, Waterloo East, Charing Cross** 🚢 **Festival Pier, London Eye Pier, Mon–Fri** 🌐 **southbankcentre.co.uk**

With a major art gallery and three world-class auditoriums for music, dance and other events lined up along the river, the Southbank Centre is one of London's pre-eminent cultural and performance venues.

London's high-profile, much-respected and visited multi-dimensional arts centre takes centre stage among the other great arts institutions on the South Bank: the National Theatre and the British Film Institute. The Southbank Centre itself comprises four main venues: the Royal Festival Hall, the Hayward Gallery, the Queen Elizabeth Hall and the Purcell Room. The centre's always buzzing, with bustling bars and restaurants slotted into and between the terraces, platforms, walkways and rooftops of this concrete complex. There are always innumerable visitors making their way to performances, primarily of classical music but also of opera, folk, world music and all kinds of contemporary leftfield genres. Comedy, talks and dance all feature too, while there is a multitude of regular festivals, seasons and weekends staged here, including the London Jazz Festival, Women of the World (WOW) Festival, the London Literature Festival and Meltdown.

↑ Crowds enjoying the sun outside the Queen Elizabeth Hall

↑ Strolling along the riverfront past the Southbank Centre, towards the monumental London Eye

1951 FESTIVAL OF BRITAIN

The 1951 Festival of Britain was timed to mark the centenary of the Great Exhibition but also to provide some optimism and cultural celebration in the aftermath of war. The wharves and factories that once stood on this site suffered considerable bomb damage during World War II, so the area was cleared for the event and a set of weird and wonderful temporary structures were erected in their place, forming a kind of cultural theme park. The one permanent structure was the Royal Festival Hall.

The South Bank

Hugging the curve of the River Thames, the Southbank Centre is a sprawling complex with the Royal Festival Hall at its heart. Just a little further along the bank are the enormous London Eye and County Hall, home to other top attractions the London Dungeon and the London Aquarium. There is plenty to entertain here, making it perfect for a gentle afternoon.

EAT

Southbank Centre Food Market
This excellent little food market is located to the rear of the Royal Festival Hall. A wide range of street eats is available, from pizzas and curries to Korean BBQ and Ethiopian vegan food, as well as treats to take home, like wine, cheese and jam.

⏰ Noon-8pm Fri, 11am-8pm Sat & noon-6pm Sun

££££

Plays at the National Theatre range from classics to modern works.

Waterloo Bridge was designed by Sir Giles Gilbert Scott.

Southbank Centre Food Market

Now surrounded by the Southbank Place development, the Shell Building is the oil company's head office.

← Skycsrapers line the South Bank near the London Eye

Hungerford Bridge's two footbridges are London's busiest.

Southbank Centre

First laid out in 1977 for the Queen's Silver Jubilee, Jubilee Gardens were remodelled for her Diamond Jubilee.

Did You Know?

The organ in the Royal Festival Hall has over 7,800 pipes.

The London Eye offers passengers a unique view of London.

County Hall houses the Sea Life London Aquarium and the London Dungeon.

The Southbank Centre Food Market takes place on Fridays, Saturdays and Sundays, in the square behind the Royal Festival Hall.

 The concrete exterior of the Hayward Gallery is well suited to the modern works that it displays within. The building's stark design is a landmark of Brutalist architecture.

 BFI Southbank, previously the National Film Theatre, was originally established to show historic films; today it offers an eclectic programme of films from around the world.

Royal Festival Hall

⚲ J6

With its 2,900-seat auditorium, this modernist building is the Southbank Centre's largest concert hall and one of the city's best classical music venues. The airy halls outside the auditorium house the free-access Clore Ballroom, where concerts are frequently staged in sight of the casual bar. The foyer is also used for exhibitions and contains a café, while the Skylon restaurant sits on the third floor. In summer, pop-up venues and bars are installed and DJ-led parties take place on the riverside terrace.

Hayward Gallery

⚲ J6

Reopened in 2018 after a lengthy refurbishment, the Hayward Gallery, an icon of 1960s Brutalist architecture with its slabby grey concrete exterior and distinctive pyramidal glass roof panels, is one of London's foremost venues for large, often provocative, contemporary art exhibitions. The gallery exhibits paintings, drawings, photography, sculpture, installation art and more, by interesting, innovative and internationally renowned artists from around the world. Paul Klee, Andreas Gursky, Bridget Riley and Anthony Caro are among the artists who have had exhibitions here.

Queen Elizabeth Hall and Purcell Room

⚲ J6

The Queen Elizabeth Hall reopened in 2018 after three years of renovations. Smaller orchestral performances, genre-bending music and dance, stand-up comedy, spoken word poetry and literary events are all staged in this relatively intimate, comfortable concert venue. The Purcell Room, in the same building, is smaller still and also hosts readings, while its music events tend to be small ensembles, piano recitals, chamber music and the like. The foyer is also regularly used as a performance venue, hosting free events day and night plus occasional club nights.

BFI Southbank

⚲ J6 ⊕ bfi.org.uk

BFI Southbank, previously the National Film Theatre, was established in 1953, and though adjacent to the Southbank Centre it's not actually part of it. It has four cinema screens and offers a huge and diverse selection of films, both British and international. It also holds regular screenings of rare and restored films and television programmes and has a free Mediatheque where the BFI's archives can be browsed.

↑ Military aircraft on display in the main atrium at the Imperial War Museum

② 🚳 🍴 🖥 🏛

IMPERIAL WAR MUSEUM

📍K8 🏠Lambeth Rd SE1 🚇Waterloo, Lambeth North, Elephant & Castle
🚆Waterloo, Elephant & Castle 🕐10am–6pm daily (last admission to the Holocaust Gallery at 5:30pm) 🚫24–26 Dec 🌐iwm.org.uk

With great creativity and sensitivity, the immersive exhibitions at the terrific Imperial War Museum provide a fascinating insight into the history of war and themes of conflict.

Inevitably the two World Wars feature heavily at the Imperial War Museum, but they are covered in innovative ways. In the First World War Galleries, there are original exhibits such as a recreated trench, while some of the most fascinating World War II exhibits relate more to the impact on the lives of people at home than to the business of fighting. One display focuses on the experiences of a London family, including the effects of food rationing and regular air raids. The Holocaust Exhibition is a particularly poignant experience, while other highly original permanent displays include Curiosities of War, which is full of unexpected items such as a wooden training horse from World War I. More conventionally, there are tanks, artillery and aircraft, including a Mark 1 Spitfire and a Harrier jet, on show in the main atrium.

> 💬 INSIDER TIP
> **Get a Guide**
>
> There is a guide book to the museum aimed specifically at children aged 7 and above. There are also daily 40-minute tours (£10, children £5) at 11am and 3pm that introduce the museum's collections. Tickets must be bought in person.

① The museum is housed in what used to be the Bethlem Royal Hospital for the Insane (commonly known as "Bedlam"), built in 1811.

② Military hardware on display includes a T-34 World War II Soviet tank captured in 1973 by Israeli forces.

③ Hanging in the atrium is the famous Battle of Britain fighter plane, the Spitfire, from 1940.

80 spokes made from 6 km (3.7 miles) of tensioned cable support the wheel.

The wheel rim was floated down the Thames in sections.

The glass capsules are mounted on the outside of the rim.

The Eye turns slowly enough that the capsules are boarded while they are moving.

↑ Illustration of the London Eye, on the South Bank

BOOKING TICKETS

Queues for the London Eye can be long, so make sure to pre-book your tickets online to secure a timed slot and to make the most of online offers. If you plan to visit more sites around the city, multi-attraction tickets, combining a trip on the Eye with a number of other London attractions, carry heavy discounts.

3

THE LONDON EYE

◉ J6 ◎ Jubilee Gardens SE1 ◎ Waterloo, Westminster ◎ From 10am daily; closing times between 6pm and 8:30pm; check website for details ◎ Two weeks in Jan for maintenance ◎ londoneye.com

Stunning views of London's historic skyline can be had from the glass capsules of the city's famous ferris wheel, the London Eye. Situated right beside the River Thames, visitors enjoy a 360-degree view of the city.

The London Eye is a 135-m- (443-ft-) high observation wheel. Opened in 2000 as part of London's millennium celebrations, it immediately became one of the city's most recognizable landmarks, notable not only for its size, but for its circularity amid the block-shaped buildings flanking it. Thirty-two capsules, each holding up to 25 people, take a gentle 30-minute round trip. On a clear day, the Eye affords a 40-km (25-mile) view over the capital in all directions and out to the countryside beyond.

↑ A capsule mid-tour with unimpeded views of the city

↑ Taking a selfie against the London skyline

EXPERIENCE MORE

4

National Theatre

📍 K6 🏛 South Bank SE1
🚇 Waterloo 🕐 9:30am-
11pm Mon-Sat (Sherling
Walkway closes 7:30pm)
🚫 24 & 25 Dec 🌐 national
theatre.org.uk

Even if you don't want to
see a play, this complex is
worth a visit, especially for a
backstage tour. These are
offered Monday to Saturday,
and it is advisable to book in
advance. You can also get a
glimpse of the backstage area
from the Sherling High-Level
Walkway (entrance near the
Dorfman Theatre), which runs
above the prop-building areas.

Sir Denys Lasdun's building
opened in 1976 after 200
years of debate: should there
be a national theatre and,
if so, where? The theatre
company was formed in
1963, under Laurence (later
Lord) Olivier. The largest of
the three theatres is named
after him; the others are the
Dorfman and the Lyttleton.
Prestigious productions are
streamed live to theatres and
cinemas all over the UK, and
occasionally the world, via the
National Theatre Live initiative,
as well as taken on tours.

5

Sea Life London Aquarium

📍 J7 🏛 County Hall,
Westminster Bridge Rd SE1
🚇 Waterloo 🕐 10am-6pm
Mon-Fri, 9:30am-7pm Sat,
Sun & public hols (last adm:
6pm) 🌐 visitsealife.com/
london

Once the home of London's
elected government, County
Hall now houses the Sea Life
London Aquarium and London
Dungeon (p228), alongside a
hotel, restaurants and other
themed attractions.

The aquarium is home to
myriad aquatic species, such
as stingrays, turtles, jellyfish,
starfish and penguins. There's
a 25-m (82-ft) glass tunnel
walkway through a tropical
ocean environment, and a
large tank housing numerous
shark species, which you can
view from several levels. Book
ahead to guarantee entry
and skip large queues.

↑ The London Eye peering over the River Thames

↑ The controversial Brutalist architecture of the National Theatre

↑ A bust of Florence Nightingale in nursing cape and bonnet

6

Florence Nightingale Museum

📍J7 🏛2 Lambeth Palace Rd SE1 🚇Waterloo, Westminster 🕐10am–5pm daily 📅1 Jan, 22-27 & 31 Dec 🌐florence-nightingale.co.uk

This determined woman captured the nation's imagination as the "Lady of the Lamp" who nursed the wounded soldiers of the Crimean War (1853–6). She founded the country's first school of nursing at old St Thomas' Hospital in 1860, and revolutionized modern nursing. She was also an advocate for women in the workplace.

Sited near the entrance to St Thomas' Hospital, this museum gives an account of Nightingale's career through displays of original documents and personal memorabilia. They illustrate her life and the developments she pioneered in health care, until her death in 1910 at the age of 90. Tours are daily at 3:30pm, plus at 11.30am on weekends.

→

Riverside shopping and refreshment at Gabriel's Wharf

7

London Dungeon

📍J7 🏛County Hall, Westminster Bridge Rd SE1 🚇Waterloo 🕐10am–5pm Mon-Fri & Sun (from 11am Thu), 10am–6pm Sat; extended hours in school holidays 🌐thedungeons.com

This scary attraction is a great hit with older children. Illustrating the most bloodthirsty events in British history with live actors and special effects, the dungeon plays strictly for terror, and screams abound during the 90-minute tour. Gory scenes recount tales of such characters as Guy Fawkes and Jack the Ripper. Don't miss the Tyrant Boat Ride along a black River Thames to find out what happened to Tudor queen Anne Boleyn and her co-conspirators.

8

Gabriel's Wharf

📍K6 🏛56 Upper Ground SE1 🚇Waterloo

This pleasant enclave of boutiques, craft shops and cafés was the product of a long and stormy debate over the future of what was once an industrial riverside area. Residents of Waterloo strongly opposed various schemes for office developments before a community association was able to acquire the site in 1984 and build cooperative housing.

Adjoining the market area is a small public garden with grass to sit on and a river pier with fine views of the City. The Oxo Tower to the east was adapted from an older power station in 1928 to surreptitiously advertise a well-known meat extract by means of its window shapes. It now houses galleries and design shops on the lower floors and a bar, restaurant and brasserie on the top floor *(p51)*.

🔺 GREAT VIEW
Waterloo Bridge

Making any Londoner's list of favourite views is this one from a busy bridge spanning the Thames. Whether you look up or down river, the scene in front of you is a reminder of the beauty of Britain's capital city.

↑ The centuries-old Lambeth Palace and its grounds

Lambeth Palace

◉ J8 ⚑ SE1 🚇 Lambeth North, Westminster, Waterloo, Vauxhall ◷ For tours only 🌐 archbishopof canterbury.org

This Grade I–listed palace has housed Archbishops of Canterbury since the 13th century and today remains the archbishop's official London residence. The chapel and its undercroft contain elements from the 13th century, but a large part of the rest of the building is far more recent. It has been frequently restored, including by Edward Blore in 1828. The Tudor gatehouse dates from 1485 and is one of the city's most familiar riverside landmarks.

The garden, planted with many mature trees, is open on the first Friday of the month in summer, while you can visit the palace year-round by pre-booking a place on a guided tour (check website).

Until the first Westminster Bridge was built, the horse ferry that operated between here and Millbank was a principal river crossing. The revenues from this ferry went to the archbishop.

Museum of Garden History

◉ J8 ⚑ Lambeth Palace Rd SE1 🚇 Waterloo, Lambeth North, Westminster ◷ 10:30am–5pm Sun–Fri, 10:30–4pm Sat ✕ First Mon of month; 23 Dec–2 Jan. 🌐 gardenmuseum.org.uk

The world's first museum of garden history is housed in the restored church of St Mary of Lambeth Palace, where it is set around a central knot garden. In the grounds are the tombs of John Tradescant, father and son, who, as well as being gardeners to Charles I and Charles II, were adventurous plant hunters. The tomb of William Bligh of HMS *Bounty*, the ship set adrift in the Pacific Ocean after the fateful mutiny, can also be seen here. Coincidentally, his vessel had been on a plant-collecting voyage.

The museum presents a history of gardening in Britain, including objects collected by the Tradescants, and an archive of garden design. It also runs a programme of exhibitions and events, and has a shop and café. During renovations in 2017, which created a new garden and opened up the church tower for the first time, a vault was discovered with 30 lead coffins.

The Old Vic

◉ K7 ⚑ Waterloo Rd SE1 🚇 Waterloo ◷ For performances and tours 🌐 oldvictheatre.com

This splendid building dates back to 1818 and changed its name to the Royal Victoria in 1833 in honour of the future queen. The theatre became a centre for music hall, the immensely popular Victorian entertainment. In 1912, Lillian Baylis became manager and from 1914 to 1923 staged all of Shakespeare's plays here.

The National Theatre *(p227)*, founded in the 1960s, was formerly based at this site. In 2003 the Old Vic Theatre Company was set up as the resident company. Though tickets are pricey, there are cheap seats for younger people. Theatre tours (which can be booked online) are fascinating, full of backstage snippets and anecdotes.

Did You Know?

Despite the fact that it was named in her honour, Queen Victoria only visited the Old Vic once, aged 14.

CHELSEA AND BATTERSEA

Chelsea was last in vogue in the 1960s when showy young shoppers, including the Rolling Stones, paraded along the King's Road. Formerly a riverside village, it first became fashionable in Tudor times, with Henry VIII liking it so much that he had a small palace (long vanished) built here. In the 18th century it featured renowned riverside pleasure gardens, painted by Canaletto. Later artists, including Turner, Whistler and Rossetti, were attracted by the river views from Cheyne Walk over to Battersea. From the mid-19th century those views featured picturesque Battersea Park, whose landscaping was enhanced in 1951 when it too was laid out as pleasure gardens for the Festival of Britain. In graceless but impressive contrast, just east of Chelsea Bridge, the colossal chimneys of Battersea Power Station clouded the skies with smoke between its opening in 1933 and its decommissioning in 1983. Decades of failed bids to make use of the vast site – including turning it into a theme park and football stadium – ensued until a Malaysian consortium bought it for £400 million in 2012. It is now part of London's largest area of urban regeneration, stretching down to Vauxhall, featuring apartment blocks, shops and restaurants.

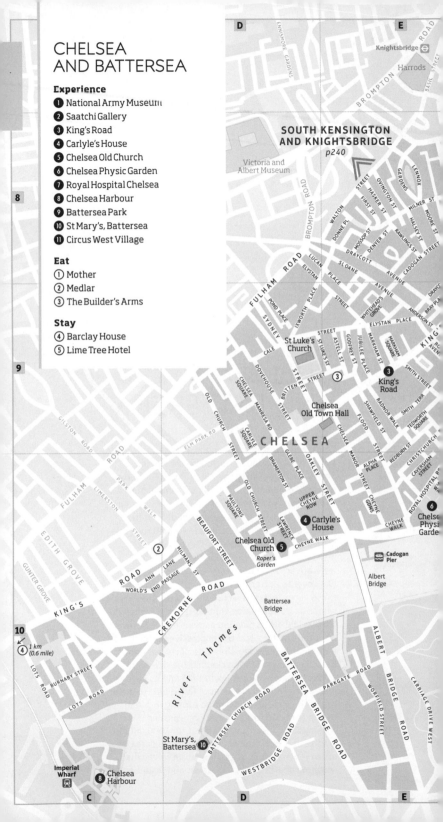

CHELSEA AND BATTERSEA

Experience
1. National Army Museum
2. Saatchi Gallery
3. King's Road
4. Carlyle's House
5. Chelsea Old Church
6. Chelsea Physic Garden
7. Royal Hospital Chelsea
8. Chelsea Harbour
9. Battersea Park
10. St Mary's, Battersea
11. Circus West Village

Eat
1. Mother
2. Medlar
3. The Builder's Arms

Stay
4. Barclay House
5. Lime Tree Hotel

SOUTH KENSINGTON AND KNIGHTSBRIDGE p240

Knightsbridge

Harrods

Victoria and Albert Museum

St Luke's Church

King's Road ③

Chelsea Old Town Hall

CHELSEA

Carlyle's House ④

Chelsea Old Church ⑤
Roper's Garden

Chelsea Physic Garden ⑥

Cadogan Pier

Albert Bridge

②

King's Road

Battersea Bridge

Battersea

River Thames

1 km (0.6 mile) ④

St Mary's, Battersea ⑩

Imperial Wharf

Chelsea Harbour ⑧

EXPERIENCE

①
National Army Museum

📍 E9 🏛 Royal Hospital Rd SW3 🚇 Sloane Square ⏰ 10am–5.30pm daily, till 8pm first Wed of month 🌐 nam.ac.uk

Adjoining the Royal Hospital Chelsea is the official museum of the British Army, with a collection that spans its 600-year history, including many uniforms, paintings and portraits. Its five galleries explore the role of the armed forces in society. As well as displays of militaria there are some thought-provoking audiovisual presentations and loads of great interactive stuff for kids.

②
Saatchi Gallery

📍 F9 🏛 Duke of York's HQ, King's Rd SW3 🚇 Sloane Square ⏰ 10am–6pm daily during exhibitions (last adm: 5:30pm) 🎫 For private events 🌐 saatchigallery.com

Set up by advertising mogul Charles Saatchi in order to showcase his impressive contemporary art acquisitions, the Saatchi Gallery has moved location several times in London. Now, however, it is firmly established in Chelsea at the Duke of York's Headquarters building, which dates from 1801. Saatchi is perhaps best known for his espousal, in the 1980s and 1990s, of the Young British Artists movement led by Damien Hirst. Today, the exhibitions of contemporary art staged here are wide-ranging and international in scope, covering everything from new Chinese artists to fashion illustration and Pop Art.

③
King's Road

📍 E9 🏛 SW3 and SW10 🚇 Sloane Square

This is Chelsea's central artery, with a wealth of upmarket high-street shops and smaller boutiques. The miniskirt revolution of the 1960s – the birth of so-called "Swinging London" – began here, with Mary Quant's first shop, Bazaar, and so have many subsequent style trends, perhaps the most famous of them being punk.

Look out for the Pheasantry at No 152, with its columns and statuary. Built in 1881 as the shopfront of a furniture-maker's premises, it now conceals a pizza restaurant.

At the top of King's Road is attractive 18th-century Sloane Square, named after Sir Hans Sloane, the wealthy physician and collector who bought the manor of Chelsea in 1712. On the east side is the Royal Court Theatre, which for over a century has fostered new drama.

STAY

Barclay House

A classy B&B in an exquisite Victorian property, with an impressive attention to detail in the three luxurious guest rooms, from the underfloor heating to the rainforest showers.

📍C10 🏠E1 Barclay Rd SW6 🌐barclayhouse london.com

£££

Lime Tree Hotel

Comfy, spotlessly maintained rooms, each individually decorated and homely, make this large boutique B&B a cut above the rest.

📍G8 🏠135 Ebury St SW1 🌐limetreehotel.co.uk

£££

Untitled by Maha Mullah in the Champagne Life exhibition at the Saatchi Gallery *(inset)*

4 NT

Carlyle's House

📍D10 🏠24 Cheyne Row SW3 🚇Sloane Square, South Kensington 🕐Mar-Oct: 11am–5pm Wed–Sun 🌐nationaltrust.org.uk

The historian Thomas Carlyle moved into this modest 18th-century house in 1834, and wrote many of his best-known books here, notably *The French Revolution*. His presence at this address made Chelsea more fashionable and the house became a mecca for literary figures, including novelists Charles Dickens and William Thackeray, poet Alfred Lord Tennyson and naturalist Charles Darwin. The house has been restored and looks as it would have done during Carlyle's lifetime.

5

Chelsea Old Church

📍D10 🏠64 Cheyne Walk SW3 🚇Sloane Square, South Kensington 🕐2–4pm Tue–Thu 🌐chelseaoldchurch.org.uk

Rebuilt after World War II, this square-towered building is a careful replica of the medieval church here that was largely destroyed in World War II. The

↑ Statue of Thomas More located outside Chelsea Old Church

glory of this church is its Tudor monuments. One to Sir Thomas More, who built a chapel here in 1528, contains an inscription he wrote (in Latin) asking to be buried next to his wife. Among other monuments is a 17th-century memorial to Lady Jane Cheyne, after whose husband Cheyne Walk was named. Outside the church is a statue in memory of More, "statesman, scholar, saint", gazing piously across the river.

6

Chelsea Physic Garden

📍E10 🏠66 Royal Hospital Rd SW3 🚇Sloane Square 🕐Apr–Oct: 11am–6pm Mon–Fri & Sun; Nov–Mar: 11am–4pm Mon–Fri 🔒Six weeks mid-Dec–Jan 🌐chelsea physicgarden.co.uk

Established by the Society of Apothecaries in 1673 to study plants for medicinal use, this garden was saved from closure in 1722 by a gift from Sir Hans Sloane, whose statue adorns it. New varieties nurtured in its glasshouses have included cotton sent to the plantations of the southern United States. Visitors to London's oldest botanic garden can see ancient trees and one of Britain's first rock gardens, installed in 1772.

The fine Georgian architecture of Chelsea

7

Royal Hospital Chelsea

📍F9 🏠Royal Hospital Rd SW3 🚇Sloane Square ⏰Museum, chapel and Great Hall: 10am-4pm Mon-Fri (no access to Hall noon-2pm) 🔒2 weeks over Christmas, public hols, for functions 🌐chelsea-pensioners.co.uk

This graceful complex was commissioned by Charles II from Christopher Wren in 1682 as a retirement home for old or wounded soldiers, who have been known as Chelsea Pensioners ever since. The hospital opened ten years later and is still home to about 300 retired soldiers, whose distinctive uniform of scarlet coat and tricorn hat dates from the 17th century. The Pensioners lead guided tours of the hospital, but only for prebooked groups.

Flanking the northern entrance are Wren's two main public rooms: the chapel, notable for its wonderful simplicity, and the panelled Great Hall. A small museum covers the history of the Chelsea Pensioners.

A statue of Charles II by Grinling Gibbons is to be found on the terrace outside,

from where there is a fine view of Battersea Power Station across the river.

8

Chelsea Harbour

📍C10 🏠SW10 🚇Fulham Broadway 🚆Imperial Wharf

This is an impressive development of modern apartments, shops, offices, restaurants, a hotel and a marina. It is near the site of Cremorne Pleasure Gardens, which closed in 1877 after more than 40 years as a venue for dances and circuses. The centrepiece of the harbour is the Belvedere, a 20-storey apartment tower with an external glass lift and a pyramid roof, topped with a golden ball on a rod that rises and falls with the tide.

9

Battersea Park

📍F10 🏠Albert Bridge Rd SW11 🚇Sloane Square then bus 137 🚆Battersea Park ⏰6:30am-10:30pm daily 🌐wandsworth.gov.uk/batterseapark

This was the second public park created to relieve the growing urban stresses of

EAT

Mother
The hip Copenhagen pizza joint has opened under the hangar-like railway arch in Circus West Village.

📍G10 🏠Circus West Village SW11 🌐mother restaurant.co.uk

££££

Medlar
Refined French cuisine in a romantic, low-key environment. Good fixed-price menus.

📍C10 🏠438 King's Rd SW10 🌐medlar restaurant.co.uk

££££

The Builder's Arms
Smart neighbourhood pub serving traditional British food. It's a congenial place to drink too.

📍E9 🏠13 Britten St SW3 🌐thebuildersarms chelsea.co.uk

££££

← The Great Hall at the Royal Hospital Chelsea, laid out for the Pensioners' lunch

Victorian Londoners – the first was Victoria Park (*p322*) in the East End. It opened in 1858 on the former Battersea Fields, a swampy area notorious for vice centred on the Old Red House, a disreputable pub.

The new park was immediately popular, especially for its man-made boating lake, with its romantic rocks, gardens and waterfalls. In 1985, the Peace Pagoda was unveiled – a 35-m- (100-ft-) high monument built by Japanese Buddhist nuns and monks and presented to the park as a gift. There is also an excellent children's zoo (entry fee), a playground, sports activities and an art gallery, the Pumphouse.

BATTERSEA POWER STATION

This is one of the London landmarks least known to visitors but best known to locals - and, of course, to Pink Floyd fans: the monstrous industrial building with its four towering smoke stacks graces the cover of their album *Animals*. Since it was decommissioned in 1983, numerous proposals for its redevelopment have come and gone. Now, finally, the colossal Grade II-listed structure is coming back into use. A new riverside park, an extension to the Thames Path, a new Tube station and a myriad of restaurants, shops and pricey housing all form part of the new district already visibly emerging.

10

St Mary's, Battersea

D10 **Battersea Church Rd SW11** **Sloane Sq then bus 19 or 219** **For services & by arrangement** **stmarysbattersea.org.uk**

There has been a church here since at least the 10th century. The present brick building dates from 1775, but the

17th-century stained glass, commemorating Tudor monarchs, comes from the former church. In 1782, the poet and artist William Blake was married in the church. Later, J M W Turner painted views of the Thames from the church tower. Benedict Arnold, who served George Washington in the American War of Independence but defected to the British side, is buried here in the crypt.

Circus West Village

G10 **Battersea Power Station** **Sloane Sq then bus 452 or 137** **Battersea Power Station** **batterseapowerstation.co.uk**

Most easily reached by boat, Circus West is the first stage of the gargantuan redevelopment of Battersea Power Station, part of the regeneration of riverside land stretching between Battersea Park and Vauxhall in between the towering power station and the train lines heading into Victoria Station. Its ongoing development, though certainly commercially driven, just about bridges the gap between the independent and corporate business worlds.

An interesting mix of restaurants, bars and shops have been installed inside the railway arches and by the new-builds gathering around the site, including a brewpub, cinema and the Village Hall performance venue.

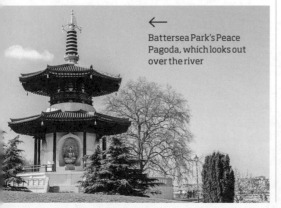

← Battersea Park's Peace Pagoda, which looks out over the river

SOUTH KENSINGTON AND KNIGHTSBRIDGE

The tone was set for Kensington from the late 17th century when William III and Mary II bought Kensington Palace. With the arrival of the royal court it soon became a highly desirable residential area, as it still is today, attracting the wealthy as well as those who sought to sell them goods. It remained largely rural until the late 18th century when a period of urban expansion slowly began, with Knightsbridge among the first spots to be developed. It was in the 1850s that the pace of transformation really exploded, the fuse lit by the Great Exhibition of 1851. Held in Hyde Park, the exhibition was the brainchild of Queen Victoria's husband, Prince Albert, who sought to demonstrate and promote British industry and invention. It was a huge success and the profits were ploughed into the creation of a permanent showcase for the arts and sciences in South Kensington. The great museums, the Royal Albert Hall and the Royal Colleges of Art and Music are all part of that legacy.

A B C

WESTBOURNE GROVE

BAYSWATER

PORCHESTER GARDENS

Bayswater

KENSINGTON,
HOLLAND PARK
AND NOTTING HILL
p260

Queensway

BAYSWATER ROAD

The Fountains

Lancaster Gate

NOTTING HILL GATE

Notting Hill Gate

12 The Diana, Princess of Wales Memorial Playground

Peter Pan Statue

The Long Water

KENSINGTON PALACE GARDENS

11 Kensington Gardens

6

THE BROAD WALK

Round Pond

LANCASTER WALK

KENSINGTON CHURCH ST

Kensington Palace **10**

Serpentine Gallery **9**

PALACE AVENUE

HOLLAND ST

FLOWER WALK

Albert Memorial **8**

KENSINGTON ROAD

PALACE GREEN

Royal College of Art **6**

Royal Albert Hall **7**

KENSINGT

PALACE GATE

HYDE PARK GATE

QUEENS GATE

JAY MEWS

EXHIBITION

7

SOUTH KENSINGTON AND KNIGHTSBRIDGE

PRINCE CONSORT ROAD

KENSINGTON GATE

QUEEN'S GATE MEWS

Royal College of Music **5**

ROAD

PRI

QUEEN'S GATE TERRACE

IMPERIAL COLLEGE ROAD

Science Museum **3**

Must Sees
1 Victoria and Albert Museum
2 Natural History Museum
3 Science Museum

GLOUCESTER

ELVASTON PLACE

QUEEN'S GATE GARDENS

QUEEN'S GATE

Natural History Museum **2**

GARDENS

Experience More
4 Brompton Oratory
5 Royal College of Music
6 Royal College of Art
7 Royal Albert Hall
8 Albert Memorial
9 Serpentine Galleries
10 Kensington Palace
11 Kensington Gardens
12 The Diana, Princess of Wales Memorial Playground
13 Marble Arch
14 Hyde Park
15 Speakers' Corner

ROAD

CROMWELL

CROMWELL PLACE

8

Gloucester Road

QUEEN'S GATE GARDENS

STANHOPE MEWS EAST

STANHOPE GARDENS

SOUTH KENSINGTON

GLOUCESTER

STANHOPE GARDENS

CLAREVILLE STREET

OLD BROMPTON ROAD

SUNNE

Shop
① Harrods

9

ROLAND GARDENS

ONSLOW GARDENS

FOULIS TERRACE

CRANLEY GARDENS

FULHAM RO

C

D

E

F

5

6

7

8

9

BAYSWATER

HYDE PARK STREET

CONNAUGHT STREET

SEYMOUR STREET

EDGWARE RD

Bond Street

Marble Arch

ROAD

CUMBERLAND GATE

Marble Arch ⑬

PARK STREET

NORTH AUDLEY ST

DUKE STREET

THE RING

Speakers' Corner ⑮

BROOK GATE

MAYFAIR AND ST JAMES'S
p86

SOUTH AUDLEY STREET

HILL

THE RING WALK

Hyde Park ⑭

GROSVENOR GATE

PARK LANE

MAYFAIR

⑨ Serpentine Sackler Gallery

SERPENTINE ROAD

The Serpentine

SERPENTINE ROAD

HAMILTON PL

Diana, Princess of Wales Memorial Fountain

Apsley House

ROTTEN ROW

ROTTEN ROW

Hyde Park Corner

Wellington Arch

ROAD

SOUTH CARRIAGE DRIVE

KNIGHTSBRIDGE

GROSVENOR PLACE

Wellington Arch

ismore rdens

KNIGHTSBRIDGE

Knightsbridge

KINNERTON ST

GROSVENOR CRESCENT

HALKIN STREET

HEADFORT PLACE

ENNISMORE GARDENS

RUTLAND GATE

KNIGHTSBRIDGE

TREVOR SQUARE

HARRIET WALK

LOWNDES SQUARE

WILTON PLACE

WILTON ROW

WILTON CRES

MONTROSE PLACE

CHAPEL STREET

GDNS

ENNISMORE GDNS MEWS

RUTLAND GATE

MONTPELIER SQUARE

TREVOR PLACE

BASIL STREET

MOTCOMB ST

BELGRAVE SQUARE

BELGRAVIA

UPPER BELGRAVE ST

EWS

MONTPELIER STREET

MONTPELIER PLACE

LANCELOT PLACE

Harrods ①

HANS CRESCENT

PAVILION RD

CADOGAN PLACE

BELGRAVE MEWS WEST

LOWNDES ST

CHESHAM PL

BELGRAVE PLACE

Brompton Oratory ④

CHEVAL PLACE

BROMPTON SQUARE

BROMPTON ROAD

BEAUCHAMP PL

OVINGTON GDNS

WALTON PLACE

HANS PLACE

PONT STREET

CHESHAM STREET

EATON

ictoria and ert Museum ①

YEOMAN'S ROW

EGERTON GDNS

BROMPTON ROAD

EGERTON TERR

SLOANE STREET

CADOGAN PLACE

EATON SQUARE

RLOE PLACE

THURLOE SQUARE

ALEXANDER PLACE

WALTON STREET

SLOANE STREET

ELIZABETH STREET

ch sington

SOUTH TERRACE

CHELSEA AND BATTERSEA
p230

CADOGAN GARDENS

HAM STREET

PELHAM CRES

FULHAM ROAD

ELYSTAN STREET

DRAYCOTT AVENUE

SLOANE AVENUE

CADOGAN

SOUTH KENSINGTON AND KNIGHTSBRIDGE

SYDNEY STREET

0 metres 400

0 yards 400

N ↑

1 ⓂⓎ🖥🛍

VICTORIA AND ALBERT MUSEUM

📍D8 🏛Cromwell Road SW7 🚇South Kensington 🕐10am–5.45pm daily (till 10pm Fri) 🗓24–26 Dec 🌐vam.ac.uk

Housed in Victorian splendour, as well as modern state-of-the-art galleries, the V&A is the world's leading museum of art and design, with its collection spanning 5,000 years of furniture, glass, textiles, fashion, ceramics and jewellery.

EXPERIENCE South Kensington and Knightsbridge

The Victoria and Albert Museum (V&A) contains one of the world's broadest collections of art and design, with exhibits ranging from early Christian devotional objects to cutting-edge furniture. Originally founded in 1852 to inspire design students as the Museum of Manufactures, it was renamed by Queen Victoria in 1899 in memory of Prince Albert. The museum has undergone extensive renovation since the early 2000s, including the opening in 2017 of a new quarter on Exhibition Road, encompassing the Sackler Courtyard and the underground Sainsbury Gallery, and an expanded Photography Centre in 2018.

↑ The grand Cromwell Road entrance to the V&A

←

The welcoming neon information desk at the museum

GALLERY GUIDE

The V&A has six levels. Level 1 houses the China, Japan and South Asia galleries, the Fashion Gallery and the Cast Courts. The British Galleries are on Levels 2 and 4. Level 3 contains the 20th Century galleries and silver, ironwork, paintings and photography. The glass display is on Level 4. The Ceramics Galleries and Furniture are on Level 6. The fantastic European galleries from 300 to 1815 are on Level 1.

↑ The reading room of the National Art Library in the V&A

Did You Know?

The V&A was the first museum to have its own restaurant. The original refreshment rooms are still in use today.

↑ Large-scale works that were once part of buildings in the Medieval & Renaissance Gallery

British Galleries

A sequence of grand rooms starting on Level 2 and continuing on Level 4 are devoted to British design and decorative arts from 1500 to 1900. The luxurious galleries chart Britain's rise from obscure island to "workshop of the world".

The galleries present the evolution of British design and the numerous influences, whether technological or aesthetic, it has absorbed from all over the world. Beautiful textiles, furniture, costumes and household objects illustrate the tastes and lifestyles of the country's ruling classes. Among the highlights are the opulent State Bed from Melville House, and a number of carefully preserved period rooms, including the stunning Rococo Norfolk House Music Room. Discovery Areas give visitors a chance to delve even deeper into the past by trying on a hoop or petticoat or viewing 3D images through a Victorian stereoscope.

Asia: China, Japan, Middle East and South Asia

The Jameel Gallery of Islamic Art in Room 42 houses a collection of objects from the early days of the Caliphs in the 7th century through to the years preceding World

Vibrant examples of stained glass in the Sacred Silver and Stained Glass galleries ↑

War I. Beautifully crafted ceramics, textiles, metalwork and glass from Iran, Egypt and Turkey show the Islamic influence on fine and decorative arts. The vast sixteenth-century Ardabil Carpet, one of the largest, oldest and most intricate in the world, is the key exhibit. Next door, the famous Tipu's Tiger automaton from Mysore and Ranjit Singh's sheet-gold-decorated throne are the highlights of the extensive South Asia collection, which ranges across 400 years from the Mughal emperors to the Raj. The China collection encompasses rare jade and ceramics pieces and a fine collection of Buddhas, dating back to the 6th century, while Japanese art is concentrated in the gallery in Room 45,

and is particularly notable for lacquerware, Samurai armour and woodblock prints.

Architecture Gallery

The Architecture Gallery features drawings, models, photographs and architectural fragments from the V&A and the Royal Institute of British Architects (RIBA) in both permanent displays and temporary exhibitions.

A superb collection of artifacts and illustrations from around the world explores key themes, such as construction techniques and the role of public buildings. Don't miss the detailed architectural scale models, including a traditional Japanese house, Modernist constructions from Ernö Goldfinger and others, and Charles Barry's Gothic plans for the Palace of Westminster, though models are often out on loan.

Europe

Ten galleries, occupying an entire wing of the museum, house some of the world's greatest treasures of medieval and Renaissance Europe. Among the many remarkable exhibits are the notebooks of Leonardo da Vinci; sculptures by Italian masters such as Donatello and Giambologna, some set in a Renaissance courtyard garden setting; the fine enamel Becket Casket (c 1180);

↑ Ancient kimonos on display in the Toshiba Gallery of Japanese Art and the reconstructed Santa Chiara Chapel, the only one of its kind outside Italy on Level 1.

The Europe collection continues in the Level 0 galleries of the opposite wing, which cover the period 1600 to 1815, and include several recreated period rooms. Room 48a on the ground floor is dedicated to the famous Raphael Cartoons – huge designs for tapestries planned for the Sistine Chapel, dating from 1515.

Another of the most famous sights at the V&A are the extraordinary Cast Courts, which have been part of the museum since its founding. They house large plaster casts of major European sculptures, such as Rome's Trajan's Column (in two pieces) and a 5-m- (16-ft-) tall reproduction of Michaelangelo's *David*, created so that visitors to the museum could see these works without travelling.

Fashion and Textiles

The popular Fashion Gallery displays items from the largest and most comprehensive collection of dress in the world. Around 100 exhibits spanning more than 250 years are arranged chronologically. They feature a magnificent mantua from the 1750s, an 1850s wedding dress with veil and shoes, a Schiaparelli evening coat embroidered with a design

→
Enamelled casket depicting the murder of Thomas Becket

by Jean Cocteau, elegant ballgowns from the 1950s; and stunning dresses from Alexander McQueen. Textiles are also found throughout the museum's collections; the Japanese gallery in particular has some exquisite kimonos and other traditional textiles.

Materials and Techniques

This group of galleries is located on Level 3. In the Silver Galleries, 3,500 pieces from 1400 to the present day are displayed in the beautifully refurbished Victorian Rooms 65 to 69. The Gilbert Collection of gold, silver and micromosaics is in Rooms 70–73.

English landscapes feature among the works in the Paintings galleries (Rooms 81, 82, 87 and 88), including scenes by Turner. The Sacred Silver and Stained Glass galleries situated in Rooms 83 and 84 display devotional treasures. The highlight of the Ironwork galleries (Rooms 113 to 114e), is the Hereford Screen, a choir screen designed by Sir George Gilbert Scott in 1862. The dazzling screen became the V&A's largest-ever conservation project.

In the Photography Centre (Rooms 99–101), there are changing displays drawn from the museum's collection of images, and you can handle antique cameras such as a 1920s Kodak Brownie.

Glass and Ceramics

The museum has the most comprehensive collection of glass and ceramics in the world. Examples of glass covering 2,000 years are largely housed in Room 131, which has a stunning glass balustrade on the staircase and mezzanine by artist Danny Lane. Displays of international contemporary glass are on display in this room and in Room 129.

The ceramics collection has an introductory gallery presenting the history and development of ceramics across the world. All of the major British pottery factories are represented.

Alexander McQueen's animal print dress Plato's Atlantis, from 2010

 HIDDEN GEM
Relax and Refresh

Be sure to visit the museum's original refreshment rooms off Room 16a (one of which was designed by William Morris). If the weather is good, don't miss a wander in the John Madejski Garden, with a coffee in hand, or pausing for breath at the Courtyard Café.

② 🖼 🍴 ☕ 🛍

NATURAL HISTORY MUSEUM

📍 D8 🏛 Cromwell Rd SW7 🚇 South Kensington 🕐 10am–5:50pm daily (till 10pm last Fri of month), last admission 5:30pm 🚫 24–26 Dec 🌐 nhm.ac.uk

A paradise for budding botanists, explorers and geologists, the superlative Natural History Museum, with its specimens, skeletons and simulators, is quite simply a national treasure and an absolute must for any visitor to the capital.

Using interactive techniques and traditional displays, life on earth and the earth itself are vividly explained at this awe-inspiring museum. And the building that houses the vast collection is a masterpiece in itself. Founded as just several of the Victorian temples to learning, it opened in 1881 and was designed by Alfred Waterhouse using revolutionary building techniques. It is built on an iron and steel framework concealed behind arches and columns, richly decorated with sculptures of plants and animals.

The museum is divided into four zones, plus the Hintze Hall, the grand centrepiece of the building dominated by a huge skeleton of a blue whale. In the Blue Zone discover Human Biology, Mammals, Dinosaurs and Images of Nature. The Green Zone has Creepy Crawlies, Fossils and the Vault. The giant escalator in the Earth Hall leads through a stunning globe to Red Zone highlights Restless Surface and Earth's Treasury. The Orange Zone includes the Darwin Centre's Cocoon and, outside, the Wildlife Garden.

① The elegant museum is set in grounds that include a peaceful wildlife garden.

② One of the museum's impressively lifelike animatronic models, a *T. rex* lurches and roars in this popular gallery. Exhibits of fossilized skeletons and eggs are also on display.

③ Life-size models are a major attraction in the vast Mammals gallery.

2   3

TOP 5 UNMISSIBLE EXHIBITS

Triceratops Skull
The gigantic skull of a plant-eating three-horned dinosaur.

Latrobe Gold Nugget
A rare crystallized gold nugget from Australia weighing 717 g (25 oz).

Butterflies
A tropical butterfly house open from March to September.

Archaeopteryx
This valuable fossil of a feathered dinosaur provided the link between birds and dinosaurs.

Earthquake Simulator
Experience the effects of an earthquake in this simulation.

Did You Know?

Kids can spend a night at the museum at Dino Snores, a monthly event for those aged 7–11

↑ The 25.5-m- (84-ft-) long skeleton of "Hope", the blue whale hanging over Hintze Hall

3 ⓧ 🍴 📷 🛍️

SCIENCE MUSEUM

📍 D8 🚪 Exhibition Rd SW7 🚇 South Kensington 🕐 10am–6pm daily (last entry 5:15pm) 📅 24–26 Dec 🌐 sciencemuseum.org.uk

Centuries of continuing scientific and technological innovation lie at the heart of the Science Museum's huge collection. Discover the science fact behind science fiction and explore humanity's achievements so far – and where we might be heading next.

From steam engines to aeroengines, space-craft to the first computers, this museum has a vast range of scientific objects. Equally important is the social context of science – what discoveries and inventions mean for day-to-day life – and the process of discovery itself. The high-tech Wellcome Wing has hands-on displays, an IMAX cinema, a 3D theatre and galleries devoted to scientific advancements.

The Science Museum's exhibits are spread over five floors. The Wellcome Wing, with four floors of interactive technology, is at the west end of the museum, accessible from the ground floor and third floor of the main building. The museum is undergoing renovations, with the spectacular new Medicine Galleries set to open on the first floor in autumn 2019; check the website for up-to-date information before you visit.

↑ The unassuming exterior of the fascinating Science Museum

💬 INSIDER TIP
Get Some Air

Though there are several places to eat in the museum, pack a picnic and walk five minutes to Hyde Park – a perfect place for kids to let off some steam.

↑ Early flying machines and fighter planes suspended over the Flight and Fly Zone galleries on the third floor

→ A child enjoying the hands-on exhibits in the immersive and imaginative Wonderlab, which has over 50 mind-boggling exhibits, shows and demonstrations

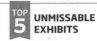

TOP 5 UNMISSABLE EXHIBITS

Apollo 10
US astronauts orbited the moon in May 1969 in the Apollo 10 capsule.

Who Am I?
Explore how your genetics and your upbringing make you who you are.

Flight Simulator
An adrenaline ride with high-definition 3D and motion effects.

Space Descent VR
A virtual reality 400-km (250-mile) journey from space back to earth.

The Garden
Hands-on galleries for younger children.

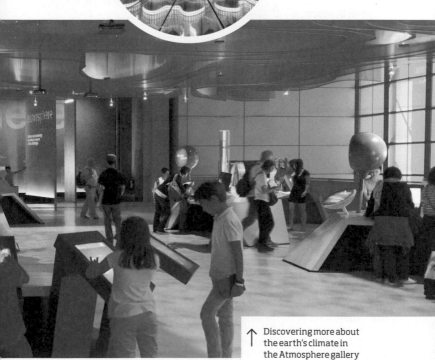

↑ Discovering more about the earth's climate in the Atmosphere gallery

←

The soaring interior of the Brompton Oratory, rich in Italianate decoration

Royal College of Art

C7 **Kensington Gore SW7** **High St Kensington, South Kensington** **For exhibitions, lectures, film screenings** **rca.ac.uk**

Sir Hugh Casson's mainly glass-fronted building (1962) is in stark contrast to the Victoriana around it. The college was founded in 1837 to teach design and practical art for the manufacturing industries. It became noted for modern art in the 1950s and 1960s, when David Hockney, Peter Blake and Eduardo Paolozzi attended.

EXPERIENCE MORE

Brompton Oratory

D8 **Brompton Rd SW7** **South Kensington, Knightsbridge** **6:30am-8pm daily (till 7:45pm Sat, from 8am Sun)** **bromptonoratory.co.uk**

Famous for its splendid musical tradition, the Italianate Oratory is a rich (some think a little too rich) monument to the English Catholic revival of the late 19th century, established by John Henry Newman (later Cardinal Newman).

The church was opened in 1884; its façade and dome were added in the 1890s, and the interior has been progressively enriched ever since. Inside, all the most eye-catching treasures predate the church – many of them were brought here from Italian churches. Giuseppe Mazzuoli carved the huge marble figures of the 12 apostles for Siena Cathedral in the late 17th century. The beautiful Lady Altar was originally created in 1693 for the Dominican church in Brescia, and the 18th-century altar in St Wilfrid's Chapel came from a church in Rochefort, Belgium.

Royal College of Music

C7 **Prince Consort Rd SW7** **South Kensington** **rcm.ac.uk**

Sir Arthur Blomfield designed the turreted Gothic palace, with Bavarian overtones, that has housed this distinguished institution since 1894. Pupils have included the composers Benjamin Britten and Ralph Vaughan Williams. The RCM is currently undergoing a £40 million redevelopment, which will include two extra performance venues and a reimagined museum (closed till 2020). Check the website for details of concerts and masterclasses hosted by the college.

Royal Albert Hall

C7 **Kensington Gore SW7** **High St Kensington, South Kensington** **For tours & performances daily** **royalalberthall.com**

Completed in 1871, this huge concert hall was modelled on

Roman amphitheatres. On the elegant red-brick exterior the only ostentation is a frieze symbolizing the triumph of arts and science. Originally planned as the Hall of Arts and Science, Queen Victoria renamed it in memory of her husband when she laid the foundation stone in 1868.

The hall is often used for classical concerts, such as the "Proms", but it also hosts other large events, like rock concerts and comedy shows. In preparation for its 150th anniversary in 2021, the hall is undergoing renovation, with a two-storey basement under excavation, but remains open.

8

Albert Memorial

📍 C7 ⬛ South Carriage Drive, Kensington Gdns SW7 ☻ High St Kensington, South Kensington
🌐 royalparks.org.uk

This grand Gothic Revival memorial to Prince Albert, Queen Victoria's beloved consort, was completed in 1872, 11 years after his death. Fittingly, it is near the site of the 1851 Exhibition, which Albert co-organized. The statue, by John Foley, shows him with an exhibition catalogue on his knee.

The Queen chose Sir George Gilbert Scott to design the monument, which stands 55 m (175 ft) high. It is loosely based on a medieval market cross – although considerably more elaborate, with a black and gilded spire, multi-coloured marble canopy, stones, mosaics, enamels, wrought iron and nearly 200 sculpted figures.

Having turned black over the years from pollution, the statue underwent a four-year renovation, and was unveiled in 1998 by Queen Elizabeth II.

Did You Know?

There are 169 carvings of notable figures from the arts in the frieze around the Albert Memorial.

---

9 🍴 🖥 🛍

Serpentine Galleries

📍 D6 ⬛ Kensington Gdns W2 ☻ Lancaster Gate, South Kensington
🕐 10am–6pm Tue–Sun
🚫 24–26 Dec & between exhibitions 🌐 serpentine galleries.org

The Serpentine Gallery houses temporary exhibitions of major and rising contemporary artists' and architects' work, excitingly transforming its space to suit the exhibits. Every summer, a temporary pavilion is commissioned from a major architect. A second building, the Serpentine Sackler Gallery, in a former gunpowder store a 5-minute walk away, displays similarly ambitious exhibits. An extension, designed by the late Zaha Hadid, houses the Chucs restaurant, and there is also an art bookshop.

The Royal Albert Hall, home to musical events across a wide variety of genres ↑

The magnificent Royal Albert Hall in South Kensington

10

Kensington Palace

📍B6 🏛Kensington Palace Gardens W8 🚇High St Kensington, Queensway, Notting Hill Gate 🕐Mar–Oct: 10am–6pm daily; Nov–Feb: 10am–4pm daily (last adm: 1 hr before closing) 🌐hrp.org.uk

Half of this spacious palace is used as royal apartments; the other half, which includes the 18th-century state rooms, is open to the public. When William of Orange and his wife Mary came to the throne in 1689, they bought a mansion, dating from 1605, and commissioned Christopher Wren to convert it into a royal palace.

The palace has seen some important royal events. In 1714, Queen Anne died here from apoplexy brought on by overeating and, on 20 June 1837, Princess Victoria of Kent was woken at 5am to be told that her uncle William IV had died and she was now queen – the start of her 64-year reign. After the death in 1997 of Diana, Princess of Wales, the gold gates to the south were deluged with bouquets in their thousands.

Visitors can explore inside the King's and Queen's state apartments, the latter little changed since it was designed for Mary in the 17th century. The palace also often displays clothes worn by many of the royals, including the Queen and Princess Diana.

11

Kensington Gardens

📍C6 🏛W8 🚇Bayswater, High St Kensington, Queensway, Lancaster Gate 🕐6am–dusk daily 🌐royalparks.org.uk

The former grounds of Kensington Palace became a public park in 1841. The gardens are full of charm, starting with Sir George Frampton's statue (1912) of J M Barrie's fictional Peter Pan, playing his pipes for the bronze fairies and animals that cling to the column below. Just north of here are many lovely ornamental fountains and statues, while to the south is George Frederick Watts' muscular horse and rider, *Physical Energy*.

Close by is a summer house designed by William Kent in 1735. The Round Pond, built in 1728, is often packed with model boats navigated by enthusiasts young and old.

In the north, near Lancaster Gate, is a dogs' cemetery, created in 1880 by the then Duke of Cambridge.

→

Passing the time aboard a rowing boat on Hyde Park's Serpentine

12

The Diana, Princess of Wales Memorial Playground

📍B6 🏛Kensington Gardens 🚇Bayswater, Queensway 🕐Daily, from 10am; closing times vary, from 4:45pm in midwinter to 7:45pm in midsummer 🌐royalparks.org.uk

The newest of Kensington Gardens' three playgrounds, on the site of an earlier playground funded by J M Barrie, takes the boy who didn't want to grow up as its theme and includes a beach cove with a 15-m (50-ft) pirates' galleon, a treehouse and a mermaid's fountain with a slumbering crocodile. Though all children under 13 must be accompanied by an adult, staff are on hand too. Many features of the playground are accessible to children with specific needs.

←

The sunken garden with reflecting pool adjoining Kensington Palace

⑬

Marble Arch

📍E5 🅰️Park Lane W1 🚇Marble Arch

John Nash designed the arch in 1827 as the main entrance to Buckingham Palace. It was, however, too narrow for the grandest coaches and in 1851 it was moved here. Historically, only senior members of the royal family and one of the royal artillery regiments are allowed to pass under it.

The arch stands near the site of the old Tyburn gallows, where until 1783 the city's most notorious criminals were hanged in front of crowds of bloodthirsty spectators.

⑭

Hyde Park

📍E6 🅰️W2 🚇Hyde Park Corner, Knightsbridge, Lancaster Gate, Marble Arch ⏰5am–midnight daily 🌐royalparks.org.uk

The ancient manor of Hyde was part of the lands of Westminster Abbey seized by Henry VIII on the Dissolution of the Monasteries in 1536. It has remained a royal park ever since. Henry used it for hunting, but James I opened it to the public in the early 17th century. The Serpentine, an artificial lake used for boating and bathing, was created when Caroline, George II's queen, dammed the flow of the Westbourne River in 1730. The Princess Diana Memorial Fountain is to the south of the Serpentine.

In its time, the park has been a venue for duelling, horse racing, demonstrations and musical performances. The 1851 Great Exhibition was held here in a vast glass palace. Come Christmas time, the festive Winter Wonderland takes over, with markets, an ice rink and a funfair.

↑ The Isis statue, one of the most recent additions to Hyde Park's statuary and buildings

⑮

Speakers' Corner

📍E5 🅰️Hyde Park W2 🚇Marble Arch

An 1872 law made it legal for anyone to assemble an audience and address them on whatever topic they chose. Since then, this corner of Hyde Park has become the established venue for budding public orators and a fair number of eccentrics. On Sunday mornings, speakers from fringe groups and one-member political parties reveal their plans for the betterment of humanity (or otherwise) while assembled onlookers heckle them.

A SHORT WALK
SOUTH KENSINGTON

Distance 2 km (1.5 miles) **Nearest Tube** South Kensington **Time** 30 minutes

This area is characterized by its world-renowned museums, which are housed in grandiose buildings celebrating Victorian self-confidence. Take a stroll from the Albert Memorial in Hyde Park, past the Royal Albert Hall, to the Victoria and Albert Museum and admire the monuments to the royal couple that made London a world capital of industry and knowledge.

David Hockney and Peter Blake are among the great artists who trained at the Royal College of Art (p252).

The former Royal College of Organists was decorated by F W Moody in 1876.

Opened in 1870, the Royal Albert Hall has a beautiful curved exterior (p252).

Historic musical instruments are exhibited at the Royal College of Music (p252).

Did You Know?

The Royal Albert Hall was partly funded by selling seats on a 999-year lease.

PRINCE

CONS

IMPERIAL COLLEGE ROAD

EXHIBIT

The Natural History Museum houses everything from dinosaurs to butterflies (p248).

CROMWELL ROAD

Visitors can experiment with interactive displays at the Science Museum (p250).

FINISH

CROMWE

| 0 metres | 100 |
| 0 yards | 100 |

N

START

The Albert Memorial was built to commemorate Queen Victoria's consort (p253).

The Albert Hall Mansions, built by Norman Shaw in 1879, started a fashion for red brick.

KENSINGTON GORE

ALBERT COURT ROAD

The Royal Geographical Society was founded in 1830. Scottish missionary and explorer David Livingstone (1813–73) was a member.

Locator Map
For more detail see p242

SOUTH KENSINGTON AND KNIGHTSBRIDGE

Imperial College is one of the country's leading scientific institutions.

ROAD

PRINCE'S GARDENS

A wealth of objects from around the globe illustrate a rich history of design and decoration at the Victoria and Albert Museum (p244).

Holy Trinity church dates from the 19th century and is located among cottages in a calm backwater.

↑ The gilded Albert Memorial gleams in the sunshine

The Brompton Oratory was built during the 19th-century Catholic revival (p252).

Brompton Square, begun in 1821, established this as a fashionable residential area.

ARDENS

KENSINGTON, HOLLAND PARK AND NOTTING HILL

Kensington remained a country village of market gardens and mansions until the 1830s. Outstanding among these mansions was Holland House, part of whose grounds are now Holland Park. The area grew up rapidly in the mid 19th century and most of its buildings date from then – mainly expensive apartments, mansion flats and fashionable shops. It was during that century that a slew of famous artists and writers settled in the area, notable among them Henry James, William Thackeray, Edward Linley Sambourne and Lord Leighton, the striking homes of the latter two, 18 Stafford Terrace and Leighton House, now open to the public. It was also during the 19th century that Notting Hill emerged as a suburb, initially attracting well-to-do residents in much the same vein as elsewhere in Kensington. By the end of World War II, however, many of the stuccoed terraced houses had been converted to multiple-occupancy tenements. They became homes, during the 1950s, to West Indian immigrant families who began arriving in the area in large numbers – their presence spawned the first Notting Hill Carnival, in 1965.

KENSINGTON, HOLLAND PARK AND NOTTING HILL

Must See

① Design Museum

Experience More

② Portobello Road
③ Holland Park
④ 18 Stafford Terrace
⑤ Leighton House
⑥ High Street Kensington
⑦ Little Venice
⑧ Notting Hill
⑨ Museum of Brands, Packaging and Advertising
⑩ St Sophia's Cathedral
⑪ Kensington Square

Eat

① Montparnasse Café
② Café Tarte
③ Holland Park Café
④ Candella
⑤ The Muffin Man Tea Shop

Stay

⑥ The Main House

REGENT'S PARK AND MARYLEBONE p274

SOUTH KENSINGTON AND KNIGHTSBRIDGE p240

1 🍴 🖥 🛍

DESIGN MUSEUM

📍 A7 🏠 224-8 Kensington High St W8 🚇 Kensington High St, Holland Park 🕐 10am-6pm daily (last entry 5pm) and till 8pm on first Fri of every month (last entry 7pm) 🌐 designmuseum.org

The Design Museum, housed in a truly unique building, is dedicated to every element of contemporary design, including architecture, transport, graphics, furniture and fashion. Its imaginatively curated temporary exhibitions usually outshine its rather small but nevertheless engaging permanent display.

Appropriately housed in what was the Commonwealth Institute, an inventively designed 1960s building, the Design Museum reopened in 2016, having moved from its previous riverside location near Tower Bridge. The building itself is a joy to behold, with its arresting interior of sweeping spaces and geometric lines all crowned by a dramatically cascading roof. Famed for this copper-plated hyperbolic parabol, the exterior was kept intact, but the interior completely re-fashioned. There is room enough for four galleries – three of them for the superlative programme of temporary exhibitions and one to house the excellent and occasionally interactive permanent collection, called Designer Maker User, which is free to explore.

The building also houses a lecture theatre, café and two appealing shops. The beautiful green woodland of Holland Park is right next door.

SHOP

Designer Shopping
The Design Museum shop is one of the best museum shops in London for the originality and diversity of its carefully selected stock. Items include clothing, stylish stationery, models and miniatures, prints, kitchenware and more.

Exhibits displayed beneath the museum's remarkable roof ↓

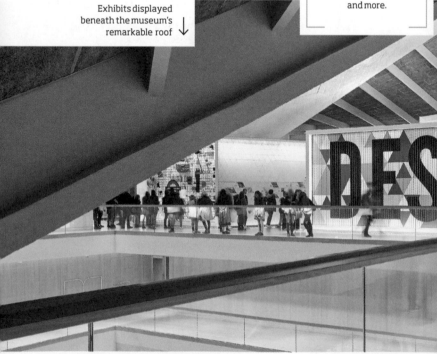

GALLERY GUIDE

The permanent exhibition, called Designer Maker User, examines some of the most iconic product designs of the modern world. It also shows a cross-section of recent innovations from the three perspectives of its title.

1 Attractive displays of innovative design feature in the permanent collection.

2 The Grade II-listed building has an unusual sweeping roof design.

3 The Design Museum is housed in the former Commonwealth Institute building, which was originally opened in 1962.

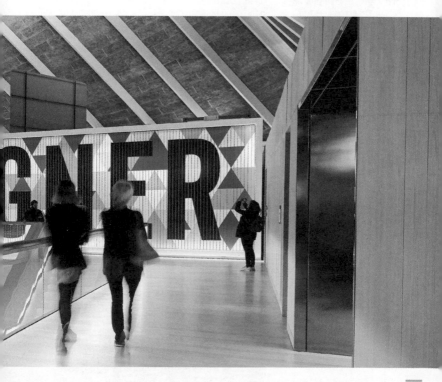

EXPERIENCE MORE

②
Portobello Road

⑨A5 ⚑W11 ⊖Notting Hill Gate, Ladbroke Grove ⏰Main market: 9am-7pm Fri & Sat; general market, bric-a-brac: 9am-6pm Mon-Wed & 9am-1pm Thu ⓦportobelloroad.co.uk

There has been a market here since 1837. Today the southern end of the road consists mostly of stalls that sell antiques, jewellery, souvenirs and other collectables. The market is extremely popular and tends to be very crowded, but it is well worth visiting, if only to experience its bustling, cheerful atmosphere. The busiest day is Saturday, when the antiques arcades are open. If you are looking for bargains, be warned – the stallholders have a sound idea of the value of what they are selling. Other markets run along the rest of the street on different days, with vintage and new clothes featured around Portobello Green, under Westway near Ladbroke Grove Tube (Fri–Sun).

③
Holland Park

⑨A7 ⚑Ilchester Place, W8 ⊖Holland Park, High Street Kensington, Notting Hill Gate ⏰7:30am-dusk daily (hours vary with season) ⓦrbkc.gov.uk

This small but delightful park, more wooded and intimate than the large royal parks to its east, Hyde Park *(p257)* and Kensington Gardens *(p256)*, was opened in 1952 on what remained of the grounds of the Jacobean Holland House – the rest had been sold off in the late 19th century for the construction of new, large houses. During its heyday in the 19th century, the mansion was a noted centre of social and political intrigue. Statesmen such as Charles James Fox mixed here with the likes of the poet Lord Byron, who met Lady Caroline Lamb here.

The house suffered heavy bomb damage during World War II, but surviving parts and outbuildings have been put to various uses: exhibitions are held in the orangery and the ice house, and the old Garden Ballroom is now a restaurant. The former front terrace of the house is often used as a backdrop for summer musical events and open-air film screenings, and theatre, opera and dance performances.

The park still contains some of the formal gardens laid out in the early 19th century. Surprisingly, there is also a Japanese garden, created for the 1991 London Festival of Japan. Look out for koi carp in the pond beneath the waterfall. Colourful peacocks roam the grounds here, and there is a well-equipped playground perfect for kids to while away an afternoon in.

Did You Know?

Lord Leighton held Britain's shortest peerage: made a baron on 24 January 1896 – he died the next day.

④
18 Stafford Terrace

⑨A7 ⚑W8 ⊖High St Kensington ⏰Wed, Sat & Sun; tours 11am, open access 2-5pm ⓦrbkc.gov.uk/subsites/museums.aspx

The former home of Linley Sambourne, built in about 1870, remains much as Sambourne furnished it – in the Victorian manner, with Oriental ornaments and heavy velvet curtains. Some rooms have William Morris wallpaper. Sambourne was a cartoonist for the satirical magazine *Punch*; drawings cram the walls of the house. It's advisable to book tours ahead.

↑ Exquisite tilework in Eastern style in Leighton House's Arab Hall

5 Leighton House

⚲ A7 🏠 12 Holland Park Rd W14 🚇 High St Kensington 🕐 10am-5:30pm Wed-Mon 🌐 rbkc.gov.uk/subsites/ museums.aspx

Lord Leighton was one of the most respected Victorian painters. His work *Flaming June* is regarded by many as the apotheosis of the Pre-Raphaelite movement. His house, built in 1864–9, has been preserved with its opulent decoration as an extraordinary monument to the Victorian aesthetics Leighton embodied. The highlight is the Arab Hall, added in 1879 to house Leighton's collection of Islamic tiles, some inscribed with text from the Koran.

There are paintings and drawings displayed, including some by Edward Burne-Jones, John Millais, G F Watts and many works by Leighton himself. There are free guided tours at 3pm on Wednesday and Sunday. Semi-regular "Leighton Lates", usually held once a month on a Friday, give visitors the chance to enjoy the house until 9pm, with complimentary live music and a glass of wine.

6 High Street Kensington

⚲ B7 🏠 W8 🚇 High St Kensington

This is one of the main shopping streets in west London, and it reflects the tastes of this affluent neighbourhood, with lots of rather conservative clothing stores and a spread of British and international high-street names. There are a good number of cafés and some decent restaurants. Holland Park and Kensington Gardens bookend the main shopping drag with green space away from the bustle.

← Stylized Japanese elegance in the Kyoto Garden, Holland Park

Colourful houses at Portobello Road, one of the city's most popular street markets

7

Little Venice

Q C4 **Q** W2 **Q** Warwick Avenue, Edgware Road

This is a charming corner of London where the western end of the Regent's Canal, the eastern end of the Grand Union Canal and the short waterway to the Paddington Basin converge. Three bridges frame a small triangle of water populated with floating cafés and even a puppet theatre – there are plenty of delightful pubs and restaurants in the nearby terraced streets too. Towpath walks will take you for miles in either direction along the canals, and narrowboats sail up to Camden Lock (p168).

8

Notting Hill

Q A6 **Q** W11 **Q** Notting Hill Gate

Now the home of Europe's biggest street carnival, most of this area was farmland until the 19th century. In the 1950s and 60s, it became a centre for the Caribbean community, many of whom lived here when they first arrived in Britain. The riotous carnival started in 1966 and takes over the area every August bank holiday weekend, when costumed parades meander through the streets.

9

Museum of Brands, Packaging and Advertising

Q A5 **Q** 111-117 Lancaster Rd W11 **Q** Ladbroke Grove **Q** 10am-6pm Tue-Sat, 11am-5pm Sun **W** museum ofbrands.com

This out-of-the-ordinary museum is at once a perm-anent exhibition for the history of product packaging in the UK, a study of the changing tastes and fashions since the Victorian period and a gleeful trip down memory lane. The sheer volume of items on display is dizzying: tins, bottles, boxes, magazines, toys, games, household appliances and much more besides. In the main exhibition space, the twisty Time Tunnel, familiar products appear multiple times, their packaging updated as the years pass. Other displays reflect past trends, like the Egyptomania of the 1920s and the militar-ization of marketing during the two World Wars. There's a section for every decade of the 20th and 21st centuries and some substantial and intriguing 19th-century displays, such as the teapots, gift sets and guides from the Great Exhibition of 1851.

NOTTING HILL CARNIVAL

The centrepiece in Europe's largest street carnival is a procession of flamboyant floats accompanied by steel bands, costumed dancers and mobile sound systems, transforming the area around Notting Hill, Ladbroke Grove and Westbourne Park into a celebration of Caribbean culture. Along the parade route are static sound systems, stages and food stalls. Born out of the black and West Indian experience in London, the carnival has expanded exponentially, and today over two million people attend.

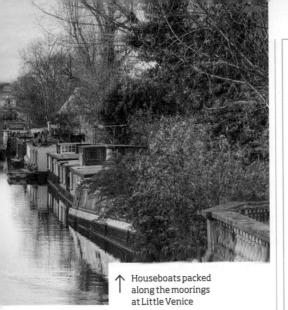

↑ Houseboats packed along the moorings at Little Venice

⑩ St Sophia's Cathedral

📍 B5 🏛 Moscow Rd W2 🚇 Queensway 🕐 2-4pm Mon, 10am-12:30pm Tue & Thu 🌐 stsophia.org.uk

The richly decorated interior of this Greek Orthodox cathedral is a riot of coloured marble and gilded mosaics. On the second Sunday of each month it's possible to visit the treasury down in the crypt. The services feature a superb polyphonic choir.

⑪ Kensington Square

📍 B7 🏛 W8 🚉 High St Kensington

This is one of London's oldest squares. It was laid out in the 1680s, and a few early 18th-century houses still remain (Nos 11 and 12 are the oldest). The renowned philosopher John Stuart Mill lived at No 18, and the Pre-Raphaelite painter and illustrator Edward Burne-Jones at No 41.

↑ One of several blue plaques commemorating notable residents of Kensington Square

EAT

Montparnasse Café
Homely French café and pâtisserie offering simple breakfasts, lunches and pastries.

📍 B7 🏛 22 Thackeray St W8

💷💷💷

Café Tarte
Nicely prepared light lunches at this friendly café - the irresistible cakes steal the show.

📍 A7 🏛 270 Kensington High St W8 🌐 cafetarte. co.uk

💷💷💷

Holland Park Café
Great location, on the edge of the picturesque park. Enjoy soups, sandwiches and cakes.

📍 A7 🏛 Holland Park, W8 🌐 cooksand partners.co.uk

💷💷💷

Candella
Teas on vintage china, dainty sandwiches and light meals.

📍 B7 🏛 34 Kensington Church St W8 🌐 candellatearoom.com

💷💷💷

The Muffin Man Tea Shop
Archetypally quaint, traditional tea shop with a hint of English village about it.

📍 B7 🏛 12 Wrights Lane W8 🌐 themuffinman teashop.co.uk.

💷💷💷

A SHORT WALK
KENSINGTON
AND HOLLAND PARK

Distance 3 km (2 miles) **Nearest Tube** High
Street Kensington **Time** 45 minutes

Although now part of central London, as recently as
the 1830s this was a country village of market gardens
and mansions. Outstanding among these was Holland
House; part of its grounds are now Holland Park. A walk
through the area takes you past many of its attractive
mid-19th century buildings, including expensive
apartments, mansion flats and fashionable shops.

Did You Know?

Holland Park was once
notorious as a location
for highway robbers.

Parts of the old formal
gardens of Holland House
feature in the delightful
Holland Park (p266).

Holland House, a
rambling Jacobean
mansion started in 1605,
was largely demolished
in the 1950s.

The Summer Ballroom,
now an upmarket
restaurant, has
parts that date
from the 1630s.

Melbury Road is lined with
large Victorian houses, long
home to celebrity residents.

The Design Museum is an
international showcase for the
many design skills at which
Britain excels (p264).

Leighton House is preserved
as it was when the Victorian
painter Lord Leighton lived
here (p267).

The Victorian letter box on
the High Street is one of the
oldest in London.

START

Drayson Mews is one of the quaint alleys that were built behind large town houses for stables. Today most have been converted into small houses.

Kensington Civic Centre, an assertive modern building by Sir Basil Spence, was completed in 1976.

No 16 Phillimore Place was home to Kenneth Grahame, author of the children's classic The Wind in the Willows from 1901 to 1908.

FINISH

Kensington High Street station

18 Stafford Terrace has a carefully preserved late Victorian interior, complete with original furnishings and draperies (p266).

Sticky Fingers, a lively café on the corner of Phillimore Gardens, is owned by Bill Wyman, former bassist of the Rolling Stones.

0 metres   100   N
0 yards   100

→
A statue in
the grounds of
Holland Park

273

REGENT'S PARK AND MARYLEBONE

The name Marylebone is a derivation of "St Mary by the Bourne", the church that once stood next to the River Tyburn (also called Tybourne), long since buried underground. Many of the street names around Marylebone, including Wigmore Street and Portland Place, are taken from ancestral connections to the Howard de Walden family whose estate still occupies more or less the entire district. The estate dates from the early 18th century but before this time the land had been in royal hands. Henry VIII established hunting grounds to the north of Marylebone, some of which became Regent's Park when it was formally laid out from 1812 by John Nash, the architect responsible for the design of much of Regency London. Along the northern perimeter of the park runs the Regent's Canal, also laid out by Nash in the early 19th century. Not long after its completion, the recently founded Zoological Society of London opened their Zoological Gardens in five acres of the park – the beginnings of London Zoo.

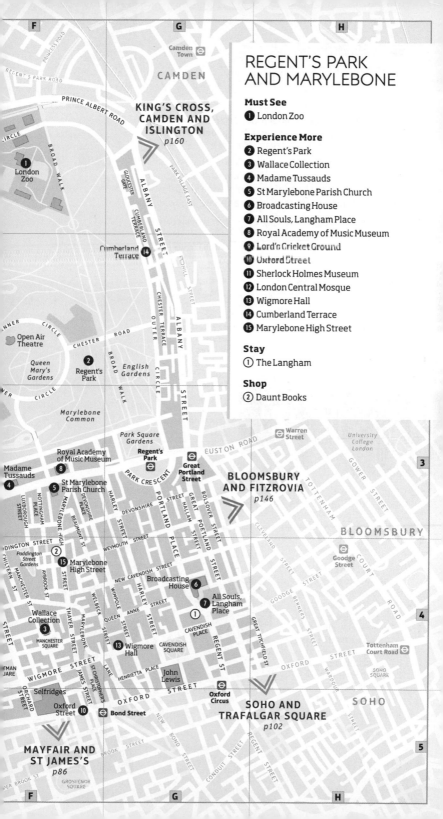

REGENT'S PARK AND MARYLEBONE

Must See
1 London Zoo

Experience More
2 Regent's Park
3 Wallace Collection
4 Madame Tussauds
5 St Marylebone Parish Church
6 Broadcasting House
7 All Souls, Langham Place
8 Royal Academy of Music Museum
9 Lord's Cricket Ground
10 Oxford Street
11 Sherlock Holmes Museum
12 London Central Mosque
13 Wigmore Hall
14 Cumberland Terrace
15 Marylebone High Street

Stay
① The Langham

Shop
② Daunt Books

① 🛝 Ⓜ ⑨ 🖥 🛍

LONDON ZOO

📍F1 🏛Regent's Park NW1 🚇Camden Town, Regent's Park 🕐Apr-Aug: 10am-6pm; Sep-Oct & Mar: 10am-5:30pm; Nov-Feb: 10am-4pm (last adm 1 hr before closing); times vary, check website 🌐zsl.org

By international standards, London Zoo is relatively small but it packs a lot in, including Sumatran tigers, Western lowland gorillas, spider monkeys, giraffes, iguanas, pythons and bird-eating tarantulas.

Despite its dense population, many of the larger animals here enjoy relatively spacious and interesting enclosures, especially since the zoo embarked on an extensive series of imaginative redevelopments in the early 2000s. Since then they have opened Penguin Beach, Gorilla Kingdom, Rainforest Life, the Meet the Monkeys and In with the Lemurs walk-through exhibits, with the Snowdon Aviary set to become a colobus monkey walk-through following a Foster + Partners reboot in 2020. The largest enclosure is the Land of the Lions, where Asiatic lions prowl around the zoo's rendering of the Gir Forest in western India. Visitors look on from walkways and an imagining of a Gujarat village, complete with train station, high street and temple ruins.

←

Entrance to the ever-popular London Zoo

STAY

Gir Lion Lodge

Wake up to the roaring of lions after spending the night at the zoo's Gir Lion Lodge, a set of comfortable, charming cabins inside the zoo. Tours of the zoo at sunset, after dark and in the morning are included, as well as a two-course dinner.

🌐zsl.org/gir-lion-lodge

£££

Children get close to a giant moth at Butterfly Paradise ↑

EXPERIENCE MORE

2

Regent's Park

📍F2 🚇NW1 🚉Regent's Park, Baker St, Great Portland St 🕐5am–dusk daily 🌐royalparks.org.uk

This area of land became enclosed as a park in 1812. John Nash designed the scheme and originally envisaged a kind of garden suburb, dotted with 56 villas in a variety of Classical styles, and a pleasure palace for the Prince Regent. In the event only eight villas – but no palace – were built inside the park (three survive round the edge of the Inner Circle).

The boating lake, which is home to many varieties of water birds, is marvellously romantic, especially when music drifts across from the bandstand. Queen Mary's Gardens are a mass of wonderful sights and smells in summer, when visitors can also enjoy a full programme of outdoor theatre, including Shakespeare, musicals and children's plays, at the Open Air Theatre nearby. The park is also renowned for its excellent sports facilities.

Nash's master plan for the park continues just beyond its northeastern edge in Park Village East and West. These elegant stucco buildings date from 1828, the same year in which London Zoo, which ranged across the north of the park, first opened.

3

Wallace Collection

📍F4 🏠Hertford House, Manchester Sq W1 🚉Bond St, Baker St 🕐10am–5pm daily 🌐wallacecollection.org

This is one of the world's finest private collections of

↑ Eighteenth-century European art in the Wallace Collection

art. It has remained intact since it was bequeathed to the government in 1897 with the stipulation that it should go on permanent public display with nothing added or removed. The product of passionate collecting for four generations of the Hertford family, it is a must for anyone with even a passing interest in the progress of European art up to the late 19th century. The house itself is magnificent, with dozens of rooms, including the superb Great Gallery, rich with period detail.

Among the 70 masterworks are Frans Hals's *The Laughing Cavalier*, Titian's *Perseus and Andromeda* and Rembrandt's *Titus*. There are several superb portraits by Reynolds, Romney and Gainsborough. Other highlights include Sèvres porcelain and sculpture by Houdon and Roubiliac. The fine European and Oriental armour collection is the second largest in the UK.

There are tours and talks daily; details are on the website, along with some excellent podcasts.

↑ Enjoying the underwater view of penguins swimming at Penguin Beach

Madame Tussauds

📍F3 🚇Marylebone Rd NW1 🚇Baker St ⏰9am-4pm Mon-Fri, 9am-5pm Sat & Sun; hours vary, check website 🌐madametussauds.com

Madame Tussaud began her wax-modelling career rather morbidly, making death masks of well-known victims of the French Revolution. In 1835 she set up an exhibition of her work in Baker Street, not far from the present site.

Traditional wax-modelling techniques are still used to recreate politicians, royals, actors, rock stars and sporting heroes, the displays changing fairly regularly to keep up with who's in and who's out.

The exhibition features "Party", where visitors can "attend" a celebrity bash; "Film", devoted to Hollywood's finest, such as Marilyn Monroe and ET; and "Royals", where you can step onto the palace balcony with Her Majesty. "Culture" has the likes of Shakespeare and Picasso, and the "Music Zone" includes Ed Sheeran, Rihanna and Lady Gaga. There are also sections dedicated to franchises such as Marvel and Star Wars, with detailed walk-in sets and a 4D Marvel film experience. "Sherlock Holmes Experience" has a theatrical sense of Victorian melodrama, and in "Spirit of London" visitors travel in stylized London taxi-cabs through momentous events in the city's history, from the Great Fire of 1666 to 1960s Swinging London.

Ticket prices are fairly steep, but cheaper if you buy online in advance. Opting for timed tickets can help reduce queuing times.

St Marylebone Parish Church

📍F3 🚇Marylebone Rd NW1 🚇Regent's Park ⏰9am-5pm Mon-Fri, 8am-4pm Sat & Sun 🌐stmarylebone.org

Noted poets Robert Browning and Elizabeth Barrett were married here in 1846 after eloping from her strict family home on nearby Wimpole Street. The large, stately church by Thomas Hardwick was built in 1817 after the former church, where Admiral Lord Nelson worshipped and where Lord Byron was christened in 1778, had become too small. Hardwick was determined that the same should not happen to his new church – so everything is on a grand scale.

→

Eric Gill's *Prospero and Ariel*, at the BBC's Broadcasting House

↑ The spacious interior of St Marylebone Parish Church

Broadcasting House

📍G4 🚇Portland Place W1 🚇Oxford Circus 🌐bbc.co.uk

Broadcasting House was built in 1931 as a suitably modern Art Deco setting for the new medium of broadcasting. Its front, curving with the street, is dominated by Eric Gill's stylized relief *Prospero and Ariel*, inspired by characters in Shakespeare's play *The Tempest*. As the invisible spirit of the air, Ariel was considered an appropriate personification of broadcasting. The character appears in two other sculptures on the western frontage, and again over the eastern entrance in the frieze *Ariel Piping to Children*.

Broadcasting House is the London headquarters of BBC news, radio, television and online departments. The only way to get a look inside is to book yourself a place, via the website, on one of the BBC's television or radio shows as a studio audience member.

A new wing added in 2005 was named after the disc jockey John Peel. Further refurbishment in 2011 created a public piazza, a BBC shop and a café that overlooks the central newsroom.

7

All Souls, Langham Place

 G4 Langham Place W1 Oxford Circus 10am-5pm Mon-Thu, 10am-2pm Fri, 9am-2pm & 5-7:30pm Sun allsouls.org

John Nash designed this church in 1824. Its quirky round frontage is best seen from Regent Street. When it was first built, the spire was ridiculed as it appeared too slender and flimsy, and the church itself was described as "one of the most miserable structures in the metropolis".

The only Nash church in London, it had close links with the BBC, based across the street at Broadcasting House; the daily service, a stalwart of the radio schedule, was broadcast from here for many years. It maintains this broadcasting tradition with a "sermon streaming" resource on its website.

Royal Academy of Music Museum

F3 Marylebone Rd NW1 Baker Street, Regent's Park 11:30am-5:30pm Mon-Fri, noon-4pm Sat ram.ac.uk

This simple museum in one of the country's finest music schools showcases the Royal Academy's collection of historical instruments. The three small rooms, staffed by student volunteers, are dispersed across three floors. On the ground floor you can find out about the history of the institution; in the Strings Gallery and the Piano Gallery upstairs are a prized Stradivari violin and viola and a 17th-century harpsichord. There's a restaurant and frequent free concerts in the revamped performance spaces.

9

Lord's Cricket Ground

D2 NW8 St John's Wood For guided tours: Jan–Feb 11am-2pm; Apr-Oct 10am-3pm; Mar, Nov & Dec 10am-2pm Last 10 days of Dec lords.org

Set up in 1814 by professional cricketer Thomas Lord, the ground can be visited on guided tours that take in the Long Room, the dressing rooms and the Marylebone Cricket Club Museum. This is full of memorabilia from cricketing history, including a stuffed sparrow killed by a cricket ball and the Ashes. This tiny urn contains, supposedly, the burned remains of a cricket bail signifying "the death of English cricket" after a notable defeat by Australia. It is still the object of ferocious competition between the two national teams. The museum explains the history of the game, and mementos of notable cricketers make it a place of pilgrimage for devotees of the sport. Tours are hourly and it is essential to book ahead; there are no tours on major match days, but ticket holders do get free access to the museum.

The late-Victorian pavilion at Lord's Cricket Ground

← Another case for the great detective unfolding in the Sherlock Holmes Museum

and is furnished exactly as described in the books. Visitors are greeted by Holmes's "housekeeper" and shown to his recreated rooms on the first floor. The shop sells souvenirs including short stories and deerstalker hats.

Did You Know?

There have been more films starring Sherlock Holmes than any other (human) character.

10

Oxford Street

♀ F5 ♠ W1 ⊖ Marble Arch, Bond St, Oxford Circus, Tottenham Court Rd �W oxfordstreet.co.uk

This is London's biggest and busiest shopping street, running from Marble Arch at the western end right along Marylebone's southern border and then beyond, dividing Soho and Fitzrovia and ending at the Centre Point tower block. The western half of the street is home to several department stores, most notably Selfridges, the largest and most famous (don't miss its magnificent Food Hall), although John Lewis, opened in 1864, predates it by half a century. Along the street's length and its shopper-clogged pavements are the UK flagship stores of brands

such as Nike, UNIQLO and Gap plus British favourites like Marks & Spencer and Topshop.

11

Sherlock Holmes Museum

♀ E3 ♠ 221b Baker St NW1 ⊖ Baker St ⊙ 9:30am-6pm daily ₩ sherlock-holmes.co.uk

Sir Arthur Conan Doyle's fictional detective lived at 221b Baker Street, an address that did not exist at the time, because Baker Street was then much shorter. This building, dating from 1815, is on what Conan Doyle would have known as Upper Baker Street, above Marylebone Road. It has been converted to resemble Holmes's flat,

12

London Central Mosque

♀ E2 ♠ 146 Park Rd NW8 ⊖ Marylebone, St John's Wood, Baker St ⊙ 10am-last prayer ₩ iccuk.org

Surrounded by trees on the edge of Regent's Park, this large, golden-domed mosque was designed by Sir Frederick Gibberd and completed in 1978. Built to cater for the increasing number of Muslim residents in and visitors to London, the mosque is capable of holding 1,800 worshippers. The main hall of worship is a plain square chamber with a domed roof and a magnificent carpet. Visitors must remove their shoes before entering the mosque, and women should remember to cover their head.

→ Immaculate Cumberland Terrace, among London's most desirable addresses

Welcoming pubs and bars offering refreshment on Marylebone High Street ↑

Wigmore Hall

📍 G4 🏠 36 Wigmore St W1
🚇 Bond St, Oxford Circus
🌐 wigmore-hall.org.uk

This appealing little concert hall for chamber music was designed by T E Collcutt, architect of the Savoy hotel, in 1900. At first it was called Bechstein Hall because it was attached to the Bechstein piano showroom; the area used to be the heart of London's piano trade. Opposite is the Art Nouveau emporium built in

1907 as Debenham and Freebody's department store – now known as Debenhams.

14

Cumberland Terrace

📍 G2 🏠 NW1 🚇 Great Portland St, Regent's Park, Camden Town

Architect James Thomson is credited with the detailed design of this, the longest and most elaborate of the Neo-Classical terraces created by John Nash that border Regent's Park. Completed in 1828, it was designed to be visible from a palace Nash planned for the Prince Regent (later George IV). The palace was never built because the prince was too busy with his plans for Buckingham Palace (p90).

15

Marylebone High Street

📍 F4 🏠 NW1 🚇 Baker St, Regent's Park, Bond St
🌐 marylebonevillage.com

This boutique-heavy high street, the most villagey part of central London, is often overlooked by visitors. Inside smart red-and-yellow brick townhouses are organic food shops, independent fashion stores and refined, often high-end restaurants, frequented by a well-dressed set of local shoppers. Must-sees are iconic design depot the Conran Shop and the incomparable Daunt Books. Nearby, St Vincent and Aybrook streets host the Marylebone Farmers' Market every Sunday (10am–2pm), one of the largest and most upmarket in London.

SHOP

Daunt Books
The most wonderful feature of this original Edwardian bookshop is its long oak galleries. Shelves carry travel guides and literature on each country.

📍 F4 🏠 83 Marylebone High St W1
🌐 dauntbooks.co.uk

A SHORT WALK
MARYLEBONE

Distance 2.5 km (1.5 miles) **Nearest Tube** Regent's Park
Time 30 minutes

Just south of Regent's Park lies the medieval village of
Marylebone (originally Maryburne, the stream by St Mary's
church). Until the 18th century it was surrounded by fields,
but these were built over as fashionable London drifted
west. The area has maintained its elegance, and your walk
will take you past the spacious houses that professionals,
especially doctors, used in the mid-19th century to receive
wealthy clients. The route also takes in Marylebone High
Street, full of interesting, high-quality food and clothes
shops, bookshops and cafés.

↑ The splendid Edwardian
interior of Daunt Books,
built in 1910

John Nash laid out Regent's
Park (p279), one of the city's
royal parks, in 1812 as a
setting for classically
designed villas and terraces.

FINISH

The Royal Academy of Music
(p281), England's first music
academy, was founded in 1822.
The present brick building, with
its own concert hall, is from 1911.

Poets Robert Browning
and Elizabeth Barrett
were married in 1846 in
St Marylebone Parish
Church (p280).

The Madame Tussauds
waxworks museum
(p280) has been
in business since
1835 and remains one
of London's most
popular attractions.

Baker Street
station

Marylebone High Street (p283) is lined with attractive
shops. At No 83 is Daunt Books with its galleried interior.
On the corner of Marylebone Lane, V V
Rouleaux is a gloriously colourful haberdashery shop.

0 metres 100

0 yards 100

N

Locator Map
For more detail see p276

REGENT'S PARK AND MARYLEBONE

Park Crescent's breathtaking façades by Nash have been preserved, although the interiors were rebuilt as offices in the 1960s. The crescent seals the north end of Nash's ceremonial route from St James's to Regent's Park via Regent Street and Portland Place.

Regent's Park station

START

Consulting rooms of eminent medical specialists have been located at Harley Street for more than a century.

In the centre of broad Portland Place is a statue of Field Marshal Sir George Stuart White, who won the Victoria Cross for gallantry in the Afghan War of 1879.

PARK SQUARE WEST

HARLEY ST

PARK CRESCENT

PORTLAND PLACE

HARLEY STREET

STREET

DEVONSHIRE STREET

UPPER WIMPOLE ST

BEAUMONT STREET

The Royal Institute of British Architects is housed in a striking Art Deco building designed by Grey Wornum in 1934.

→ Enjoying café life along the pleasant Marylebone High Street

HAMPSTEAD AND HIGHGATE

These rather exclusive north London neighbourhoods, perched on either side of the vast, bucolic Hampstead Heath, were distinct villages centuries before they were swallowed up by the metropolis, a quality still tangible to this day. There has been a settlement in Highgate since at least the early Middle Ages, when an important staging post on the Great North Road from London was established, with a gate to control access. Hampstead is known to have existed as far back as the 10th century. From around the 17th century both became fashionable retreats from the capital, an allure only partially dampened in the 19th century by their own urban expansion, the arrival of the railway and the encroachment of the city. They also share illustrious literary and artistic connections, though Hampstead's arguably have the edge, with the likes of John Keats having set up home there. Though they may have lived in Hampstead, many of the city's intellectuals are buried in Highgate's cemetery – among them political theorist Karl Marx.

HAMPSTEAD AND HIGHGATE

Must Sees
1. Hampstead Heath
2. Highgate Cemetery

Experience More
3. Flask Walk and Well Walk
4. Burgh House
5. Fenton House
6. Church Row
7. 2 Willow Road
8. Downshire Hill
9. Keats House
10. Freud Museum

Drink
1. The Spaniards Inn
2. The Southampton Arms
3. The Holly Bush

① 🍴 ☕

HAMPSTEAD HEATH

📍 X3 🏠 Hampstead NW3, NW5 🚇 Belsize Park, Hampstead, Kentish Town, Golders Green 🚉 Hampstead Heath, Gospel Oak 🕐 24 hrs daily 🌐 Hampstead Heath: cityoflondon.gov.uk; Kenwood House: english-heritage.org.uk

A favourite green space among Londoners, Hampstead Heath is the largest of inner London's parklands, though it is too wild and wonderfully unkempt to be considered a proper park.

The sprawling heath, separating the hilltop villages of Hampstead and Highgate, brings a slice of the countryside to the city, with large tracts of wild woodlands and meadows rolling over hills and around ponds and lakes. Covering an area of 8 sq km (3 sq miles), its natural habitats attract a wealth of wildlife, including bats and some 180 species of birds. There are also all kinds of landscaped areas, most notably the Hill Garden, a charming Edwardian garden once the grounds to Lord Leverhulme's house, but now its raised pergola walkway, flowering plants and beautiful formal pond are open to all. Among the many other features of the heath are Vale of Health, an isolated village tucked inside the southern boundary, and the picturesque Viaduct Pond.

Kenwood House

This magnificent white Neo-Classical mansion, its walls hung with paintings by old masters, overlooks splendidly landscaped grounds high on the edge of the north side of the heath. This is one of the most picturesque parts of the whole area, with two large and lovely ponds, sweeping lawns and trails through the woodlands. There has been a house here since 1616, but the present villa was remodelled by

→

View over London from the green environs of Hampstead Heath

↑ Taking a dip in the men's bathing pond (there are women's and mixed ponds too)

🏔 GREAT VIEW
Hillside Heights

Parliament Hill, in the southeast corner of the heath, provides one of the most spectacular views over the capital, taking in the Shard, the skyscrapers of the City, the dome of St Paul's Cathedral and Canary Wharf.

Statue by Henry Moore in the grounds of Kenwood House →

↑ Grand Kenwood House, on the edge of Hampstead Heath

Robert Adam in 1764 for the Earl of Mansfield. Adam transformed the interior and most of his work has survived, including the highlight, the resplendent library, with its ceiling paintings, opposing apses and Corinthian columns. Precious paintings in Kenwood's collection include works by Vermeer, Van Dyck, Hals, Reynolds, Gainsborough and Rembrandt – one of his self-portraits is the star attraction of the collection. The house features a tearoom and café with a lovely garden seating area. In summer there are ticketed, open-air concerts in the grounds, though many people pack a picnic and sit nearby to listen.

↑ Elegant rooms filled with old master paintings

2 ⟨⟩ ⟨⟩

HIGHGATE CEMETERY

📍 Z2 🚇 Swain's Lane N6 🚉 Archway 🕐 Check website for opening hours 🌐 highgatecemetery.org

Opened in 1839, this is London's best-known cemetery, most famous for epitomizing the Victorian obsession with death and the afterlife.

The two leafy sections of Highgate Cemetery, divided by a country lane, are full of flowerbeds, statues, elaborate tombs and overgrown gravestones, bathed in a light suitably subdued by the shade from the small forests of trees. For Victorians, preoccupied with death and insistent on burial rather than cremation, this was the graveyard of choice, where you could lie shoulder to shoulder with poets, artists and intellectuals. Both sections contain the graves of numerous iconic figures but it is the West Cemetery which is the more atmospheric, and architecturally interesting. Its showpiece is the restored Egyptian Avenue, a street of family vaults styled on ancient Egyptian tombs, leading to the Circle of Lebanon, a ring of vaults topped by a cedar tree.

↑ Statue of an angel, one of many found among the tombs and trees

Did You Know?

The cemetery contains over 53,000 graves and more than 170,000 people have been buried here.

Karl Marx's tomb in its ↑ tranquil surroundings in Highgate Cemetery

TOP 5 **FIVE NOTABLE RESIDENTS**

Karl Marx (1818-83)
German political philosopher.

George Eliot (1819-80)
The pen name of Mary Ann Evans, author of *Middlemarch*.

Douglas Adams (1952-2001)
Author of the cult-classic *The Hitchhiker's Guide to the Galaxy*.

Christina Rossetti (1830-94)
Romantic poet.

Malcolm McLaren (1946-2010)
Manager of the notorious Sex Pistols.

↑ Fenton House, whose treasures can be explored in the summer months

EXPERIENCE MORE

3

Flask Walk and Well Walk

📍 W3 🏠 NW3
🚇 Hampstead

Flask Walk is named after the Flask pub. Here, in the 18th century, the area's therapeutic spa water was put into flasks and sold to visitors or sent to London. The water, rich in iron salts, came from nearby Well Walk, where a disused fountain now marks the site of the well. There have been many notable residents of Well Walk: artist John Constable, novelists D H Lawrence and J B Priestley, and the poet John Keats. At the High Street end, Flask Walk is narrow and lined with old shops. Beyond the Flask pub it broadens into a row of fine Regency houses.

4

Burgh House

📍 W3 🏠 New End Sq NW3
🚇 Hampstead 🕐 Noon-5pm
Wed-Fri & Sun 🕐 3 weeks
at Christmas 🌐 burgh
house.org.uk

Since 1979, an independent trust has run Burgh House as the Hampstead Museum, which illustrates the history of the area and some of its notable residents. The museum owns a significant art collection, including a work by the Bloomsbury Group painter Duncan Grant, along with furniture and archive material on the area. There is a display about Hampstead as a spa in the 18th and 19th centuries. In the 1720s, Dr William Gibbons, chief physician to the spa, lived at this address.

5   (NT)

Fenton House

📍 V3 🏠 20 Hampstead
Grove NW3 🚇 Hampstead
🕐 Mar-Oct: 11am-5pm
Wed-Sun & public hols
🌐 nationaltrust.org.uk

Built in 1686, this splendid William and Mary house is the oldest mansion in Hampstead. It contains several exhibitions: the Benton-Fletcher collection of early keyboard instruments – a harpsichord dating from 1612 is said to have been played by Handel – and a collection of porcelain. The instruments are kept in full working order and concerts are sometimes given. The porcelain was largely accumulated by Lady Binning who, in 1952, left the house and its contents to the National Trust.

↑ The buildings of Church Row, Hampstead, a perfect slice of Georgian history

⑥ Church Row

♀V4 ⚑NW3 ⊖Hampstead

Church Row is one of the most complete Georgian streets in London. Much of its original detail has survived, notably the ironwork. At the west end is St John's, Hampstead's parish church, built in 1745. The iron gates are earlier and come from Canons Park in Edgware, Middlesex. Inside the church is a bust of poet John Keats. Artist John Constable's grave is in the churchyard, and a long list of other Hampstead luminaries are buried in the adjoining cemetery.

⑦ 2 Willow Road

♀W3 ⚑NW3 ⊖Hampstead ⊟Hampstead Heath ◷Mar–Oct: 11am–5pm Wed–Sun (tours only before 3pm) �🌐nationaltrust.org.uk

The striking modernist 1930s home of Hungarian architect Ernö Goldfinger – designer of a number of Brutalist London tower blocks – is preserved almost exactly as he designed and lived in it, complete with many of his beguiling possessions. The relatively plain, unremarkable façade makes the sleek, stylish yet warm interior all the more memorable. Steps from the ground floor delicately fan out in a spiral leading up to the open-plan, beautifully efficient living space. Bathed in a natural light perfect for

↑ The Regency façade of St John's Downshire Hill, completed in 1823

viewing Goldfinger's precious 20th-century art collection, the geometrically designed rooms are full of innovative touches – removable walls, for example, that allow interior spaces to be reconfigured.

⑧ Downshire Hill

♀W4 ⚑NW3 ⊖Hampstead

A beautiful street of mainly Regency houses, Downshire Hill lent its name to a group of artists, including Stanley Spencer and Mark Gertler, who would gather at No 47 between the two World Wars. The same house had been the meeting place of Pre-Raphaelite artists, among them Dante Gabriel Rossetti and Edward Burne-Jones. A more recent resident, at No 5, was the late Jim Henson, the creator of *The Muppets*.

The church on the corner (the second Hampstead church to be called St John's) was built in 1823 to serve the Hill's residents. Inside, it still has its original box pews.

Keats House

W4 **10 Keats Grove NW3** **Hampstead, Belsize Park** **Hampstead Heath** **11am–5pm Wed–Sun** **Christmas week** **cityoflondon.gov.uk/keats**

Originally two semi-detached houses built in 1816, the smaller one became Keats's home in 1818, when a friend persuaded him to move in. Keats spent two productive years here: perhaps his most celebrated poem *Ode to a Nightingale* was said to have been written under a plum tree in the garden. The Brawne family moved into the larger house a year later and Keats became engaged to their daughter, Fanny. However, the marriage never took place: Keats died of consumption in Rome before two years had passed. He was only 25 years old. A copy of one of Keats's love letters to Fanny, the engagement ring he offered her and a lock of her hair are among the mementos exhibited at the house, whose displays were revamped for its 200th anniversary in 2018. Visitors are also able to see copies of some of Keats's manuscripts, part of a collection that serves as a tribute to his life and work. Thirty-minute tours begin at 1:30pm and 3pm.

Did You Know?

The Freud Museum has a collection of contemporary art open for public viewing.

Freud Museum

V5 **20 Maresfield Gdns NW3** **Finchley Rd** **Noon–5pm Wed–Sun** **1 Jan, 25–26 Dec** **freud.org.uk**

In 1938, Sigmund Freud, the founder of psychoanalysis, fled from Nazi persecution in Vienna to this Hampstead house. Making use of the possessions he brought with him, his family recreated the atmosphere of his Vienna consulting rooms.

After Freud died in 1939 his daughter Anna (who was a pioneer of child psychoanalysis) kept the house as it was, and in 1986 it was opened as a museum dedicated to her father. On display is the couch on which patients lay for analysis. A series of 1930s home movies shows Freud with his dog as well as more distressing footage of Nazi attacks on his apartment. There's a bookshop and free tours or talks take place at

2pm on Wednesdays. In 2016 Anna Freud was commemorated with her own blue plaque on the house, joining that of her father; it is the only 19th-century building in the city to have been awarded the rare "double blue" accolade. Other properties with two blue plaques include 29 Fitzroy Square (*p156*) and the Handel and Hendrix house (*p99*).

DRINK

The Spaniards Inn

Dickensian pub on Hampstead Heath with a colourful 500-year history, a beer garden for summer and an open fire in winter.

W1 **Spaniards Rd NW3** **thespaniards hampstead.co.uk**

The Southampton Arms

A relaxed traditional pub with a dinky beer garden, offering a superior range of ales from independent breweries.

Y3 **139 Highgate Rd NW5** **thesouthampton arms.co.uk**

The Holly Bush

A cosy 18th-century pub with low ceilings on a charming backstreet in Hampstead. Great pub grub too.

V3 **22 Holly Mount NW3** **hollybush hampstead.co.uk**

 ←
A stained-glass skylight illuminating the library of Keats House

A SHORT WALK
HAMPSTEAD

Distance 1.5 km (1 mile) **Nearest Tube** Hampstead
Time 30 minutes

Perched awkwardly on a hilltop, with its broad heath to the north, Hampstead has kept its village atmosphere and sense of being outside the city. This has attracted artists and writers since Georgian times and has made it one of London's most desirable residential areas. Its mansions and town houses are perfectly maintained, and a stroll through Hampstead's narrow streets is one of London's quieter pleasures.

A welcome retreat from the city, Hampstead Heath's broad open spaces include bathing ponds, meadows and lakes (p290).

Whitestone Pond takes its name from the old white milestone nearby.

Admiral's House dates from about 1700. Built for a sea captain, its name derives from its external maritime motifs. No admiral ever actually lived in it.

Grove Lodge was home to novelist John Galsworthy (1867–1933), author of The Forsyte Saga, for the last 15 years of his life.

Summer visitors should seek out the late 17th-century Fenton House and its exquisite walled garden, which are well hidden in the jumble of streets near the heath (p293).

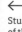

← Stunning views of the city from a hillside on Hampstead Heath

0 metres 100
0 yards 100

↑ Browsing the characterful shops on Flask Walk

Locator Map
For more detail see p288

No 40 Well Walk is where artist John Constable lived while working on his many Hampstead pictures (p293).

Built in 1702 but much altered since, Burgh House contains an intriguing local history museum and a café overlooking the small garden (p293).

Flask Walk is an alley of charming specialist shops that broadens into a residential village street (p293).

Hampstead station

The Everyman Cinema has been an arthouse cinema since 1933.

The tall houses on Church Row are rich in original detail. Notice the superb ironwork on what is probably London's finest Georgian street (p294).

GREENWICH AND CANARY WHARF

In the mid-15th century, Henry IV's son Humphrey, Duke of Gloucester and the brother of Henry V, first established the royal foothold in Greenwich when he built himself the Palace of Placentia, originally known as Bella Court. Henry VIII was born in the palace, as were his daughters, Mary and Elizabeth. The palace was demolished at the end of the 17th century and the land where it stood is now occupied by the Old Royal Naval College; the royal hunting grounds are now the gorgeous Greenwich Park. The buildings of the Naval College, the centrepiece of the UNESCO World Heritage Site referred to as Maritime Greenwich, started life as Greenwich Hospital, a home for wounded and retired sailors opened in 1692. The conversion to a Royal Navy college in 1873 cemented an already well-established maritime heritage in Greenwich, one shared by Canary Wharf over the river, the site of the historic docklands since the early 19th century.

GREENWICH AND CANARY WHARF

Experience

1 Cutty Sark
2 National Maritime Museum
3 Greenwich Park
4 Royal Observatory
5 The Queen's House
6 Old Royal Naval College
7 Ranger's House - the Wernher Collection
8 Greenwich Foot Tunnel
9 The Fan Museum
10 The O2 Arena
11 Emirates Air Line
12 Museum of London Docklands
13 Canary Wharf

Eat & Shop

1 Greenwich Market

Drink

2 Trafalgar Tavern

O

Around Greenwich

12 Museum of London
Docklands

13 Canary Wharf

Canary Wharf

The O2 Arena

10 North Greenwich

11 Emirates Air Line

Royal Victoria

London City Airport

Pontoon Dock

Thames Barrier

MILLWALL

River Thames

Mudchute

Woolwich Dockyard

Charlton

Westcombe Park

CHARLTON

Area of main map

GREENWICH

0 km   1

0 miles   1

N

8

2 CRANE ST

PARK ROW

HIGH BRIDGE

EASTNEY STREET

HOSKINS ST

OLD WOOLWICH ROAD

TRAFALGAR ROAD

FEATHERS PLACE

PARK ROW

PARK VISTA

Maze Hill

MAZE HILL

HUMBER ROAD

VANBRUGH HILL

FOYLE ROAD

9

5 The Queen's House

WESTCOMBE PARK ROAD

VANBRUGH FIELDS

10

3 Greenwich Park

Greenwich Park

THE AVENUE

Flamstead House

4 Royal Observatory

Planetarium

Astronomy Centre

GREAT CROSS AVENUE

MAZE HILL

VANBRUGH PARK

BLACKHEATH AVENUE

BOWER AVENUE

CHARLTON WAY

MAZE HILL

11

CHESTERFIELD ROAD

GENERAL WOLFE ROAD

CADE ROAD

Ranger's House – the Wernher Collection

7

WALK

SHOOTERS HILL ROAD

0 metres   200

0 yards   200

N

O

↑ The structure holding the copper hull of the impressive *Cutty Sark*

EXPERIENCE

1 Cutty Sark

Q N9 **A** King William Walk SE10 **⊜** Cutty Sark DLR **⊜** Greenwich Pier **⊙** 10am–5pm daily (last adm: 4:15pm) **⊘** 24–26 Dec **w** rmg.co.uk

This majestic vessel is a survivor of the clippers that crossed the Atlantic and Pacific oceans in the 19th century. Launched in 1869 as a tea carrier, it was something of a speed machine in its day, returning from Australia in 1884 in just 83 days – 25 days faster than any other ship. It made its final voyage in 1938 and was put on display here in 1957. In 2006 the *Cutty Sark* was closed to visitors for renovation work, which suffered a major setback in May 2007 when the ship was severely damaged by fire. It was reopened by the Queen in spring 2012, fully restored and slightly raised in a glass enclosure. Visitors can explore the cargo decks and sleeping quarters below deck, take the ship's wheel, and be entertained by tales from the costumed "crew". There are interactive displays on navigation and life on board.

2 National Maritime Museum

Q N9 **A** Romney Rd SE10 **⊜** Cutty Sark DLR **⊜** Greenwich **⊙** 10am–5pm daily **⊘** 24–26 Dec **w** rmg.co.uk

This substantial museum, which was built in the 19th century as a school for sailors' children, celebrates Britain's

→ Portrait of a young Nelson, National Maritime Museum

3

Greenwich Park

📍 010 🅰 SE10 🚇 Cutty
Sark DLR, Greenwich
DLR 🚆 Greenwich,
Maze Hill, Blackheath
🕐 6am–6pm or dusk
🌐 royalparks.org.uk

Originally the grounds of a
royal palace and still a Royal
Park, Greenwich Park was
enclosed in 1433 and its
brick wall built in the reign
of James I. Later, in the 17th
century, the French royal
landscape gardener André Le
Nôtre was invited to redesign
the park. The broad avenue,
rising south up the hill, was
part of his plan. It's a steep
climb up the hilltop but one
well-rewarded by sweeping
views across London and
more green space to explore.

4

Royal Observatory

📍 010 🅰 Greenwich Park
SE10 🚇 Cutty Sark DLR
🚆 Greenwich 🕐 10am–5pm
daily (to 6pm Easter & Jun–
Sep) 📅 24–26 Dec 🌐 rmg.
co.uk

The meridian (0° longitude)
that divides Earth's eastern
and western hemispheres
passes through here, and
millions of visitors come to be
photographed standing with
a foot on either side of it.
In 1884, Greenwich Mean
Time became the basis of
time measurement for most
of the world. Here you can
journey through the history
of time, explore how scientists
first began to map the stars
and see world-changing
inventions, including the UK's
largest refracting telescope.
Visitors can even touch a 4.5-
billion-year-old asteroid.

→

The onion dome of the Royal
Observatory Greenwich,
housing a colossal telescope

seafaring heritage, from early
British trade through its
emergence as a leading
maritime nation to the
expeditions of Captain Cook,
and from the Napoleonic Wars
through to the modern day.
Unveiled in 2018, its new East
Wing galleries support an
impressive array of historical
objects. In the Tudor and
Stuarts Seafarers gallery, a
digital recreation brings a
Deptford royal dockyard from
1690 to life, while the Polar
Worlds section draws together
artifacts from the quests of
Shackleton and Scott in the
Arctic and Antarctic.

In the Nelson, Navy, Nation
gallery, the star exhibit is the
uniform that Lord Horatio
Nelson was wearing when he
was shot at the Battle of
Trafalgar in October 1805.
Rather more spectacular is
the royal barge built for Prince
Frederick in 1732, decorated
with gilded mermaids and his
Prince of Wales feathers on
the stern. Throughout the
museum there are numerous
activities for children, such as
navigating a ship around the
world on a huge floor map.

The stately original building,
Flamsteed House, was
designed by Christopher Wren
for the first Astronomer Royal,
John Flamsteed. It contains
original instruments belonging
to his successors, including
Edmond Halley, as well as the
celebrated sea clocks of John
Harrison, including the H4 –
arguably the most important
timepiece ever made. There is
also a state-of-the-art
planetarium here, the only
one in London. There is an
entry charge for Flamsteed
House and the planetarium
shows; the Astronomy Centre
is free.

5

The Queen's House

📍 O9 🏠 Romney Rd SE10 🚇 Cutty Sark DLR 🚆 Greenwich ⏰ 10am–5pm daily 📅 24–26 Dec 🌐 rmg.co.uk

The Queen's House was designed by Inigo Jones and completed in 1637. It was originally intended to be the home of Anne of Denmark, wife of James I, but she died while it was still being built and it was finished for Charles I's queen consort, Henrietta Maria. After the English Civil War it was briefly occupied by Henrietta as dowager queen, but was not much used by the royal family after that. From 1821 to 1933 the Royal Hospital School was housed here.

Period highlights include the square Great Hall, enlivened by Turner Prize-winner Richard Wright's gold-leaf ceiling, added during refurbishment in 2016, and the spiral cantilevered "tulip staircase", which curves sinuously upwards without a central support. The main focus of interest for visitors, though, is the superb art collection of the National Maritime Museum.

6

Old Royal Naval College

📍 N9 🏠 King William Walk SE10 🚇 Cutty Sark DLR, Greenwich DLR 🚆 Greenwich, Maze Hill ⏰ 10am–5pm daily; grounds: 8am–11pm daily 📅 24–26 Dec & some Sat 🌐 ornc.org

A landmark of Greenwich, these ambitious buildings by Christopher Wren were built on the site of the old 15th-century royal palace, where Tudors Henry VIII, Mary I and Elizabeth I were born, to house naval pensioners. At its peak, the then hospital was home to some 2,700 veterans. The Painted Hall, which was

> These ambitious buildings by Christopher Wren were built on the site of the old 15th-century royal palace, where Henry VIII, Mary I and Elizabeth I were born.

intended as a dining room for the retired seamen, was opulently decorated by Sir James Thornhill in the early 18th century. The tremendous ceiling mural is the largest figurative painting in the country. In 1805, the hall was the location of a lavish lying-in-state ceremony for Lord Horatio Nelson, who was killed at the Battle of Trafalgar.

The hall reopened in 2019 following an extensive conservation and cleaning project, with a new entrance via the vaulted King William Undercroft – itself restored to something close to its original Baroque splendour. Ceiling tours, which need to be booked in advance, climb to the top of an observation deck to view the painting's detail at close hand. There are also free guided walking tours of the site several times a day, for which no booking is

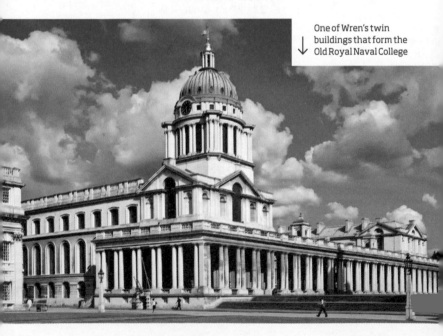

One of Wren's twin buildings that form the Old Royal Naval College

→

Statue by Bergonzoli and Chinese-themed tapestries at the Ranger's House

required. They start from the visitor centre and last about 45 minutes.

In 1873, the hospital was acquired by the Naval College in Portsmouth and remained a training post for officers until 1997. It also trained thousands of Wrens during World War II.

There is a relaxed pub next to the visitor centre with a huge terrace overlooking the *Cutty Sark*, but visitors are also welcome to picnic in the grounds – provided that they dispose of litter thoughtfully.

7

Ranger's House - the Wernher Collection

📍 O11 🚶 Chesterfield Walk, Greenwich Park SE10 🚈 Cutty Sark DLR 🚉 Blackheath 🕐 Apr-Oct: 11am-5pm Sun-Wed 🌐 english-heritage.org.uk

The Wernher Collection is located in the Ranger's House (1688), an elegant building southeast of Greenwich Park (*p303*). It is an enchanting array of over 700 pieces accumulated by Sir Julius Wernher, who made a fortune from South African mines, in the late 19th century. The collection is displayed in 12 rooms and includes paintings, jewellery, furniture and porcelain. Highlights include Renaissance masterworks by Hans Memling and Filippo Lippi, over 100 Renaissance jewels, and an opal-set lizard pendant jewel. The tour ends with a viewing of the fantastic sculpture of a woman and angel by 19th-century artist Giulio Bergonzoli. Tours are the best way to see the site. It is advisable to book ahead – check the website for details.

8

Greenwich Foot Tunnel

📍 N9 🚶 Between Greenwich Pier SE10 and Isle of Dogs E14 🚈 Island Gardens, Cutty Sark DLR 🚉 Greenwich Pier 🕐 24hrs daily

This 370-m- (1,200-ft-) long tunnel was opened in 1902 to allow south London labourers to walk to work in Millwall Docks. It is well worth making the crossing from Greenwich for the wonderful views, once above ground, back across the river, of Christopher Wren's Royal Naval College and of Inigo Jones's Queen's House.

Matching round red-brick terminals, with glass domes, mark the top of the lift shafts

---

200,000

White glazed tiles were needed to line the Greenwich Foot Tunnel.

on either side of the river. Both ends of the tunnel are close to stations on the Docklands Light Railway (DLR). Although there are security cameras, the tunnel can be eerie at night.

9

The Fan Museum

📍 N10 🚶 12 Croom's Hill SE10 🚉 Greenwich 🕐 11am-5pm Tue-Sat, noon-5pm Sun 🕐 1 Jan, 24-26 Dec 🌐 thefanmuseum.org.uk

One of London's most unusual museums owes its existence and appeal to the enthusiasm of Helene Alexander, whose personal collection of about 4,000 fans from the 17th century onwards has been augmented by donations. A small permanent exhibition looks at types of fans and fan-making, while the collection is rotated in temporary displays. On some days, afternoon tea is served in the orangery.

🔟 ⑂ 🖥 🏛
The O2 Arena

📍 O8 🏢 North Greenwich SE10 🚇 North Greenwich 🕐 9am-late 🌐 theo2.co.uk

The former Millennium Dome was the focal point of Britain's celebration of the year 2000. Controversial from its earliest days, it is nonetheless an amazing feat of engineering. Its canopy is made from 100,000 sq m (109,000 sq yards) of Teflon-coated spun glass-fibre, and is supported by over 70 km (43 miles) of steel cable rigged to a dozen 100-m (328-ft) masts. Now London's largest indoor concert venue, the O2 also has bars, restaurants, a cinema and IndigO2, a smaller venue. You can also don climbing gear and ascend the outside along a long, bouncy walkway to the very top.

1️⃣1️⃣ ⑂
Emirates Air Line

📍 O8 🏢 Western Gateway E16/Edmund Halley Way SE10 🚇 Royal Victoria DLR, North Greenwich 🕐 7am-11pm Mon-Fri, 8am-11pm Sat, 9am-11pm Sun (to 9pm Sun-Thu Oct-Mar) 🌐 emiratesairline.co.uk

This cable car, crossing the Thames between the Royal Victoria Dock and the O2, provides spectacular views

Did You Know?

Sponsored by airline Emirates, the construction of the cable car cost a whopping £60 million.

during the five-minute trip. It's a magnificent way to cross the river. Travelcards or Oyster Pay as you go provide a 25 per cent discount. In the evenings the "flights" slow down, giving you more time to enjoy the panorama of city lights.

1️⃣2️⃣ ⑂ 🖥 🏛
Museum of London Docklands

📍 O8 🏢 No 1 Warehouse, West India Quay E14 🚇 Canary Wharf, Westferry 🕐 10am-6pm daily 🌐 museumoflondon.org. uk/museum-london-docklands

Occupying a late Georgian warehouse, this museum tells the story of London's docks and their links from Roman times to the present. A highlight is the recreation

↑ The Emirates cable car and the O2 Arena – the roof of which can be climbed *(inset)*

of the dark and dangerous "Sailortown" of Wapping in the 1850s.

Canary Wharf

⑬08 🚇E14 ⓔCanary Wharf, West India Quay DLR

London's most ambitious commercial development opened in 1991, when the first tenants moved into the 50-storey One Canada Square. At 235 m (700 ft), it continues to dominate the city's eastern skyline with its pyramid-shaped top. The tower stands on what was the West India Dock, closed, like all the London docks, between the 1960s and the 1980s, when trade moved to Tilbury. Today, Canary Wharf is thriving, with a major shopping complex, cafés and restaurants.

THE THAMES BARRIER

In 1236, the Thames rose so high that people rowed across Westminster Hall; London flooded again in 1663, 1928 and in 1953. Something had to be done, and in 1984 the Thames Barrier, 520 m (1,700 ft) across, was unveiled. Its 10 gates swing up to 1.6 m (6 ft) above the level reached by the tide in 1953, and have been used over 180 times. Some boat tours go to the barrier, and there's also a small visitor centre.

A SHORT WALK
GREENWICH

Distance 1.5 km (1 mile) **Nearest Tube** Cutty Sark DLR **Time** 25 minutes

This historic town, with illustrious royal and naval connections, is a UNESCO World Heritage Site. In Tudor times it was the site of a palace enjoyed by Henry VIII, near a fine hunting ground. The old palace is gone, but your walk will take you past Inigo Jones's exquisite Queen's House, built for James I's wife. The route also takes in museums, shops, cafés and markets, Wren's architecture and the magnificent Royal Park, making this an enjoyable short stroll.

START

Greenwich Pier is a boarding point for boats to Westminster, the O2 and the Thames Barrier.

Greenwich Foot Tunnel (p305) is one of two remaining tunnels under the Thames that were built solely for pedestrians.

Clipper ships such as the Cutty Sark (p302) once traded across the oceans.

Greenwich Market, in the heart of Greenwich, sells crafts, antiques and books (p303).

Did You Know?

The Old Royal Naval College had a starring role in Marvel's *Thor: The Dark World*.

There has been a church on the spot on which St Alfege Church stands since 1012.

KING WILLIAM WALK

COLLEGE APPROACH

GREENWICH CHURCH STREET

NELSON ROAD

STOCKWELL STREET

← *Cutty Sark*, impressively restored and raised to allow visitors to explore above and below deck

Locator Map
For more detail see p300

George II Statue

The Old Royal Naval College (p304), a stately structure by Wren, was built in four parts so that the Queen's House could keep its river view.

FINISH

The Painted Hall contains 18th-century murals by Sir James Thornhill, who painted the interior of the dome of St Paul's Cathedral.

ROMNEY ROAD

On his return from Italy, the Queen's House (p304) was the first building Inigo Jones designed in the Palladian style.

Real and model boats, digital displays and instruments like an 18th-century compass illustrate naval history at the National Maritime Museum (p302).

↑ John Rysbrack's George II statue (1735), depicting the king as a Roman emperor

| 0 metres | 100 | N |
| 0 yards | 100 | ↑ |

A deer in Richmond Park

Must Sees

① Queen Elizabeth Olympic Park

② Hampton Court

③ Kew Gardens

④ Warner Bros. Studio Tour: The Making of Harry Potter

Experience More

⑤ BAPS Shri Swaminarayan Mandir

⑥ Victoria Park

⑦ Alexandra Palace

⑧ William Morris Gallery

⑨ Charlton House

⑩ Sutton House

⑪ Eltham Palace

⑫ Horniman Museum

⑬ Wimbledon Lawn Tennis Museum

⑭ Wimbledon Windmill Museum

⑮ Dulwich Picture Gallery

⑯ Dulwich Park

⑰ Brixton

⑱ Richmond Park

⑲ Ham House

⑳ Orleans House Gallery

㉑ Marble Hill House

㉒ Richmond

㉓ Syon House

㉔ Musical Museum

㉕ Osterley Park House

㉖ Pitzhanger Manor House and Gallery

㉗ London Museum of Water & Steam

㉘ Fulham Palace

㉙ Chiswick House

㉚ Hogarth's House

BEYOND
THE CENTRE

London's high and mighty once sought refuge
from the city in their country manor houses,
located a short distance away from the centre.
Consumed by the rapid expansion of the Victorian
era, these stately homes and royal estates became
intertwined with sprawling suburbs, leading
to the boroughs of today. Postwar immigration
contributed to the identity of each of London's
neighbourhoods – from the West Indian
population in Brixton to the Hindu community
in Neasden – and their local characters continue
to evolve as the regeneration of the city and
gentrification pushes ever further outward.

❶ Ⓜ Ⓨ ▢

QUEEN ELIZABETH OLYMPIC PARK

▢ E20 ⊖ Hackney Wick, Stratford, Pudding Mill Lane ▭ 308, 339, 388, 108 ▤ Stratford International ⊙ 24 hrs daily; information point 10am–3pm daily Ⓦ queenelizabetholympicpark.co.uk

Home of the 2012 London Olympic Games, this east London site was transformed from an area of industrial wasteland into a world-class sporting hub with top-quality sporting venues.

As the only city to have hosted the Olympic Games three times – in 1908, 1948 and 2012 – London is justifiably proud of its place in Olympic history. The main site for the 2012 Olympics and Paralympics was a 225-hectare (560-acre) area of former industrial land stretching along the River Lea in east London. The main attractions today are immediately familiar to anyone who watched the events: a series of large, functional but striking venues dotted amid meandering waterways and surrounded by quintessentially English wildflower gardens. Renamed the Queen Elizabeth Olympic Park to commemorate the Queen's Diamond Jubilee in 2012, the site has been transformed into a permanent leisure attraction. There is plenty to see and do, particularly if you catch one of the numerous events hosted here, including big sporting occasions and live music, or want to try out some sports. The former media hub, Here East, is now home to tech start-ups, restaurants and cafés.

1. The 6,000-seat velodrome is an iconic building in the Olympic Park and contains the fastest cycling track in the world.

2. The pools at the London Aquatics Centre lie beneath the curving roof of this attractive building.

3. Visible from all over the Olympic Park, the ArcelorMittal Orbit tower gives visitors great views.

❶

Lee Valley VeloPark

⊙ 9am–10pm Mon–Fri, 8am–10pm Sat, 8am–9pm Sun; book taster sessions online in advance Ⓦ visitleevalley.org.uk

The Velodrome is the hub of a large cycling activity centre, with BMX and road tracks, and mountain-bike trails. Visitors can book taster sessions.

❷

London Aquatics Centre

⊙ 6am–10:30pm daily; check online for swim sessions and events Ⓦ londonaquatics centre.org

Architect Zaha Hadid was inspired by the flow of water for her sweeping design for the Aquatics Centre. Everyone can swim in the competition and training pools here.

❸

ArcelorMittal Orbit

⊙ 11am–4pm Mon–Fri, 10am–6pm Sat & Sun Ⓦ arcelormittalorbit.com

Designed by artist Anish Kapoor, the twisting steel tower is part sculpture, part viewing platform, with a thrilling 178-m (580-ft) slide.

INSIDER TIP
From the Water
To see the best of the park, take a 45-minute guided boat tour (Easter–Oct). Check *leeandstort boats. co.uk* for details.

↑ The centrepiece stadium, set amid lush meadow land and waterways

Lee Valley Hockey and Tennis Centre

Mountain bike trails

①

Tumbling Bay Playground, a children's play area

Wetlands area

Underpass to Stratford International station

Here East is home to cafés, bars and restaurants.

The Copper Box Arena is an indoor sports arena.

②

③

The London Stadium hosts sporting and music events, and is the home of West Ham United FC.

→

The vast and varied Queen Elizabeth Olympic Park

2 ⊘ Ⓜ 🍴 ☕ 🛍

HAMPTON COURT

🏠 East Molesey, Surrey KT8 9AU 🚇 Hampton Court 🛳 Hampton Court pier
(summer only) 🕐 Check website for opening hours 🌐 hrp.org.uk

**With its impressively preserved palace, beautifully manicured
gardens and location on the River Thames, the former stomping
ground of Tudor king Henry VIII makes for an irresistible attraction.**

Glorious Hampton Court began life in 1514 as the
riverside country house of Cardinal Wolsey,
Henry VIII's Archbishop of York. Later, in 1528, in
the hope of retaining royal favour, Wolsey offered
it to the king. Hampton Court was twice rebuilt
and extended, first by Henry himself and then, in
the 1690s, by King William and Queen Mary, who
employed Christopher Wren as architect. There is
a striking contrast between Wren's Classical royal
apartments and the Tudor turrets, gables and
chimneys elsewhere. The inspiration for the
gardens comes largely from the time of William
and Mary, who created a vast, formal Baroque
landscape, with avenues and exotic plants.

FLOWER SHOW

The world's biggest flower show takes
place every year at Hampton Court in July.
Displays are on either side of Long Water
and focus on growing your own food. Book
tickets at rhs.org.uk.

↑ The sunken Pond Garden,
once a pond that stored fish
for Henry VIII's table

↑ Spectacular Hampton Court, seen from the Privy Garden

← An example of the formal and ordered style of the palace gardens

→ Fresh produce from the Kitchen Garden, sold to visitors once a week

Timeline

1528
▲ Wolsey gives the palace to Henry VIII to try to keep favour with the king

1647
▲ Charles I imprisoned by Oliver Cromwell

1734
▲ William Kent decorates the Queen's Staircase

1992
▲ State apartments damaged by a fire in 1986 are reopened

Exploring the Palace

As a historic royal palace, Hampton Court bears traces of many of the kings and queens of England from Henry VIII to the present day. The building itself is a harmonious blend of Tudor and English Baroque architecture. Inside, visitors can see the Great Hall, built by Henry VIII, as well as the state apartments of the Tudor court. Many of the Baroque state apartments, including those above Fountain Court, are decorated with furniture, tapestries and old masters from the Royal Collection.

Did You Know?

Anne Boleyn was gambling on a match of tennis here when she was arrested and taken to the Tower (p178).

The Tudor Chapel Royal, refitted by Wren, except for the gilded vaulted ceiling.

Queen's Guard Chamber

Haunted Gallery

Hung with tapestries beneath a hammer-beam roof, the Tudor Great Hall is sumptuously decorated.

① The Tudor kitchen prepared up to 1,000 meals a day for the court, which often included dishes of game, pies, lamb, venison and swan – at a time when most people only ever ate stored or preserved meat.

② The King's Staircase has wall paintings by William Kent, recreating the court of George I with real people of the time.

③ The Great Hall was used as a banqueting room and a theatre – William Shakespeare's King's Men performed here for James I over Christmas and New Year in 1603–4.

→

The vast Hampton Court with its mix of Tudor and English Baroque architecture

CARDINAL WOLSEY

Thomas Wolsey (c 1475–1530), who was simultaneously a cardinal, Archbishop of York and Lord Chancellor, was, after the king, the most powerful man in England. However, when he was unable to persuade the pope to allow Henry VIII to divorce his first wife, Catherine of Aragon, Wolsey fell from royal favour. He died while making his way to face trial for treason.

Queen's Presence Chamber

Wren's east façade

Fountain Court overlooked by the state apartments

Queen's Gallery with a marble chimneypiece

King's Great Bed Chamber

An astronomical clock is atop the entrance to Clock Court

The grand King's Staircase leads up to the state apartments

Immaculately manicured
flowerbeds in front of the
iconic Palm House ↑

3 🏷️ 🚫 🍴 ☕ 🛍️

KEW GARDENS

🏠 Royal Botanic Gardens, Richmond TW9 3AB 🚇 Kew Gardens 🚉 Kew Bridge
🕐 Gardens: Jan 10am–4:15pm, Feb 10am–5pm, Mar & Oct 10am–6pm, Apr & Sep
10am–7pm, May–Aug 10am–8pm, first 3 weeks Nov 10am–4pm, late Nov–Dec 10am–
3:30pm; Kew Palace & Great Pagoda: Apr–Sep 10:30am–5:30pm; Queen Charlotte's
Cottage: Apr–Sep: 11am–4pm Sat, Sun & public hols 🚫 24–25 Dec 🌐 kew.org

The Royal Botanic Gardens, Kew, are
a World Heritage Site. Given to the
nation in 1841, they display about
30,000 plants.

Kew's reputation was first established by
the British naturalist and plant hunter,
Sir Joseph Banks, who worked here in the late
18th century. The former royal gardens were
created by Princess Augusta, the mother of
George III, on the 3.6 ha (9-acre) site in 1759.
The Palm House was designed by Decimus
Burton in the 1840s and this famous jewel
of Victorian engineering houses exotic plants
in tropical conditions.

↑ Fine views from up in the canopy
on the Treetop Walkway

HIDDEN GEM
Hive of Activity

An unusual construction set in a wildflower meadow, The Hive gives visitors a multi-sensory experience of life inside a beehive.

↑ The 1762 Great Pagoda, standing almost 50 m (164 ft) high

Map of Kew Gardens showing the main sights ↓ and places to visit

Queen Charlotte's Cottage

Waterlily Pond

River Thames

Sackler Crossing

Minka House

Azalea Garden

Brentford Gate entrance

Kew Palace

Nash Conservatory

Elizabeth Gate entrance

Duke's Garden

Great Pagoda

Lion Gate Entrance

Temperate House

King William's Temple

Victoria Gate entrance

Palm House

Princess of Wales Conservatory

WARNER BROS. STUDIO TOUR: THE MAKING OF HARRY POTTER

⌂ Studio Tour Drive, Leavesden WD25 7LR ⧐ Watford Junction (shuttle buses run from the station every 20 mins) ⏲ 9:30am-8pm Mon-Fri, from 8:30am Sat, Sun & school holidays (final tour begins 6:45pm) ⓦ wbstudiotour.co.uk

Walk the streets of Diagon Alley, enjoy a frothing glass of Butterbeer and admire the animatronics behind your favourite characters – this behind-the-scenes and in-the-scenes tour is an absolute must for budding wizards and witches.

Housed in a building adjacent to the studios where all eight of the Harry Potter films were created, the Making of Harry Potter tour brings you up close to the original sets, props, models and costumes used in the world-famous films. Visitors can wander into the imposing Great Hall at Hogwarts, walk up Diagon Alley, sneak into Dumbledore's office, explore the

←

The front entrance of the Warner Bros. Studio Tour: The Making of Harry Potter

The iconic set of Platform 9¾, departure point for the Hogwarts Express ↓

Did You Know?

The Harry Potter novels have sold more than 500 million copies, in 80 languages.

Diagon Alley, home to the wand shop Ollivanders and Weasley's Wizard Wheezes

Forbidden Forest and admire the Hogwarts Express locomotive at Platform 9¾. Just as impressive as the real-life sets is the huge, jaw-droppingly detailed scale model of Hogwarts School, used for the exterior shots in the films.

There's much more to marvel at throughout the tour, from costumes for the students at Beauxbatons Academy and the Yule Ball to Harry's broomstick and Hagrid's motorcycle, as well as animatronic creatures, including Buckbeak, a 6-m- (20-ft-) wide Aragog and a full-size Basilisk head. Secrets of the special and visual effects departments reveal how the Invisibility Cloak works and what role the green screen played. As you might expect, the three shops on site offer a huge range of take-home souvenirs.

↑ The office of Albus Dumbledore, first created for *Harry Potter and the Chamber of Secrets*

EAT

The Studio Café
Enjoy classic British fare at this quite basic canteen. Breakfast is well catered for, with the Full English setting you up for the day. At lunch, tuck into hot or cold meals - soups, salads, sandwiches and the like.

£££

Backlot Café
This is the place to stop for Butterbeer, whether as a drink or an ice cream. There is basic hot food available here too.

£££

EXPERIENCE MORE

BAPS Shri Swaminarayan Mandir

🏠 105-119 Brentfield Rd NW10 🚇 Harlesden then bus 224 (or Stonebridge Park and bus 112) 🕐 Daily; Mandir and Haveli: 9am–6pm; Deities: 9am, 11am, 11.45am–12.15pm & 4–6pm (to 5pm Sat) 🌐 london mandir.baps.org

Right out in northwest London, not far from Wembley Stadium, stands one of the most incongruous – and beautiful – religious buildings in the city, often known simply as the Neasden Temple. The intricately carved Hindu temple was completed in 1995, after a small army of volunteers from the local community banded together to raise funds and build it. Thousands of tonnes of Bulgarian limestone and Italian Carrara marble were shipped to India to be carved, then assembled on site like a giant jigsaw. The result is a staggeringly detailed, intricately carved temple. When the Mandir's inner sanctum is not closed for prayer, you can inspect some

of the shrines to the deities close-up. The I laveli, the cultural education centre, features yet more beautiful carving, this time in Burmese teak and English oak.

Leave any large bags at the security desk across the road, dress modestly (with your shoulders, upper arms and knees covered) and leave your shoes in the cloakroom before you enter the main building.

Victoria Park

🏠 Grove Rd E3 🚇 Bethnal Green 🚆 Hackney Wick, Cambridge Heath 🚌 277, 425 🕐 7am–dusk

Victoria Park opened in 1845 as London's first public park. The venue for many political rallies in the 19th century and beyond, it became known as the "People's Park" and remains hugely popular. There are boats for hire on one of its two lakes, as well as gardens, cafés, playgrounds, splash pools, tennis courts and a skate park. It's part of the largest belt of green space in the East End. Footpaths along the Hertford Union and Regent's canals hug two of its borders, linking up with the River Lea on its journey around the Olympic Park.

Alexandra Palace

🏠 Alexandra Palace Way N22 🚆 Alexandra Palace 🚇 Wood Green then bus W3 🕐 Daily 🌐 alexandrapalace.com

Built as the People's Palace in 1873, Alexandra Palace has a slightly chequered history – it has burned down twice, once just 16 days after it opened, and again in 1980. From 1936 until 1956 the BBC's television studios were housed at Alexandra Palace, and in 1936 the first television transmission took place from here. Affectionately known as Ally Pally, the large, ornate Victorian halls now host a wide variety of events, from

DRINK

Crate Brewery
This canalside brewery is the place to go to sample the east London hipster scene: post-industrial styling and great craft beer.

🏠 Queens Yard, Hackney Wick E9 🌐 cratebrewery.com

trade and antiques fairs to large-scale concerts. Set in parkland, the building sits majestically exposed on a hill, so the views are spectacular, and it's a good spot for fireworks and funfairs (the website has details of events). There's a permanent ice rink and the grounds have a pitch-and-putt golf course, a boating lake and playgrounds.

8
William Morris Gallery

📍 Lloyd Park, Forest Rd E17
🚇 Walthamstow Central
🕐 10am–5pm Tue–Sun
🚫 25 & 26 Dec, 1 Jan
🌐 wmgallery.org.uk

The most influential designer of the Victorian era, born in 1834, lived in this 18th-century house as a young man. It is now a beguiling and well-presented museum giving a full account of William Morris the artist, designer, writer, craftsman and socialist. It has examples of his work and that of other members of the Arts and Crafts movement – tiles

←

Victoria Park, part of a 3 km (1.5-mile) band of green space that opens up east London

by William De Morgan and paintings by members of the Pre-Raphaelite Brotherhood.

Interactive exhibits introduce visitors to techniques such as hand-printing and dyeing. There are regular special exhibitions, workshops and lectures.

9
Charlton House

📍 Charlton Rd SE7
🚉 Charlton 🕐 9am–10pm Mon–Fri, 9am–5pm Sat
🚫 Public hols 🌐 greenwich-heritage.org/visit/charlton-house

Completed in 1612 for Adam Newton, tutor to Prince Henry, Charlton House is the best-preserved Jacobean mansion in London, for enthusiasts of that period. It is now used as a community centre, but many of the original ceilings and fireplaces survive, as does the carved main staircase and parts of the wood panelling. Other ceilings have been restored using the original moulds. The grounds contain a summer house reputedly designed by architect Inigo Jones, and a mulberry tree said to have been planted by James I in 1608.

↑ The exquisite, and intricately detailed (inset), BAPS Shri Swaminarayan Mandir

10
Sutton House

📍 2–4 Homerton High St E9
🚇 Bethnal Green then bus 253 🕐 Hours vary, check website 🚫 Christmas, Jan (check website)
🌐 nationaltrust.org.uk

One of the very few Tudor merchants' houses in London to have survived in something like its original form, Sutton House was built in 1535 for Ralph Sadleir, a courtier to Henry VIII. Though the front was altered in the 18th century, the Tudor fabric remains surprisingly intact, including brickwork, fireplaces and wood panelling. The house has spent time as a school and an anarcho-punk squat, a history explored on regular tours; check website for times.

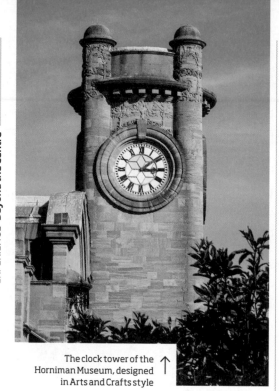

The clock tower of the Horniman Museum, designed in Arts and Crafts style ↑

conservatory, a bandstand, nature trails and a sunken garden as well as a Butterfly House (for a fee) and Animal Walk, a small petting zoo.

13

Wimbledon Lawn Tennis Museum

⌂ Church Rd SW19 ⊖ Southfields ⏰ 10am-5pm daily 🚫 1 Jan, 24-26 Dec 🌐 wimbledon.com

Even those with only a passing interest in the sport will find plenty to enjoy here. The museum explores tennis's development from its early incarnation in the 1860s as a diversion for country house parties to the sport it is today. Equipment and tennis fashion from the Victorian era are on display and visitors can watch clips and recent matches in the video theatre. It's advisable to book ahead to take one of the tours, which include a visit to Centre Court.

14

Wimbledon Windmill Museum

⌂ Windmill Rd SW19 ⊖⇄ Wimbledon then bus 93 ⏰ Apr-Oct: 2-5pm Sat, 11am-5pm Sun & public hols 🌐 wimbledon windmill.org.uk

Built in 1817, the mill on Wimbledon Common now houses a museum exploring windmills, rural life and local history. Boy Scout founder Robert Baden-Powell wrote

11

Eltham Palace

⌂ Court Yard SE9 ⇄ Eltham then a 15-minute walk ⏰ Apr-Sep: 10am-6pm Sun-Fri (till 5pm Oct, till 4pm Mar); Nov-Feb: 10am-4pm Sun only; daily at half-term 🌐 english-heritage.org.uk

This unique property lets visitors relive the grand life of two very different eras. In the 14th century English kings spent Christmas in a splendid palace here. The Tudors used it as a base for deer-hunting, but it fell into ruin after the English Civil War (1642–8). In 1935 Stephen Courtauld, of the wealthy textile family, restored the Great Hall and, next to it, he built a house described as "a wonderful combination of Hollywood glamour and Art Deco design". The palace has been superbly restored – especially the circular glass-domed entrance hall. The lush grounds are particularly lovely, especially the carp-filled moat and the 1930s garden.

12

Horniman Museum

⌂ 100 London Rd SE23 ⇄ Forest Hill ⏰ 10am-5:30pm daily; animal walk: 12:30-4pm daily; gardens: 7:15am-sunset Mon-Sat, 8am-sunset Sun and public hols 🚫 24-26 Dec 🌐 horniman.ac.uk

Frederick Horniman, a tea merchant, had this museum built in 1901 to house the curios he had collected on his travels in the 1860s. It features a music gallery, an aquarium and world culture displays, but the highlight is a natural history gallery that contains a remarkable collection of taxidermy and skeletons, including the famous Horniman Walrus. The gardens have a Victorian

> ### Did You Know?
>
> In 2018 the *New York Times* named the Horniman one of the "10 coolest museums in the world".

Watching Wimbledon

Visiting during the Wimbledon Championships? Try for ground-day tickets (several thousand are on sale each day) to see action on the outside courts. Once in, you could snap up resale tickets too.

part of *Scouting for Boys* here in 1908, and there are display cases of early memorabilia from the scouting and Girl Guide movements.

The mill came out of service in 1864, but you can see some of the original workings on the upper floors, as well as try your hand at grinding grain on old mortars and querns, an activity popular with young children. There are also some beautifully crafted cutaway models of this and other mills.

15

Dulwich Picture Gallery

📍 Gallery Rd SE21 �æ West Dulwich, North Dulwich 🕐 10am-5pm Tue-Sun & bank hols 🚫 1 Jan, 24-26 Dec 🌐 dulwichpicture gallery.org.uk

England's oldest public art gallery, which opened in 1817, was designed by Sir John Soane (*p138*). Its imaginative use of skylights made it the prototype of most galleries created since. It was built to house the royal collection of the King of Poland, who had been forced to abdicate in 1795. The superb collection has works by Rembrandt (his *Jacob III de Gheyn* has been stolen from here four times), Canaletto, Poussin, Watteau, Raphael and Gainsborough. The building houses Soane's mausoleum to Desenfans and Bourgeois, the art dealers who built the collection.

16

Dulwich Park

📍 College Road SE21 �æ West Dulwich 🚌 P4, P13 🕐 7.30am-dusk

Just across the road from Dulwich Picture Gallery, this park was opened in 1890 on land previously owned by Dulwich College, the public school whose buildings lie to the south of the park. This is one of the prettiest of the borough parks, with paths weaving around colourful flowerbeds, sports courts and pitches, a bowling green, a central boating lake and a duck pond. Dog walkers are confined to the perimeter, making the central lawns pleasant for play and picnicking in the warmer months. At weekends the outer loop fills with kids and adults messing around on the novelty bikes rented out by the park's resident cycle hire firm, London Recumbents.

← Visitors exploring the superb Dulwich Picture Gallery

Relaxing on the riverside next to the 18th-century stone-arch Richmond Bridge

Multinational flags in Brixton Village, one of a pair of colourful covered market arcades ↑

Brixton

 SW2, SW9 Brixton

The unofficial capital of south London, Brixton has been characterized since the 1950s by one of the city's largest West Indian communities. Brixton Market loops around the centre along Electric Avenue, Pope's Road and Station Road, and is packed full of stalls selling Caribbean produce alongside arts, crafts, clothing and the usual market bric-a-brac. Brixton Village and Market Row, neighbouring market arcades, are filled with independent traders and an eclectic mix of food hotspots, including Mexican, Japanese, Korean and Spanish. Despite the march of gentrification, Brixton fiercely protects its roots and remains a brilliantly energetic part of the city.

Richmond Park

Richmond TW10
Richmond then bus 65 or 71 24 hours daily (7:30am–8pm Nov & Feb) royalparks.org.uk

In 1637, Charles I built a 13-km (8-mile) wall round the royal park to enclose it as a hunting ground. Today the vast park is a beautiful national nature reserve and deer still graze warily among the chestnuts, birches and oaks. They have learned to coexist with the human visitors who stroll here on fine weekends.

In late spring, the highlight is the Isabella Plantation with its spectacular azaleas, while the Pen Ponds are popular with optimistic anglers. (Adam's Pond is for model boats.) The rest of the park is covered with heath, bracken and trees (some hundreds of years old). Richmond Gate, in the northwest corner, was designed by John Soane (p138).

EAT

Franco Manca
Arguably London's love affair with sourdough pizza started here, at the original Franco Manca. Simple menu, perfect pizzas.

4 Market Row SW9 franco manca.co.uk

££££

---

in 1798. Nearby is Henry VIII Mound, which offers superb views across the Thames Valley, with a tree-framed sightline towards the City and St Paul's (p174). The Palladian White Lodge, built in 1729, is now home to the famed Royal Ballet School.

Ham House

Ham St, Richmond
Richmond then bus 65 or 371 Noon–4pm daily; gardens: Feb–Oct: 10am–5pm daily (Nov–Jan: til 4pm) 24 & 25 Dec nationaltrust.org.uk

This magnificent house by the Thames was built in 1610, but its heyday came when the Countess of Dysart inherited it from her father, who had been Charles I's "whipping boy" (in his boyhood he took the punishment for the future king's misdemeanours). From 1672, she and her husband, a confidant of Charles II, modernized the house, and it was regarded as one of Britain's finest. The garden has been

→

Syon House, built as a square around a central courtyard

lovingly restored to its 17th-century form. In summer and on winter weekends, a foot passenger ferry runs from here to Marble Hill House and Orleans House at Twickenham.

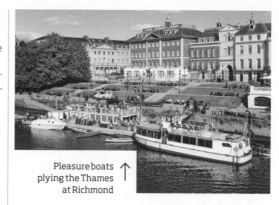
Pleasure boats plying the Thames at Richmond

 20

Orleans House Gallery

Orleans Rd, Twickenham ✉🚊 St Margaret's or Richmond then bus 33, 490, H22, R68 or R70 🕐10am–5pm Tue–Sun; gardens: 9am–dusk daily 🚫1 Jan, Good Fri, 24–26 Dec 🌐orleanshousegallery.org

This gallery occupies what remains of Orleans House, named after Louis Philippe, Duke of Orleans, who lived there from 1815 to 1817. The beautifully restored Octagon Room was designed by James Gibbs for James Johnston in 1720. The gallery displays the Richmond Borough art collection, and there is also a community arts centre.

  21

Marble Hill House

Richmond Rd, Twickenham 🚊 St Margaret's 🕐Apr–Oct: for guided tours only, check website; park and café: daily year-round 🚫Public hols 🌐english-heritage.org.uk

Built in 1729 for George II's mistress, Henrietta Howard, the house and its grounds have been fully restored to its

Georgian appearance. The house has a collection of paintings by William Hogarth and a depiction of the river and house in 1762 by artist Richard Wilson, who is widely regarded as the father of English landscape painting. A £4-million grant has been secured to renovate the park, set to be restored to their 18th-century appearance.

  22

Richmond

TW10 ✉🚊Richmond

This attractive London suburb took its name from the palace that Henry VII built here in 1500. Many early 18th-century houses survive near the Thames and off Richmond Hill, notably Maids of Honour Row, built in 1724. The beautiful view of the river from the top of the hill has been captured by many artists, and is largely unspoiled.

23

Syon House

London Rd, Brentford ✉Gunnersbury then bus 237 or 267 🕐Mid-Mar–Oct: 11am–5pm Wed–Thu, Sun & public hols; gardens: mid-Mar–Oct: 10:30am–5pm daily 🌐syonpark.co.uk

The Earls and Dukes of Northumberland have lived here for 400 years – it is the only large mansion in the London area still in hereditary ownership. The interior was remodelled in 1761 by Robert Adam and is considered one of his masterpieces. The five Adam rooms house original furnishings and a collection of old master paintings.

The 80-ha (200-acre) park, landscaped by Capability Brown, includes a lovely 16-ha (40-acre) garden with more than 200 species of rare trees. The park's Great Conservatory inspired Joseph Paxton's designs for the Crystal Palace.

24

Musical Museum

399 High St, Brentford
🚇Kew Bridge 🚇Gunners-
bury, South Ealing then bus
237 or 267 🕐10:30am-5pm
Tue, Fri-Sun & bank hols
🌐musicalmuseum.co.uk

The collection, arranged
over three floors, chiefly
comprises large self-playing
instruments, including player
(automatic) pianos and organs,
miniature and cinema pianos,
and what is apparently the
only surviving self-playing
Wurlitzer organ in Europe.

25

Osterley Park House

🏠Jersey Rd, Isleworth
🚇Osterley 🕐Mar-Oct:
11am-5pm daily; Nov-Feb:
11am-4pm daily (partial
opening); garden: mid-Feb-
Nov 10am-5pm daily (till
4pm in winter); park: 7am-
7:30pm (later in summer)
🌐nationaltrust.org.uk

Osterley is ranked among
Robert Adam's finest works,
and its colonnaded portico
and ornate stuccowork

demonstrate why. Much of the
furniture is by Adam; the
garden and temple are by
William Chambers, architect
of Somerset House.

26

Pitzhanger Manor House and Gallery

🏠Mattock Lane W5
🚇Ealing Broadway
🕐House: 10am-4:30pm
Tue-Sun & public hols;
10am-3pm Sat; park:
7:30am-dusk daily 🚫Public
hols 🌐pitzhanger.org.uk

Sir John Soane, architect of
the Bank of England, rebuilt
this manor house in 1804 as
his own country residence.
There are clear echoes of his
elaborately constructed town
house in Lincoln's Inn Fields
(p138). Soane retained two of
the principal formal rooms:
the drawing room and the
dining room, designed in 1768
by George Dance the Younger,
with whom Soane had worked.

Pitzhanger reopened in
2019 following a £12-million
conservation project, which
returned the house and
garden to Soane's vision, with a
skylit gallery for exhibitions.

27

London Museum of Water & Steam

🏠Green Dragon Lane,
Brentford 🚇Kew Bridge,
Gunnersbury then bus
65, 237 or 267 🕐10am-
4pm Wed-Sun, daily in
school hols 🌐water
andsteam.org.uk

This 19th-century water
pumping station near the
north end of Kew Bridge is
now a museum of steam
power and water. Its main
exhibits are five giant Cornish
beam engines that pumped
water here from the river, to
be distributed across London.
The earliest engines, dating
from 1820, are similar to those
built to pump water out of
Cornish mines. Visitors can see
them working some weekends
and on public holidays (times
are posted on the website).
The Waterworks gallery tells
the story of London's water

←

Gobelins tapestry from the
"Loves of the Gods" series at
Osterley Park House

↑ Part of the Knot Garden at Fulham Palace *(inset)*, originally created by Bishop Blomfield in 1831

supply, in lots of interactive detail, and there's an outdoor area where children can play with the water features.

28

Fulham Palace

🏠 Bishops Ave SW6
🚇 Putney Bridge
🕐 Summer: 12:30–4:30pm Mon–Thu, noon–5pm Sun & bank hol Mon; winter: 12:30–3:30pm Mon–Thu, noon–4pm Sun; park: daylight hours daily 🕐 Good Fri, 25 & 26 Dec 🌐 fulhampalace.org

The home of the Bishops of London from the 8th century until 1973, the oldest surviving parts of Fulham Palace date from the 15th century. The palace stands in its own land-scaped gardens, which comprise a delightful walled garden and a botanical garden. The museum's collection of paintings and artifacts spans two rooms restored to their original Georgian look. Plans are in place to redevelop the site further. Tours are given four to five times each month; check the website for days and times, and also for details of talks and concerts held here.

29

Chiswick House

🏠 Burlington Lane W4
🚇 Chiswick 🕐 Apr–Oct: 10am–5pm Wed–Mon & bank hols; gardens: 7am–dusk daily 🌐 chiswick houseandgardens.org.uk

Completed in 1729 to the design of its owner, the third Earl of Burlington, this is a fine example of a Palladian villa. Burlington revered Palladio and his disciple Inigo Jones, and statues of both stand outside. Built around a central octagonal room, the house is packed with references to ancient Rome and Renaissance Italy.

Chiswick was Burlington's country residence and this house was built as an annexe to a larger, older house (since demolished). It was designed for recreation and entertaining – Lord Hervey, Burlington's enemy, dismissed it as "too little to live in and too big to hang on a watch chain". Some of the ceiling paintings are by William Kent, who also contributed to the garden design.

The house was an asylum from 1892 until 1928, when lengthy restoration began. The layout of the garden, now a public park, is much as Burlington designed it.

Free tours of the house are included with admission on Sundays at 2.30pm.

DRINK

The Bell and Crown

Lots of riverside outdoor seating and a rustic interior are found here.

🏠 11–13 Thames Rd, Chiswick W4

The City Barge

Great food and beer is available here daily, and the Saturday brunch is legendary.

🏠 27 Strand-on-the-Green, Chiswick W4

Bull's Head

Cosy pub with good Sunday roasts as well as riverside picnic benches.

🏠 15 Strand-on-the-Green, Chiswick W4

30

Hogarth's House

🏠 Hogarth Lane W4
🚇 Turnham Green 🕐 Noon–5pm Tue–Sun & bank hol Mon 🕐 1 Jan, Good Fri, Easter Sun, 24–26 Dec 🌐 hounslow.info/arts/hogarthshouse

When the painter William Hogarth lived here from 1749 until his death in 1764, he called it "a little country box by the Thames" and painted bucolic views from its windows – he had moved here from Leicester Square *(p115)*. It has now been turned into a small museum and gallery, filled with engraved copies of the moralistic cartoon-style pictures with which Hogarth made his name. Salutary tales such as *Marriage à la Mode, An Election Entertainment* and many others can all be seen here.

NEED TO KNOW

Transport in London city centre

Before You Go 334

Getting Around 336

Practical Information 340

BEFORE YOU GO

Forward planning is essential to any successful trip. Be prepared for all eventualities by considering the following points before you travel.

AT A GLANCE

CURRENCY
Pound Sterling
(GBP)

AVERAGE DAILY SPEND

SAVE	SPEND	SPLURGE
£75	£125	£200

BOTTLED WATER	COFFEE	BEER	DINNER FOR TWO
£1	£2.80	£5	£70

CLIMATE

 The longest days occur May–Aug, while Oct–Feb sees the shortest daylight hours.

 Temperatures average 22°C (75°F) in summer. Winter can be very cold and icy.

 The heaviest rainfall is in October and November, but showers occur all year round.

ELECTRICITY SUPPLY

Power sockets are type G, fitting three-pronged plugs. Standard voltage is 230 volts.

Passports and Visas

For a stay of up to six months for the purpose of tourism, citizens of the US, Canada, Australia and New Zealand do not need a visa to enter the country. New arrangements for EU citizens, currently able to settle permanently, are likely to be put in place after the UK leaves the EU. Consult your nearest British embassy or check the **UK Government** website for up-to-date visa information specific to your home country.
UK Government
W gov.uk/check-uk-visa

Travel Safety Advice

Visitors can get up-to-date travel safety information from the UK Foreign and Commonwealth Office, the US State Department, and the Department of Foreign Affairs and Trade in Australia.
Australia
W smartraveller.gov.au
UK
W gov.uk/foreign-travel-advice
US
W travel.state.gov

Customs Information

An individual is permitted to carry the following within the EU for personal use:

Tobacco products: 800 cigarettes, 400 cigarillos, 200 cigars or 1 kg of smoking tobacco.

Alcohol: 10 litres of spirits, 20 litres of fortified wines, 90 litres of wine and 110 litres of beer.

Cash: If you plan to enter or leave the EU with €10,000 or more in cash (or the equivalent in other currencies) you must declare it to the customs authorities.

These regulations may be subject to change once post-Brexit arrangements are put in place by the government, so consult the UK Government website for the most up-to-date customs information. If travelling outside the EU limits vary so check restrictions before you set off.

Insurance

It is wise to take out an insurance policy covering theft, loss of belongings, medical problems, cancellation and delays.

Emergency treatment is usually free from the National Health Service, and there are reciprocal arrangements with other EEA countries, Australia, New Zealand and some others (check the **NHS** website for details).

Specialist care, drugs and repatriation are costly. Residents of EEA countries should carry a European Health Insurance Card (**EHIC**), which allows treatment for free or at a reduced cost.

It is advisable for visitors from outside the EEA, Australia and New Zealand to arrange their own comprehensive medical insurance.

EHIC
w gov.uk/european-health-insurance-card
NHS
w nhs.uk

Vaccinations

No inoculations are needed for the UK.

Money

Major credit and debit cards are accepted in most shops and restaurants, while prepaid currency cards are accepted in some. Contactless payments are widely accepted in London, including on public transport. However, it is always worth carrying some cash, as many smaller businesses and markets still operate a cash-only policy. Cash machines are conveniently located at banks, train stations, shopping areas and main streets.

Booking Accommodation

London offers a huge variety of accommodation to suit any budget, including luxury five-star hotels, family-run B&Bs and budget hostels.

Lodgings can fill up and prices become inflated during during the summer, so it's worth booking well in advance.

A comprehensive list of accommodation to suit all needs can be found on **Visit London**, London's official tourist information website.
Visit London
w visitlondon.com

Travellers with Specific Needs

Accessibility information for public transport is available from the TFL website *(p337)*.

In the City, Westminster, Camden and Kensington and Chelsea, a disabled driver badge allows you to park in blue-badge bays only.

The Visit London website offers handy tips on the city's accessibility provisions. **AccessAble** has a useful searchable online directory.

Museums and galleries offer audio tours, which are useful to those with impaired vision. **Action on Hearing Loss** and the **Royal National Institute for the Blind** can also offer useful information and advice.

AccessAble
w accessable.org.uk
Action on Hearing Loss
w actionhearingloss.org.uk
The Royal National Institute for the Blind
w rnib.org.uk

Language

London is a multicultural city, in which you will hear many languages spoken. Many attractions and tour companies offer foreign language tours.

Closures

Mondays Some museums and tourist attractions are closed for the day.
Sundays Most shops close early or for the day.
Public holidays Schools and public services are closed for the day; some shops, museums and attractions either close early or for the day.

PUBLIC HOLIDAYS 2020	
1 Jan	New Year's Day
10 Apr	Good Friday
13 Apr	Easter Monday
4 May	Bank Holiday
25 May	Bank Holiday
31 Aug	Bank Holiday
25 Dec	Christmas Day
28 Dec	St Stephen's Day

GETTING
AROUND

London has one of the busiest public transport systems in Europe; understanding how it works will help you make the most of your trip.

Arriving by Air

Five airports serve London: Heathrow, Gatwick, Stansted, Luton and London City. With the exception of London City Airport, all are situated a significant distance from central London, with good transport connections to the city centre. For the best rates, book tickets in advance. For a list of transport options, approximate journey times and travel costs for transport to and from London's airports, see the table opposite.

Train Travel

International Train Travel

St Pancras International is the London terminus for Eurostar, the high-speed train linking the UK with the Continent.

You can buy tickets and passes for multiple international journeys via **Eurail** or **Interrail**; advance reservations are usually not required but always check that your pass is valid on the service on which you wish to travel before attempting to board.

Eurostar run a regular service from Paris, Brussels and Amsterdam to London via the Channel Tunnel.

Eurotunnel operates a drive-on-drive-off train service between Calais and Folkestone, in the south of England.

Eurail
W eurail.com
Eurostar
W eurostar.com
Eurotunnel
W eurotunnel.com
Interrail
W interrail.eu

Domestic Train Travel

The UK's railway system is complicated and can be confusing. Lines are run by several different companies, but they are coordinated by **National Rail**, which operates a joint information service.

London has eight main railway termini serving different parts of Britain (Charing Cross, Euston, King's Cross, London Bridge, St Pancras,

GETTING TO AND FROM THE AIRPORT

Airport	Transport to London	Journey Time	Price
London City	DLR	30 mins	from £2.80
	Taxi	30 mins	from £25
London Heathrow	Heathrow Express	15 mins	from £22
	London Underground	50 mins	from £3.10
	National Express Coach	1 hr	from £6
	Taxi	1 hr	from £50
London Stansted	Stansted Express	50 mins	from £7
	National Express Coach	1 hr 50 mins	from £5
	Taxi	1 hr 10 mins	from £75
London Gatwick	Gatwick Express	30 mins	£17.80
	London Thameslink	40 mins	from £11
	National Express Coach	1 hr 50 mins	from £5
	Taxi	1 hr 10 mins	from £60
London Luton	Bus & London Thameslink	45 mins	from £17.40
	National Express Coach	1hr 20 mins	from £5
	Taxi	1hr 10 mins	from £70

Paddington, Waterloo and Victoria). There are also over 300 smaller London stations.

Each main terminus is the starting point for local and suburban lines that cover the whole of southeast England.

London's local and suburban train lines are used by hundreds of thousands of commuters every day. For visitors, rail services are most useful for trips to the outskirts of London and areas of the city without nearby Underground connections (especially in south London). If you are planning to travel outside of the capital, always try to book rail tickets in advance.

National Rail
W nationalrail.co.uk

Long-Distance Bus Travel

Coaches from European and UK destinations arrive at Victoria Coach Station. The biggest operator in the UK is **National Express**. **Eurolines** is its European arm, offering a variety of coach routes to London from other European

cities. Fares start from around £12 and vary depending on distance. Book in advance.

Eurolines
W eurolines.eu

National Express
W nationalexpress.com

Public Transport

Most public transport in London is coordinated by Transport for London (**TFL**), London's main public transport authority.

Timetables, ticket information, transport maps and more can be found on their website.

TFL
W tfl.gov.uk

Fare Zones

TFL divides the city into six charging zones for Underground, Overground and National Rail services, radiating out from Zone 1 in the centre. On buses, there is a flat fare for each trip, no matter how far you travel.

Tickets

Tube and rail fares are expensive, especially individual tickets. If you expect to make multiple trips around the city in a short space of time, you can buy a one-day off-peak Travelcard, which gives unlimited travel on all systems after 9:30am on weekdays (or any time on Saturday, Sunday and public holidays) within Zones 1–4 or 1–6 for a flat fee.

If you wish to travel more freely, purchase a pay-as-you-go Oyster card or Visitor Oyster card (valid for all London zones), which you can preload and top up with credit (note that a £5 deposit is required when buying an Oyster card and you will need one card per person). You can also use contactless credit or debit cards in the same way as the Oyster card. It is cheaper to pay as you go using contactless or Oyster as fares are subject to daily and weekly caps.

When using public transport, you "touch in" with your card on a yellow card reader, and the corresponding amount is deducted. On Underground, DLR and Overground trains, you must also remember to "touch out" where you finish your journey, or you will be charged a maximum fare, though the excess can usually be reclaimed via the website if you forget. Prices are higher during peak times: 6:30–9:30am and 4–7pm Mon–Fri.

Buy Travelcards and Oyster cards at Underground and local rail stations, or any shop that has the TFL "Ticket Stop" sticker in the window. You can also buy them from TFL before arriving; delivery is available to over 60 countries. Many smaller stations do not have staffed ticket counters, just self-service machines.

The Underground and DLR

The London Underground (commonly referred to as "the Tube") has 11 lines, all named and colour-coded, which intersect at various stations. The construction of an additional line, the Elizabeth line, is currently underway. Following setbacks, this will open in 2020 at the earliest.

Some lines, like the Jubilee, have a single branch; others, like the Northern, have more than one, so it is important to check the digital boards on the platform and the destination on the front of the train.

Trains run every few minutes 7:30–9:30am and 4–7pm, and every 5–10 minutes at all other times. The Central, Jubilee, Northern, Victoria and Piccadilly lines offer a 24-hour service on Fridays and Saturdays. All other lines operate 5am–12:40am Mon–Sat; reduced hours Sun.

The DLR (Docklands Light Railway) is an overground network of trains that run from the City to stops in east and southeast London, including City Airport. It operates 5:30–12:30am Mon–Sat; 7am–11:30pm Sun, with trains departing every 3 minutes.

Stations with disabled access are marked on Tube maps, which are located on all trains and at every station.

The Overground

Marked on Tube maps by an orange line, the Overground connects with the Underground and main railway stations at various points across the city. It operates in much the same way as the Underground, and covers most areas of the city without nearby Underground connections.

Bus

Slower but cheaper than the Tube, buses are also a good way of seeing the city as you travel.

Bus routes are displayed on the TFL website and on maps at bus stops. The destination and route number is indicated on the front of the bus and the stops are announced on board.

Buses do not accept cash so a ticket, Oyster card or contactless payment is required.

A single fare costs £1.50, while unlimited bus travel caps out at £4.50 – just use the same card each time you use the bus to reach the daily cap.

The hopper fare allows you to make a second bus journey for free within an hour of travel. Travel is free on buses for under-16s as long as they carry a Zip Oyster card. Apply for one on the TFL website at least four weeks before you are due to arrive.

The Night buses (indicated by the letter "N" added before the route number) run on many popular routes from 11pm until 6am, generally 3–4 times per hour up to 2 or 3am. They cost slightly more than regular buses.

Taxis

London's iconic black cabs can be hailed on the street, booked online or over the phone, or picked up at taxi ranks throughout the city. The yellow "Taxi" sign is lit up when the taxi is free. The driver's cab licence number should be displayed in the back of the taxi.

All taxis are metered, and fares start from £3. Taxi apps such as Uber also operate in London.

The following services can be booked by phone or online:
Dial-a-Cab
w dialacab.co.uk
Gett Taxis
w gett.com/uk
Licensed London Taxi
w licensedlondontaxi.co.uk

Driving

EU driving licences issued by any of the EU member states are valid throughout the European Union. This situation may change following the UK's departure from the EU. If visiting from outside the EU, you may need to apply for an International Driving Permit. Check with your local automobile association before you travel, or consult the UK Driver and Vehicle Licensing Agency (**DVLA**).

DVLA

w gov.uk/driving-nongb-licence

Driving in London

Driving in London is not recommended. Traffic is slow moving, parking is scarce and expensive, and in central London there is the added cost of the **Congestion Charge** – an £11.50 daily charge for driving in central London 7am–6pm Mon–Fri.

In the event of an accident, contact the **AA** for roadside assistance.

AA

w theaa.com

Congestion Charge

w tfl.gov.uk/modes/driving/congestion-charge

Parking

Parking is prohibited at all times wherever the street is marked with double yellow or red lines by the kerb.

If there is a single yellow line, parking is normally allowed from 6:30pm–8am Mon–Sat and all day Sun, but exact hours vary, so always check the signs along each street before leaving your vehicle. Where there is no line at all, parking is free at all times, but this is rare in central London. Rental car drivers are still liable for parking fines.

Car Rental

To rent a car in the UK you must be 21 or over (or in some cases, 25) and have held a valid driver's licence for at least a year.

Driving out of central London will take about an hour in any direction, more during rush hours; if you want to tour the countryside, it can be easier to take a train to a town or city outside London and rent a car from there.

Rules of the Road

Drive on the left. Seat belts must be worn at all times by the driver and all passengers. Children up to 135 cm tall or the age 12 or under must travel with the correct child restraint for their weight and size.

Mobile telephones may not be used while driving except with a "hands-free" system, and third-party insurance is required by law.

Overtake on the outside or right-hand lane, and when approaching a roundabout, give priority to traffic approaching from the right, unless indicated otherwise. All vehicles must give way to emergency services vehicles.

It is illegal to drive in bus lanes during certain hours. See roadside signs for restrictions.

The drink-drive limit (*p340*) is strictly enforced.

Cycling

You need a strong nerve to cycle in London's traffic, but it can be a great way to see the city. **Santander Cycles**, London's self-service cycle hire, has docking stations in central London. Bikes can also be rented from the **London Bicycle Tour Company** and other rental companies throughout the city.

Be aware that drink-drive limits (*p340*) also apply to cyclists.

Santander Cycles

w tfl.gov.uk/modes/cycling/santander-cycles

London Bicycle Tour Company

w londonbicycle.com

Walking

Walking is a rewarding way to get around in London. The centre is not large, and you will be surprised at how short the distance is between places that seem far apart on the Tube.

Boats and Ferries

Car ferries from Calais and Dunkirk arrive in Dover, around 2 hours' drive from London.

Passenger and car-ferry services also sail from other ports in northern France to the south of England, as well as from Bilbao and Santander in Spain to Portsmouth or Plymouth.

Ferry services also run to other ports around the country from the Netherlands and the Republic of Ireland.

London by Boat

Some of London's most spectacular views can be seen from the River Thames.

MBNA Thames Clippers runs river services every 20 minutes on catamarans between Westminster or Battersea Power Station and North Greenwich in both directions, via the London Eye, Bankside and Tower Bridge, with some boats continuing east to Woolwich. The Tate Boat, or RB2, is also operated by MBNA Thames Clippers and runs between the Tate Britain and Tate Modern museums.

Standard tickets cost £8.40 in the central zone, but discounted fares apply if bought online or when using a Travelcard, contactless or Oyster. Discounted fares on the Tate Boat are also available if bought at either Tate or on Millbank or Bankside piers.

A number of providers offer river tours and experiences on the Thames, with numerous options available, from dining experiences to hop-on-hop-off services.

MBNA Thames Clippers

w thamesclippers.com

River Tours

w tfl.gov.uk/modes/river/about-river-tours

PRACTICAL
INFORMATION

A little local know-how goes a long way in London. Here you will find all the essential advice and information you will need during your stay.

EMERGENCY NUMBERS

GENERAL EMERGENCY

999

TIME ZONE
GMT/BST
British Summer
Time (BST) runs
29 Mar–24 Oct 2020
EST -5; AEDT +11

TAP WATER
Unless otherwise
stated, tap water
in the UK is safe
to drink.

TIPPING

Waiter	10-12.5%
Hotel Porter	£1 per bag
Housekeeping	£1-2 per day
Concierge	£1-2
Taxi Driver	10%

Personal Security

Pickpockets work crowded tourist areas. Use your common sense and be alert to your surroundings. If you are unfortunate enough to have anything stolen, report the crime as soon as possible to the nearest police station. Get a copy of the crime report in order to claim on your insurance.

Contact your embassy if you have your passport stolen, or in the event of a serious crime or accident.

Health

For minor ailments go to a pharmacy or chemist. These are plentiful throughout the city; chains such as Boots and Superdrug have branches in almost every shopping district or in the city.

If you have an accident or medical problem requiring non-urgent medical attention, you can find details of your nearest non-emergency medical service on the NHS website (p335). Alternatively, you can call the NHS helpline number at any hour on 111, or go to your nearest Accident and Emergency (A&E) department.

You may need a doctor's prescription to obtain certain pharmaceuticals; the pharmacist can inform you of the closest doctor's surgery or medical centre where you can be seen by a GP (general practitioner).

EU citizens can receive emergency medical treatment in the UK free of charge (p335); however, this situation may change following the UK's departure from the EU.

Visitors from outside the EU may have to pay upfront for medical treatment and reclaim on insurance at a later date.

Smoking, Alcohol and Drugs

The UK has a smoking ban in all public places, including bars, cafés, restaurants, public transport, train stations and hotels.

The UK legal limit for drivers is 80 mg of alcohol per 100 ml of blood, or 0.08 per cent BAC (blood alcohol content). This is roughly equivalent to one small glass of wine or a pint of regular-strength lager; however, it is best to avoid drinking altogether if you plan to drive. The possession of illegal drugs is prohibited and could result in a prison sentence.

ID

There is no requirement for visitors to carry ID, but in the case of a routine check you may be asked to show your passport and visa documentation. It is always useful to carry a photocopy of your passport ID page.

Local Customs

Always stand to the right on escalators or stairwells. Allow passengers to exit before you board public transport. On the Tube, it is customary to offer your seat to passengers who are less able-bodied, pregnant or elderly.

Visiting Churches and Cathedrals

Dress respectfully: cover your torso and upper arms. Ensure shorts and skirts cover your knees.

Mobile Phones and Wi-Fi

Free Wi-Fi hotspots are widely available in the city centre. Cafés and restaurants will give you their Wi-Fi password on the condition that you make a purchase.

Visitors travelling to the UK with EU tariffs are able to use their devices abroad without being affected by data roaming charges. Users will be charged the same rates for data, SMS services and voice calls as they would pay at home. This situation may change once the UK has left the EU.

Post

Standard post in the UK is handled by Royal Mail. There are Royal Mail post office branches located throughout London, which are generally open from 9am–5:30pm Mon–Fri and until 12:30pm Sat.

You can buy 1st-class, 2nd-class and international stamps in post offices, shops and supermarkets. Distinctive red post boxes are located on main streets throughout the city.

Taxes and Refunds

VAT (Value Added Tax) is charged at 20% and almost always included in the marked price. Stores offering tax-free shopping display a distinctive sign and (for non-EU residents) will provide you with a VAT 407 form to validate when you leave the country.

Discount Cards

London can be a very expensive city, but there a number of ways in which costs can be reduced, and many museums are free. Students and under-18s pay lower admission to many exhibitions, and holders of an ISIC (International Student Identity Card) or IYTC (International Youth Travel Card) are eligible for a range of other discounts.

A number of visitor passes and discount cards are available online and from participating tourist offices. These cards are not free, so consider carefully how many of the offers you are likely to take advantage of before buying one. For a full list of the options available, consult the **Visit London** website.

One such card is the **London Pass**, which offers free entry to more than 80 of the city's top attractions, fast-track entry to some busier sights, money-off selected tours and discounts in participating shops and restaurants, with the option of adding unlimited travel.

London Pass
w londonpass.com
Visit London
w visitlondon.com

APPS

Citymapper
Covers all urban modes of transport, including cycling and walking routes, to help you navigate the city.

TFL Oyster
Top up and manage your Oyster card on the go with this app from TFL.

Trainline
Use this app to find the cheapest train tickets and check journey times.

Visit London
Includes offline maps, area guides plus exclusive deals and offers.

INDEX

Page numbers in **bold** refer to main entries

2 Willow Road **294**
18 Stafford Terrace **266**
19 Princelet Street **199**

A

Accommodation
    booking 335
    see also Hotels
Air travel
    arriving by air 336
    getting to/from airports 337
Albert Memorial **253**, 259
Albert, Prince 34, 244
    Albert Memorial **253**, 259
Alcohol 334, 340-41
Alexandra Palace **322-3**
All Hallows by the Tower **186**
All Souls, Langham Place **281**
Ambulances 340
Angel Islington **169**
Apps 341
Apsley House **98-9**
ArcelorMittal Orbit (Kapoor) **312**
Architecture 11
    London on the Roof **50-51**
ATMs 335
Auction houses **98**

B

Ballet 46, 125
    see also Entertainment
Bank of England Museum **184**,
    191
Bankside see Southwark and
    Bankside
Bankside Gallery **210-11**
Banqueting House **82**, 85
BAPS Shri Swaminarayan
    Mandir 32, **322**, 323
Barbican Centre **182-3**
Barbican Estate 182, **183**
Bars see Pubs and bars
Battersea see Chelsea and
    Battersea
Battersea Park **238-9**
Battersea Power Station **239**
Bedford Square 158
Beefeaters 178-9
Bermondsey Street **213**
Berwick Street Market **116-17**
Beyond the Centre 25, **310-31**
    map 311
    pubs and bars 322, 331
    restaurants 321, 328

BFI Southbank **223**
Big Ben 76, **80**, 85
Bloomsbury and Fitzrovia 19,
    36, **146-59**
    A Short Walk: Bloomsbury
        158-9
    map 148-9
    pubs and bars 157
    restaurants 157
    shopping 155
Bloomsbury Group 55, **154**, 293
Bloomsbury Square **154**, 159
Boat Race 39, 59
Boats
    London by boat 339
    Queen Elizabeth Olympic
        Park 313
    Serpentine 257
    Thames Clipper 41, 339
Boleyn, Anne 35, 180, 228
Bond, James 129
Books, London for Bookworms
    54-5
Bookshops 54-5, 100, 116, 155,
    283
Borough Market 10, 57, **211**, 215
Brick Lane 32, **197**
British Film Institute 45, 220
    BFI Southbank **223**
British Library 55, **164**
British Museum **150-53**, 158
    tours 150
Brixton **328**
Broadcasting House **280-81**
Brompton Oratory **252**, 259
Brompton Square 259
Buckingham Palace **90-91**, 96
Budgeting 334
Bunhill Fields **197**
Burgh House **293**, 297
Burlington Arcade 97, 100
Bus travel 338
    long-distance 337

C

Cafés see Restaurants
Calendar
    A Year in London **58-9**
    Sporting 39
Camden see King's Cross,
    Camden and Islington
Camden Market **168**
Camley Street Natural Park
    37, **165**
Canary Wharf 41, **307**
    see also Greenwich and
        Canary Wharf
Car ferries 339
Carlyle, Thomas 95
    Carlyle's House **235**
Car rental 339
Cash 334, 335

Cathedrals
    St Paul's Cathedral 51, 63,
        174-7, 190
    St Sophia's Cathedral **271**
    Southwark Cathedral **210**,
        215
    Westminster Abbey **72-5**, 84
    Westminster Cathedral 51, **83**
    see also Churches
Cemeteries
    Bunhill Fields **197**
    Highgate Cemetery **292-3**
    St Pancras Old Church and
        Graveyard **164-5**
Cenotaph, the **81**, 85
Changing the Guard 35, 90, 91
Chapels
    Lady Chapel (Westminster
        Abbey) 74, 75
    Queen's Chapel **97**
    Wesley's Chapel-Leysian
        Mission **196**
Charing Cross Road **116**
Charles Dickens Museum 54, **155**
Charlton House **323**
Charterhouse **189**
Chelsea and Battersea 22,
    230-39
    hotels 235
    map 232-3
    restaurants 238
Chelsea Harbour **238**
Chelsea Old Church **235**
Chelsea Physic Garden **235**
Children, London for Families
    52-3
Chinatown 33, **112-13**
Chiswick House 36, **331**
Christ Church, Spitalfields **199**
Churches
    All Hallows by the Tower **186**
    All Souls, Langham Place **281**
    Brompton Oratory **252**, 259
    Chelsea Old Church **235**
    Christ Church, Spitalfields **199**
    concerts 46
    etiquette 341
    Holy Trinity Church 259
    St Alfege 308
    St Andrew, Holborn **143**
    St Bartholomew-the-Great
        187
    St Bride's **141**, 174
    St Clement Danes **140**, 145
    St Ethelreda's Church **143**
    St George's, Bloomsbury **155**,
        159
    St James Garlickhythe 190
    St James's Church 95, 101
    St John's Downshire Hill 294
    St John's Smith Square 46, **83**
    St Katharine Cree **189**
    St Lawrence Jewry 188

Churches (cont.)
St Leonard's Church **200**
St Margaret's Church **80–81**, 84
St Martin-in-the-Fields 46, **114**
St Mary Abchurch 191
St Mary Aldermary 190
St Marylebone Parish Church **280**, 284
St Mary-le-Bow 174, **185**, 190
St Mary-le-Strand **128**
St Mary's, Battersea **239**
St Mary Woolnoth 191
St Nicholas Cole Abbey 190
St Pancras Old Church and Graveyard **164–5**
St Paul's Church **125**, 131
St Stephen Walbrook 174, **185**, 191
Temple Church 137
see also Cathedrals; Chapels
Churchill, Winston 64, 80, 176
Churchill War Rooms **81**, 84
Church Row **294**, 297
Cinemas **44–5**, 50
Circus West Village **239**
The City 20, **170–91**
A Short Walk: The City 190–91
map 172–3
pubs and bars 187
restaurants 189
City Hall 40, **213**
Cleopatra's Needle **128**
Climate 334
Clink Prison Museum **212**, 215
Closures 335
Coach travel 337
Columbia Road Market 10, **200**
Coronation 73, 75, 181
County Hall 222, 227
Courtauld Gallery 124, **125**
Covent Garden Piazza and Central Market **122–3**, 130–31
Covent Garden and the Strand 18, **118–31**
A Short Walk: Covent Garden 130–31
maps 120–21
pubs and bars 128
restaurants 123, 124, 127
Credit/debit cards 335
Cricket 39
Lord's Cricket Ground **281**
Crime 340
Crown Jewels 178, 179, 181
Cumberland Terrace **283**
Currency 334
Customs regulations 334
Cutty Sark **302**, 308
Cycling 339
Lee Valley VeloPark **312**

D

Dennis Severs' House **198**
Design Museum **264–5**, 272
Diana, Princess of Wales 94, 176, 256
Diana Memorial Playground 52–3, **256**
Dickens, Charles 54, 110, 137, 139, 142, 235
Charles Dickens Museum 54, **155**
Discounts
cards and passes 341
children 53
public transport 338
theatre tickets 46, 115
Downing Street **81**, 85
Downshire Hill **294**
Drink see Food and drink; Pubs and bars
Driving 338–9
Dr Johnson's House **142**
Drugs 341
Dulwich Park **325**
Dulwich Picture Gallery **325**

E

Electricity supply 334
Elgin Marbles 153
Elizabeth II, Queen 34, 94
Buckingham Palace 90–91
Coronation 73, 75
Diamond Jubilee 312
Kensington Palace 256
Eltham Palace **324**
Emergency numbers 340
Emirates Air Line **306**
Entertainment
Barbican Centre **182–3**
BFI Southbank **223**
for children 53
Kings Place **165**
London Coliseum **129**
London for Film Buffs **44–5**
London for Live Shows **46–7**
London on the Roof **50–51**
National Theatre 220, 222, **227**, 229
O2 Arena **306**
The Old Vic **229**
Purcell Room 220, **223**
Queen Elizabeth Hall 220, **223**
Rich Mix **200–201**
Rose Playhouse **211**
Royal Albert Hall 46–7, 64, **252–3**, 258
Royal Festival Hall 220, 221, 222, **223**
Royal Opera House 122, **125**, 131

Entertainment (cont.)
Sam Wanamaker Playhouse 208, 209
Savoy Theatre 126
Shakespeare's Globe **208–9**, 214
Southbank Centre 65, **220–23**
Theatreland 12, **129**
Theatre Royal Drury Lane 125, 131
Wigmore Hall **283**
Estorick Collection of Modern Italian Art **168**
Etiquette 341
Eurotunnel 336

F

Fan Museum **305**
Faraday, Michael, Faraday Museum **99**
Fenton House **293**, 296
Ferries 339
Festival of Britain (1951) 65, **221**
Festivals and events 11, 33
A Year in London **58–9**
film festivals 45, 58, 59
food festivals 56
Notting Hill Carnival 11, 32–3, 59, **270**
Southbank Centre 220
Sporting Calendar 39
Film
London for Film Buffs **44–5**
Warner Bros. Studio Tour: The Making of Harry Potter **320–21**
Fire service 340
Fitzrovia see Bloomsbury and Fitzrovia
Fitzroy Square **156**
Flask Walk **293**, 297
Fleet Street **140**, 145
Florence Nightingale Museum **228**
Food and drink
London for Foodies **56–7**
pub food 43
Top 5 London Food Hubs 57
see also Pubs and bars; Restaurants
Football 38–9
Fortnum & Mason **95**, 100
Foundling Museum **156–7**
Freud, Sigmund, Freud Museum **295**
Fulham Palace **331**

G

Gabriel's Wharf **228**
Gatwick Airport 336, 337

Geffrye Museum **201**
Gherkin, the 187
Golden Hinde II 215
Granary Square **165**
Grant Museum of Zoology **157**
Gray's Inn 136, **137**
Great Court (British Museum) 152, 153
Great Exhibition 64, 221, 257
Green Park **97**
Greenwich and Canary Wharf 24, **298–309**
 A Short Walk: Greenwich 308–9
 map 300–301
 pubs and bars 305
 restaurants 303
 shopping 303
Greenwich Foot Tunnel 41, **305**, 308
Greenwich Park **303**
Grosvenor Square **99**
Guards Museum **83**
Guildhall **188**

H

Ham House **328–9**
Hammersmith Bridge 40
Hampstead Heath **290–91**, 296
Hampstead and Highgate 24, **286–97**
 A Short Walk: Hampstead 296–7
 map 288–9
 pubs and bars 295
Hampton Court 35, 40, **314–17**
Hampton Court Flower Show 314
Handel & Hendrix in London **99**
Harley Street 285
Harrods 48, 49
Hatton Garden **143**
Hayward Gallery 220, **223**
Health 340
 insurance 335
 vaccinations 335
Heathrow Airport 336, 337
Henry VII 62, 329
 Westminster Abbey 74
Henry VIII 35, 74, 82, 95, 189
 armour 181
 birthplace 304, 308
 Green Park 97
 Hampton Court 314–17
 Henry VIII Mound 328
 Hyde Park 257
 National Portrait Gallery 110
 St James's Palace 94, 100
Highgate *see* Hampstead and Highgate
Highgate Cemetery **292–3**
 Top 5 Notable Residents 293

High Street Kensington **267**, 272
Historic buildings
 2 Willow Road **294**
 18 Stafford Terrace **266**
 19 Princelet Street **199**
 Admiral's House 296
 Albany mansion 100
 Apsley House **98–9**
 Bankside power station 206–7
 Banqueting House **82**, 85
 Battersea Power Station **239**
 Bethlehem Royal Hospital for the Insane ("Bedlam") 225
 Broadcasting House **280–81**
 Burgh House **293**, 297
 Burlington House 92
 Carlyle's House **235**
 Central Hall 84
 Charlton House **323**
 Charterhouse **189**
 Chatham House 94
 Chiswick House 36, **331**
 Churchill War Rooms **81**, 84
 Clarence House 100
 Dennis Severs' House **198**
 Dover House 85
 Dr Johnson's House **142**
 Elizabeth Tower 76, 80
 Fenton House **293**, 296
 Flamsteed House 303
 Great Pagoda (Kew Gardens) 319
 Guildhall **188**
 Ham House **328–9**
 Holland House 266, 272
 Inns of Court **136–7**, 144–5
 Jewel Tower 77, **80**, 84
 Keat's House **295**
 Kenwood House **290–91**
 Leighton House **267**, 272
 livery halls **185**
 Mansion House **184**, 191
 Marble Hill House **329**
 Marlborough House **96–7**
 Old Curiosity Shop **139**, 144
 Old Royal Naval College **304–5**, 309
 Orleans House 328
 Osterley Park House **330**
 Peace Pagoda (Battersea Park) 239
 Pitzhanger Manor House and Gallery **330**
 Queen's House **304**, 309
 Ranger's House **305**
 Royal Exchange **184**, 191
 Royal Hospital Chelsea **238**
 Somerset House **124–5**
 Spencer House **94**, 100
 Sutton House **323**
 Syon House 36, **329**
 Tower of London 35, **178–81**

Historic buildings (cont.)
 Ye Olde Cheshire Cheese **142–3**
 see also Cathedrals; Chapels; Churches; Libraries; Museums and galleries; Palaces
History **60–65**
HMS *Belfast* **213**
Hogarth, William 109, 114, 115, 157, 189, 329
 Hogarth's House **331**
Holborn and the Inns of Court 18, **132–45**
 A Short Walk: Lincoln's Inn 144–5
 map 134–5
 pubs and bars 141
 shopping 142
Holland Park 53, **266**, 272–3
 see also Kensington, Holland Park and Notting Hill
Horniman Museum **324**
Horse Guards Parade 35, **82**, 85
Hotels
 booking 335
 Chelsea and Battersea 235
 Kensington, Holland Park and Notting Hill 267
 Mayfair and St James's 99
 Regent's Park and Marylebone 278
 Ritz Hotel 96, 100
 Savoy Hotel **126**
 Whitehall and Westminster 80
Household Cavalry Museum **83**
Houses of Parliament 13, 64, **76–7**, 85
Hoxton **198**
Huguenots 196, **199**
Hungerford Bridge 41, 222
Hunterian Museum **139**, 144
Hyde Park 36, 53, **257**

I

Ice rinks
 Alexandra Palace 323
 Hyde Park 257
 Somerset House 125
ID 341
Imperial College 259
Imperial War Museum **224–5**
Inner Temple 136, **137**
Inns of Court **136–7**, 144–5
 see also Holborn and the Inns of Court
Institute of Contemporary Arts **96**
Insurance 335
Islington *see* King's Cross, Camden and Islington

Itineraries **26-31**
 2 Days 28-9
 7 Days 30-31
 24 hours 26-7

J

Jewel Tower 77, **80**, 84
Jewish Museum **169**
Johnson, Samuel 46, 131, 140
 Dr Johnson's House **142**
Jones, Inigo
 Banqueting House 82, 85
 Charlton House summer
  house 323
 Covent Garden 122
 Queen's Chapel 97
 Queen's House **304**, 309

K

Keats, John 293
 Keat's House **295**
Kensington Gardens 36, 52-3,
 256
Kensington, Holland Park and
 Notting Hill 23, **260-73**
 A Short Walk: Kensington and
  Holland Park 272-3
 hotels 267
 map 262-3
 restaurants 271
 shopping 274
Kensington Square **271**
Kenwood House **290-91**
Kew Gardens 36, **318-19**
 map 319
King's Cross, Camden and
 Islington 19, **160-69**
 map 162-3
 restaurants 164
King's Cross Station 165
Kings Place **165**
King's Road **234**
Knightsbridge see South
 Kensington and
 Knightsbridge
Knights Templar 136, **137**, 145

L

Lambeth Palace **229**
Language 335
Leadenhall Building (the
 "Cheesegrater") 187
Leadenhall Market **188**
Leather Lane Market **143**
Lee Valley VeloPark **312**
Leicester Square **115**
Leighton House **267**, 272
LGBT+
 Pride in London 59
 Soho 117

Libraries
 British Library 55, **164**
 London Library 95
 Wellcome Library 156
Lincoln's Inn 136, **137**
 A Short Walk 144-5
Lincoln's Inn Fields **139**, 144, 145
Literature **54-5**
Little Venice **270**
Livery halls **185**
Local customs 341
London Aquatics Centre 312
London Bridge 41, 215
London Central Mosque 32, **282**
London City Airport 336, 337
London Coliseum **129**
London Dungeon 227, **228**
London Eye 65, 222, **226-7**
London Film Festival 45, 58
London Film Museum **129**
London Marathon 39, 59, 96
London Museum of Water &
 Steam **330-31**
London Silver Vaults **143**
London Transport Museum **127**,
 131
London Underground 64, 338
London Zoo **278-9**
Lord's Cricket Ground **281**
Luton Airport 336, 337

M

Madame Tussauds **280**, 284
Mall, the **96**
Mansion House **184**, 191
Maps
 A Short Walk: St James's
  100-101
 A Short Walk: Southwark
  214-15
 A Short Walk: Bloomsbury
  158-9
 A Short Walk: The City 190-91
 A Short Walk: Covent Garden
  130-31
 A Short Walk: Greenwich
  308-9
 A Short Walk: Hampstead
  296-7
 A Short Walk: Kensington and
  Holland Park 272-3
 A Short Walk: Lincoln's Inn
  144-5
 A Short Walk: Marylebone
  284-5
 A Short Walk: South
  Kensington 258-9
 A Short Walk: Whitehall and
  Westminster 84-5
 Beyond the Centre 311
 Bloomsbury and Fitzrovia
  148-9

Maps (cont.)
 Chelsea and Battersea 232-3
 the City 172-3
 Covent Garden and the
  Strand 120-21
 Explore London 14-15
 Greenwich and Canary Wharf
  300-301
 Hampstead and Highgate
  288-9
 Holborn and the Inns of Court
  134-5
 Kensington, Holland Park and
  Notting Hill 262-3
 Kew Gardens 319
 King's Cross, Camden and
  Islington 162-3
 Mayfair and St James's 88-9
 Regent's Park and
  Marylebone 276-7
 Shoreditch and Spitalfields
  194-5
 Soho and Trafalgar Square
  104-5
 South Bank 218-19, 222
 South Kensington and
  Knightsbridge 242-3
 Southwark and Bankside
  204-5
 Whitehall and Westminster
  70-71
Marble Arch **257**
Marble Hill House **329**
Markets 10
 antiques market
  (Bermondsey Square) 213
 Berwick Street Market
  116-17
 Borough Market 10, 57, **211**,
  215
 Brick Lane 197
 Brixton Market 33, 328
 Camden Lock Market 49
 Camden Market **168**
 Columbia Road Market 10,
  200
 Covent Garden Piazza and
  Central Market **122-3**, 131
 Greenwich Market 303, 308
 Leadenhall Market **188**
 Leather Lane Market **143**
 Marylebone Farmers' Market
  283
 Old Spitalfields Market 49,
  196
 Petticoat Lane **196-7**
 Portobello Road 49, **266**
 Smithfield Market **186-7**
 Southbank Centre Food
  Market 57
 street food 57
 Top 5 London Markets 49
Marlborough House **96-7**

Marylebone
  A Short Walk: Marylebone
    284-5
  see also Regent's Park and
    Marylebone
Marylebone High Street **283**,
  284, 285
Mayfair and St James's 17,
  86-101
  A Short Walk: St James's
    100-101
  hotels 99
  map 88-9
  restaurants 96
Medical care 340
Middle Temple 136, **137**
Millennium Bridge 175, 214
Millennium Dome 65, 306
Mobile phones 341
Monarchy **34-5**
Money 335
Monument **186**
Multiculturalism **32-3**, 65
Museums and galleries 10
  Bank of England Museum
    184, 191
  Bankside Gallery **210-11**
  British Museum **150-53**, 158
  Charles Dickens Museum 54,
    155
  Churchill Museum 81
  Clink Prison Museum **212**, 215
  Courtauld Gallery 124, **125**
  Cutty Sark **302**, 308
  Design Museum **264-5**, 272
  Dulwich Picture Gallery **325**
  Estorick Collection of Modern
    Italian Art **168**
  Fan Museum **305**
  Faraday Museum **99**
  Fashion and Textile Museum
    213
  Florence Nightingale
    Museum **228**
  for children 52
  Foundling Museum **156-7**
  Freud Museum **295**
  Geffrye Museum **201**
  Grant Museum of Zoology **157**
  Guards Museum **83**
  Guildhall Art Gallery 188
  Hampstead Museum 293
  Handel & Hendrix in London
    99
  Hayward Gallery 220, **223**
  HMS Belfast **213**
  Hogarth's House **331**
  Horniman Museum **324**
  Household Cavalry Museum
    83
  House of Illustration 165
  Hunterian Museum **139**, 144
  Imperial War Museum **224-5**

Museums and galleries (cont.)
  Institute of Contemporary
    Arts **96**
  Jewish Museum **169**
  London Dungeon 227, **228**
  London Film Museum **129**
  London Museum of Water &
    Steam **330-31**
  London Transport Museum
    127, 131
  Madame Tussauds **280**, 284
  MCC Museum 39, 281
  Museum of Brands,
    Packaging and Advertising
    270
  Museum of Comedy 155
  Museum of Freemasonry **127**
  Museum of Garden History
    229
  Museum of London **183**
  Museum of London
    Docklands **306-7**
  Museum of Music 252
  Museum of the Order of St
    John **189**
  Musical Museum **330**
  National Army Museum **234**
  National Gallery **106-9**
  National Gallery of Art 44
  National Maritime Museum
    302-3, 309
  National Portrait Gallery
    110-11
  Natural History Museum 34,
    248-9, 258
  Old Operating Theatre **210**
  Orleans House Gallery **329**
  Photographers' Gallery **117**
  Pitzhanger Manor House and
    Gallery **330**
  Pollock's Toy Museum **156**
  Postal Museum **156**
  Queen's Gallery, the **91**
  Ranger's House - the
    Wernher Collection **305**
  Royal Academy of Arts **92-3**,
    100
  Royal Academy of Music
    Museum **281**
  Saatchi Gallery **234**
  Science Museum 52, **250-51**,
    258
  Serpentine Galleries **253**
  Sherlock Holmes Museum
    282
  Sir John Soane's Museum
    138-9
  Somerset House **124-5**
  Tate Britain **78-9**
  Tate Modern 65, **206-7**,
    214
  V&A Museum of Childhood
    201

Museums and galleries (cont.)
  Victoria and Albert Museum
    244-7, 259
  Wallace Collection **279**
  Wellcome Collection **156**
  Whitechapel Gallery **198-9**
  White Cube Bermondsey
    213
  William Morris Gallery **323**
  Wimbledon Lawn Tennis
    Museum **324**
  Wimbledon Windmill Museum
    324-5
Music
  live 46
  Musical Museum **330**
  Royal Academy of Music
    284
  Royal Academy of Music
    Museum **281**
  Royal College of Music **252**,
    258
  see also Entertainment
Musical Museum **330**
Musicals 47

N

Nash, John
  All Souls, Langham Place
    281
  Buckingham Palace 90
  Clarence House 110
  Cumberland Terrace 283
  Marble Arch 257
  Pall Mall 94
  Park Crescent 285
  Piccadilly Circus 115
  Regent's Park **279**, 284
  Trafalgar Square 114
National Army Museum **234**
National Gallery **106-9**
  Top 5 Paintings 108
National Maritime Museum
  302-3, 309
National Portrait Gallery **110-11**
  lunchtime lectures 110
National Theatre 220, 222, **227**,
  229
Natural History Museum 34,
  248-9, 258
  Top 5 Unmissable Exhibits
    248
Nature reserves
  Camley Street Natural Park
    37, **165**
  Walthamstow Wetlands 37
Neal Street **126**, 130
Neal's Yard **126**, 130
Nightlife
  Soho 117
  see also Entertainment; Pubs
    and bars

Notting Hill **270**
  see also Kensington, Holland
    Park and Notting Hill
Notting Hill Carnival 11, 32–3, 59,
  270

O

O2 Arena **306**
Old Bailey 141, **187**
Old Compton Street 117
Old Curiosity Shop, the **139**, 144
Old Operating Theatre **210**
Old Royal Naval College **304–5**,
  309
Old Spitalfields Market 49, **196**
Old Vic, The **229**
Olympic Games 38, 65
  Queen Elizabeth Olympic Park
    38, **312–13**
Olympic Stadium 313
One Canada Square 307
Opening hours 335
Opera 46, 125, 129
Orleans House Gallery **329**
Osterley Park House **330**
Oxford Street 48, **282**
Oyster Card 338

P

Palaces
  Alexandra Palace **322–3**
  Buckingham Palace **90–91**
  Eltham Palace **324**
  Fulham Palace **331**
  Hampton Court 35,
    314–17
  Kensington Palace **256**
  Kew Palace 35
  Lambeth Palace **229**
  Palace of Westminster **76–7**,
    80
  St James's Palace **94**, 100, 101
Pall Mall **94**, 101
Parking 339
Parks and gardens 12
  Battersea Park **238–9**
  Burlington Gardens 92
  Chelsea Physic Garden **235**
  Coram's Fields 53, 157
  for children 52–3
  Fulham Palace **331**
  Green Park **97**
  Greenwich Park **303**
  Hampstead Heath **290–91**,
    296
  Hampton Court 314–15
  Holland Park 53, **266**, 272–3
  Hyde Park 36, 53, **257**
  Inns of Court 136–7
  Jubilee Gardens 222

Parks and gardens (cont.)
  Kensington Gardens 36, 52–3,
    256
  Kew Gardens 36, **318–19**
  Lincoln's Inn Fields **139**, 144,
    145
  London for Green Spaces
    36–7
  Queen Elizabeth Olympic Park
    38, **312–13**
  Regent's Park 53, **279**, 284
  Richmond Park **328**
  rooftop gardens 51
  St James's Park 36, 53, **95**, 96
  Sky Garden **187**
  Syon House 329
  Victoria Embankment
    Gardens **128**
  Victoria Park 239, **322**
  see also Nature reserves
Parliament Hill 290
Parliament Square **81**
Passports 334
Personal security 340
Petticoat Lane **196–7**
Pharmacies 340
Photographers' Gallery **117**
Piccadilly Circus 101, **114–15**
Pickpockets 340
Pitzhanger Manor House and
  Gallery **330**
Police 340
Pollock's Toy Museum **156**
Portobello Road 49, **266**
Postal Museum **156**
Postal services 341
Potter, Harry 165
  Warner Bros. Studio Tour
    320–21
Prices
  average daily spend 334
  public transport 336, 337
  tipping 340
Primrose Hill **169**
Proms, the 46–7, 59, 253
Public holidays 335
Public transport 337–8
  children 53
  etiquette 341
  prices 336
Pubs and bars 13
  Beyond the Centre 322, 331
  Bloomsbury and Fitzrovia 157
  the City 187
  Covent Garden and the
    Strand 128
  Greenwich and Canary Wharf
    305
  Hampstead and Highgate 295
  Holborn and the Inns of Court
    141
  London on Tap **42–3**
  music 47

Pubs and bars (cont.)
  rooftop 50
  Soho and Trafalgar Square
    116
  Southwark and Bankside 211,
    215
  Top 4 Historic Pubs 43
  Ye Olde Cheshire Cheese
    142–3
Purcell Room 220, **223**

Q

Queen Anne's Gate **82**
Queen Elizabeth Hall 220, **223**
Queen Elizabeth Olympic Park
  38, **312–13**
Queen's Chapel **97**
Queen's Gallery, the **91**
Queen's House **304**, 309

R

Rail travel 336–7, 338
Ranger's House – the Wernher
  Collection **305**
Reading Room (British Museum)
  152, 153
Regent's Canal 165, 168, 270,
  322
Regent's Park 53, **279**, 284
Regent's Park and Marylebone
  23, **274–85**
  A Short Walk: Marylebone
    284–5
  hotels 278
  map 276–7
  shopping 283
Regent Street 48
Remembrance Sunday 59, 81
Restaurants 13
  Beyond the Centre 321, 328
  Bloomsbury and Fitzrovia 157
  Chelsea and Battersea 238
  Chinatown 113
  the City 189
  Covent Garden and the
    Strand 123, 124, 127
  Greenwich and Canary Wharf
    303
  Kensington, Holland Park and
    Notting Hill 271
  King's Cross, Camden and
    Islington 164
  London for Foodies **56–7**
  Mayfair and St James's 96
  Michelin-starred 56, 57
  riverside 41
  rooftop 51
  Shoreditch and Spitalfields
    197
  Soho and Trafalgar Square
    113, 115

Restaurants (cont.)
South Kensington and
Knightsbridge 247
Southwark and Bankside 212
see also Food and drink
Rich Mix **200-201**
Richmond 10, **329**
Richmond Park **328**
Ritz Hotel 96, 100
Rooftop venues **50-51**
Rose Playhouse **211**
Rosetta Stone 150, 151, 153
Royal Academy of Arts **92-3**, 100
Royal Academy of Music
Museum **281**
Royal Albert Hall 46-7, 64,
252-3, 258
Royal Botanic Gardens, Kew see
Kew Gardens
Royal College of Art **252**, 258
Royal College of Music **252**, 258
Royal Courts of Justice (the Law
Courts) **141**, 145
Royal Exchange **184**, 191
Royal Festival Hall 220, 221,
222, **223**
Royal Greenwich Observatory
303
Royal Hospital Chelsea **238**
Royal Mews **91**
Royal Opera House 122, **125**,
131
Royalty **34-5**
Rugby 39
Rules of the road 336, 339
Russell Square 55, **154-5**, 159

S

Saatchi Gallery **234**
Safety
personal security 340
travel safety advice 334
St Andrew, Holborn **143**
St Bartholomew-the-Great **187**
St Bride's **141**, 174
St Clement Danes **140**, 145
St Ethelreda's Church **143**
St George's, Bloomsbury **155**,
159
St James's see Mayfair and St
James's
St James's Palace **94**, 100, 101
St James's Park 36, 53, **95**, 96
St James's Square **94-5**, 101
St John's Smith Square 46, **83**
St Katharine Cree **189**
St Katherine Docks **188-9**
St Leonard's Church **200**
St Margaret's Church **80-81**, 84
St Martin-in-the-Fields 46, **114**
St Marylebone Parish Church
280, 284

St Mary-le-Bow 174, **185**, 190
St Mary-le-Strand **128**
St Mary's, Battersea **239**
St Pancras International 64,
164
St Pancras Old Church and
Graveyard **164-5**
St Paul's Cathedral 51, 63, **174-7**,
190
St Paul's Church **125**, 131
St Sophia's Cathedral **271**
St Stephen Walbrook 174, **185**,
191
Savoy Hotel **126**
Science Museum 52, **250-51**,
258
Top 5 Unmissable Exhibits
251
Sea Life London Aquarium 222,
227
Senate House 55, 158
Serpentine Gallery **253**
Serpentine, the 257
Seven Dials **126**, 130
Shaftesbury Avenue **116**
Shakespeare's Globe **208-9**,
214
Shakespeare, William 62, 98,
137, 164
Hampton Court 316
National Portrait Gallery 110
Rose theatre 211
Shakespeare's Globe **208-9**,
214
statue (Leicester Square) 115
Westminster Abbey 74
Shard, the 51, 187, **212-13**
Sherlock Holmes Museum **282**
Shopping
auction houses **98**
Bloomsbury and Fitzrovia 155
bookshops 54-5, 100, 116,
155, 283
for children 52
Greenwich and Canary Wharf
303
Holborn and Inns of Court 142
Kensington, Holland Park and
Notting Hill 274
London in Fashion **48-9**
London Silver Vaults **143**
Mayfair and St James 95
Regent's Park and
Marylebone 283
shopping arcades **97**
Shoreditch and Spitalfields
200
Shoreditch and Spitalfields 20,
192-201
map 194-5
restaurants 197
shopping 200
Sir John Soane's Museum **138-9**

Sky Garden **187**
Smithfield Market **186-7**
Smoking 340
Soane, John **139**, 165, 184, 325,
330
Soho and Trafalgar Square 17,
102-17
map 104-5
pubs and bars 116
restaurants 113, 115
Somerset House **124-5**
South Bank 12, 21, **217-29**
map 218-19
Southbank Centre 65, **220-23**
South Kensington and
Knightsbridge 22, **240-59**
A Short Walk: South
Kensington 258-9
map 242-3
restaurants 247
Southwark and Bankside 21,
202-15
A Short Walk: Southwark
214-15
map 204-5
pubs and bars 211
restaurants 212
Southwark Bridge 214
Southwark Cathedral **210**, 215
Speakers' Corner **257**
Specific needs, travellers with
335
Speed limit 338
Spencer House **94**, 100
Spitalfields see Shoreditch and
Spitalfields
Sports and outdoor activities
ice rinks 125, 257, 323
Lee Valley VeloPark **312**
London for Sports Fans **38-9**
Lord's Cricket Ground **281**
Queen Elizabeth Olympic Park
38, **312-13**
swimming 257, 290, 312
Stansted Airport 336, 337
Summer Exhibition (Royal
Academy) 92, **93**
Sutton House **323**
Swimming
Hampstead Heath 290
London Aquatics Centre 312
Serpentine 257
Syon House 36, **329**

T

Tap water 340
Tate Britain **78-9**
Tate Modern 65, **206-7**, 214
interactive art **206**
Taxes 341
Taxis 338
Telephone services 341

Temple Bar Memorial **140–41**, 145
Tennis 39, 325
  Wimbledon Lawn Tennis Museum **324**
Thames Barrier 10, **307**
Thames Path 10, 40
Thames, River
  boats 339
  flooding 307
  London on the River **40–41**
  the South Bank **222**
Theatre
  for children 53
  West End 12, 47, 115, 116, **129**
  see also Entertainment
Tickets
  London Eye 226
  public transport 338
  theatre 46, 115
  Wimbledon 325
Time zone 340
Tipping 340
Tobacco 334
Tower Bridge 40, 41, 64, **186**
Tower Hill 178, 186
Tower of London 35, **178–81**
Trafalgar Square **114**
  see also Soho and Trafalgar Square
Train travel 336–7, 338
Travel
  getting around 336–9
  safety advice 334
Trooping of the Colour 11, 34–5, 58, 82
Tube, the 64, 338
Turner Prize **79**

U

Upper Street **169**

V

V&A see Victoria and Albert Museum
V&A Museum of Childhood **201**
Vaccinations 335
VAT refunds 341
Victoria and Albert Museum **244–7**, 259
Victoria Embankment Gardens **128**
Victoria Park 239, **322**

Victoria, Queen 34, 64, 75, 90, 140
  Albert Memorial 253
  The Old Vic 229
  Royal Albert Hall 253
  Victoria and Albert Museum 244
Visas 334

W

Walks
  A Short Walk: St James's 100–101
  A Short Walk: Southwark 214–15
  A Short Walk: Bloomsbury 158–9
  A Short Walk: The City 190–91
  A Short Walk: Covent Garden 130–31
  A Short Walk: Greenwich 308–9
  A Short Walk: Hampstead 296–7
  A Short Walk: Kensington and Holland Park 272–3
  A Short Walk: Lincoln's Inn 144–5
  A Short Walk: Marylebone 284–5
  A Short Walk: South Kensington 258–9
  A Short Walk: Whitehall and Westminster 84–5
  Capital Ring 37
  getting around London 339
  Thames Path 10, 40
Wallace Collection **279**
Warner Bros. Studio Tour: The Making of Harry Potter **320–21**
Websites 341
Wellcome Collection **156**
Wellington Arch **98**
Well Walk **293**, 297
Wesley's Chapel-Leysian Mission **196**
West End Theatre 12, 47
Westminster see Whitehall and Westminster
Westminster Abbey **72–5**, 84
  Coronation 73, 75
  evensong 72

Westminster Cathedral 51, **83**
Whispering Gallery (St Paul's Cathedral) 176, 177
Whitechapel Gallery **198–9**
Whitehall and Westminster 16, **68–85**
  A Short Walk: Whitehall and Westminster 84–5
  hotels 80
  map 70–71
Wi-Fi 341
Wigmore Hall **283**
Wildlife
  Camley Street Natural Park 37, **165**
  children's zoo (Battersea Park) 239
  city farms 53
  London Zoo **278–9**
  Sea Life London Aquarium 222, **227**
  Walthamstow Wetlands 37
William Morris Gallery **323**
Wimbledon 39, 58, 324
Wimbledon Lawn Tennis Museum **324**
Wimbledon Windmill Museum **324–5**
World War I 64, 81
  War Memorial (Borough High Street) 215
World War II 64–5
  Churchill War Rooms **81**
  HMS Belfast **213**
Wren, Christopher 63, **174**
  Flamsteed House 303
  Hampton Court 314, 316
  Kensington Palace 256
  Marlborough House 96
  Old Royal Naval College 304–5, 309
  Royal Hospital Chelsea **238**
  St Andrew, Holborn 143
  St Bride's 141, 174
  St Clement Danes 140, 145
  St James's Church 95, 100
  St Lawrence Jewry 188
  St Mary-le-Bow 174, 185, 190
  St Paul's Cathedral 174, 176–7
  St Stephen Walbrook 174, 185, 191

Y

Ye Olde Cheshire Cheese **142–3**

ACKNOWLEDGMENTS

The publisher would like to thank the following for their kind permission to reproduce their photographs:

Key: a-above; b-below/bottom; c-centre; f-far; l-left; r-right; t-top

123RF.com: bloodua 282tl; Alexey Fedorenko 273br; flik47 153clb; Allan Gregorio 59cl; Christian Mueller 23tc, 260-1; Michael Spring 59tr.

4Corners: Maurizio Rellini 2-3, 8-9b; Alessandro Saffo 21bl, 216-7.

Alamy Stock Photo: age fotostock / Lluís Real 44-5t; Alan King engraving 179bl; Andrew Orchard sports photography 38tr; Arcaid Images / Diane Auckland 127bl, / Richard Bryant 198tr, 267tl; ART Collection 317tr; Colin Bain 136-7b; Rob Ball 46-7t; John Baran 174cr; Richard Barnes 38b; Peter Barritt 257cr; Guy Bell 302-3t, 321tl; Nigel Blacker 124-5t; Eden Breitz 210tr; Michael Brooks 96-7b; Matthew Bruce 330cra, 330-1t; Jason Bryan 307cr; Colin Burdett 250cr; Paul Carstairs 223tr; Matthew Chattle 99tc; Chronicle 61tr, 65tr, 74bc, 75bl; Classic Image 177tl; Vera Collingwood 293t; Danielle Connor 25, 310; Lindsay Constable 56-7b; csimagebase 37b; Ian Dagnall 181bl, 36bl, 244cra. DavidCC 185tl; De Luan 74br; Kathy deWitt 142bl; Chris Dorney 251tl; dpa picture alliance archive 75br; Everett Collection Inc 73br; Exflow 266-7b; eye35.pix 318-9t; Malcolm Fairman 152-3b; Andrew Fare 60t; John Farnham 290clb; Tony Farrugia 49cla; Nicola Ferrari 20cb, 192-3; Fotomaton 270br; Paris Franz 111tl; Garden Photo World / David C Phillips 21tl, 202-3; Marc Gascoigne 32-3t; Goss Images 28bl; Granger Historical Picture Archive 61br, 74ca; 77ca; robertharding / Chris Mouyiaris 199tr; Alex Hare 303br; Cath Harries 43br, 142t; Heritage Image Partnership Ltd 75bc, 77tc, 178br, 181crb, 181br; Jeremy Hoare 294bc; Angelo Hornak 177cl, 177cr, 177bl; Ianni Dimitrov Pictures 90-1b; Yanice Idir 117tc; imageBROKER / Helmut Meyer zur Capellen 244br, i/ Werner Lang 320cl; Imagedoc 39cl, 52bl; Imageplotter 58bl; incamerastock 49crb, 225tl; INTERFOTO 64br, 77tl; Jansos 12bl, 22tl, 230-1; Benjamin John 58ca, 93br, 158cl, 280t; Johnny Jones 53cr; Bjanka Kadic 244clb; Sung Kuk Kim 47b; Norman Krimholtz 168bc; Elitsa Lambova 151tl; Peter Lane 282-3b; LatitudeStock 223cla; Chris Lawrence 18bl, 132-3; Lebrecht Music & Arts 108br, 177tr, 181c; Geraint Lewis 209cla; LH Images 278cl; London Picture Library 19tl, 146-7; Londonstills.com 291tr; M.Sobreira 228br; mauritius images GmbH / Steve Vidler 106clb, 181cra, 184tr, 201cr, 212t, 302br; Neil McAllister 74cla; Meibion 42-3t; Trevor Mogg 10bl, 56-7t; Luciano Mortula 34bl; ilpo musto 280br; adam parker 39tl; Pawel Libera Images 35bl; Mark Phillips 154-5t; Photopat / Tate Modern, London / SUPERFLEX © 2018 One

Two Three Swing! 206-7b; picture 228tl; The Picture Art Collection 108tl; Enrico Della Pietra 18tl, 118-9, 999t; PjrWindows 18bl, 132-3; PjrTravel 177ftl, 229t; PjrWindows 143tl; Portrait Essentials 139tl; Laurence Prax 113tl; Prisma by Dukas Presseagentur GmbH 55tr, 151tr; RayArt Graphics 17cb, 102-3; RealyEasyStar / Rodolfo Felici 129t; Richard Wareham Fotografie 40-1t; robertharding / Adam Woolfitt 77br; Roger Cracknell 01 / classic 238t; Grant Rooney 41crb, 123clb, 197tr, 223tl; Amanda Rose 34ca; Peter Scholey 184b, 234cl; Scott Hortop Travel 101br, 156tl; Adrian Seal 196t; Marco Secchi 90bl, 111c; Alex Segre 30tl, 54-5b, 291cra, 297tl, 322br, 325b; Ian Shaw 211t; Mick Sinclair 271bc; Kumar Sriskandan 43cl, 96t, 153tr; Robert Stainforth 98-9b; Stockimo / Neil Juggins 224-5b; Stockinasia 326-7; Adam Stoltman 65br; Sunshine 320-1b; Homer Sykes 155br, 294t; Erik Tham 8clb, 106-7; Roger Tillberg 208clb; Tim Gartside London 35cr; travelibUK 74cl; travelpix 244-5; Trevor Smithers ARPS 136-7t; Simon Turner 50br; Pat Tuson 37cr, 271bl; V. Dorosz 291tl; V&A Images 330bl; Steve Vidler 49tl, 181br; Steve Vidler 295bl; Monica Wells 165tl; Tim E White 57cl; Mark Wiener 181crb; World History Archive 60-1cla, 179br; Gregory Wrona 17tl, 33br, 86-7, 329tr; Chris Yates 48tl; Marc Zakian 169crb; Justin Kase zninez 223tr; Zoonar / Michal Bednarek 128b; Zoonar GmbH 235tr.

AWL Images: Jon Arnold 236-7; David Bank 66-7; Alan Copson 82br; PhotoFVG 239cra; Alex Robinson 23cb, 274-5, 283t; Mark Sykes 252tl; Travel Pix Collection 16, 68-9.

Barbican Centre: Max Colson 182br.

Bridgeman Images: Christie's Images 315bl; Mirrorpix 77cra; Royal Academy of Arts, London / Joshua Reynolds Self portrait (c.1779-80) oil on panel (1723-92) 93tl, / Michelangelo Buonarroti Tondo Taddei (16th century) 93tr; Universal History Archive / UIG 63br.

Coca Cola London Eye: Dave Bennet 225cl.

Courtesy of BFI: 45cl.

Image courtesy of the Saatchi Gallery, London: Steve White / Installation of Champagne Life exhibition 234-5b.

Depositphotos Inc: georgios 64bl; jovannig 26cr; masterlu 51b, 174-5.

Dorling Kindersley: Max Alexander 52-3t.

Dreamstime.com: Igor Abramovych 227crb; Absente 151cra; Adeliepenguin 285br; Andersastphoto 150-1b, 268-9; Anizza 59cr; Anyaivanova 114b; Rafael Ben Ari 152cla; Aivita Arika 215tl; Anthony Baggett 99cb, 139b;

Front flap:
Alamy Stock Photo: Enrico Della Pietra t; Jansos bl; **AWL Images:** Alex Robinson cla; **Dreamstime. com:** Michal Bednarek cb; **Getty Images:** oversnap cra; **iStockphoto.com:** oversnap br.

Sheet map cover:
Getty Images: Joe Daniel Price.

Cover images:
Front and Spine: **Getty Images: Joe Daniel Price.**
Back: **AWL Images:** Nadia Isakova c, Alex Robinson tr; **Depositphotos Inc:** masterlu cl; **Getty Images:** Joe Daniel Price b.

For further information see: www.dkimages.com

Penguin Random House

Main Contributors Matt Norman, Michael Leapman, Alice Park
Senior Editor Ankita Awasthi Tröger
Senior Designer Owen Bennett
Project Editor Alice Fewery
Project Art Editors Dan Bailey, Toby Truphet, Hansa Babra, Ankita Sharma, Priyanka Thakur
Design Assistant William Robinson
Factchecker Darren Longley
Editors Rebecca Flynn, Lucy Sienkowska, Danielle Watt, Louise Abbott, Natalie Baker
Proofreader Debra Wolter
Indexer Helen Peters
Senior Picture Researcher Ellen Root
Picture Research Harriet Whitaker, Marta Bescos
Illustrators Brian Delf, Trevor Hill, Robbie Polley, Ann Child, Gary Cross, Tim Hayward, Arghya Jyoti Hore, Fiona M Macpherson, Janos Marffy, David More, Chris Orr, Richard Phipps, Rockit Design, Michelle Ross, John Woodcock.
Senior Cartographic Editor Casper Morris
Cartography Andrew Heritage, Zafar ul Islam Khan, Suresh Kumar, James Mills-Hicks, John Plumer, Ashutosh Ranjan Bharti, Deshpal Singh Dabas
Jacket Designers Maxine Pedliham, Bess Daly
Jacket Picture Research Susie Peachey
Senior DTP Designer Jason Little
DTP Coordinator George Nimmo
Senior Producer Stephanie McConnell
Managing Editor Hollie Teague
Art Director Maxine Pedliham
Publishing Director Georgina Dee
This edition updated by Edward Aves, Matthew Grundy Haigh, Bharti Karakoti, Azeem Siddiqui, Lauren Whybrow, Tanveer Zaidi

First edition 1993

Published in Great Britain by Dorling Kindersley Limited, 80 Strand, London, WC2R 0RL

Published in the United States by DK Publishing, 1450 Broadway, Suite 801, New York, NY 10018

Copyright © 1993, 2019 Dorling Kindersley Limited
A Penguin Random House Company
18 19 20 21 10 9 8 7 6 5 4 3 2 1

A CIP catalog record for this book is available from the British Library.

A catalog record for this book is available from the Library of Congress.

ISSN: 1542 1554
ISBN: 978-0-2413-6874-9

Printed and bound in China.

www.dk.com

MIX
Paper from responsible sources
FSC™ C018179
www.fsc.org

The information in this DK Eyewitness Travel Guide is checked regularly.
Every effort has been made to ensure that this book is as up-to-date as possible at the time of going to press. Some details, however, such as telephone numbers, opening hours, prices, gallery hanging arrangements and travel information, are liable to change. The publishers cannot accept responsibility for any consequences arising from the use of this book, nor for any material on third party websites, and cannot guarantee that any website address in this book will be a suitable source of travel information. We value the views and suggestions of our readers very highly. Please write to: Publisher, DK Eyewitness Travel Guides, Dorling Kindersley, 80 Strand, London, WC2R 0RL, UK, or email: travelguides@dk.com